OLDER AUTISTIC ADULTS

In Their Own Words:

The Lost Generation

BY

WILMA WAKE, PH.D., LCSW

ERIC ENDLICH, PH.D.

ROBERT S. LAGOS

FUTURE HORIZONS

Dedication

This book is dedicated to all elders who are on the autism spectrum – or suspect they are. We especially dedicate it to the 150 incredible people who completed our questionnaire with deep honesty and commitment, and to the hundreds of others who at least started filling out the questionnaire, asked questions, or urged us on.

ACKNOWLEDGMENTS

This work has been supported by many in numerous ways, for which we are grateful. Philip Wylie encouraged our research from the beginning and helped develop our questionnaire. Sara Heath helped us to access material about the study that she and Philip had done. Dr. Wenn Lawson helped us explore resources. We are deeply indebted to AANE [Asperger/Autism Network] for support and inspiration throughout this research. We especially appreciate the support from Executive Director, Dania Jekel, MSW, and Grace Myhill, MSW, Director of The Peter M. Friedman Neurodiverse Couples Institute of AANE. We have heartfelt appreciation to the AANE Maine support group, which has sustained and encouraged us for years. Neuropsychologist Dr. Laura Slap-Shelton has provided technical support, resources, and encouragement. Brooke White Ober, MS, CCC-SLP, and Aaron Ober, MD, helped us locate research material. Patricia Burke, MSW; LCSW, has helped in understanding ethical and clinical issues for therapy. Paula Smith at the Autism Research Centre [University of Cambridge] helped us access the U.K. population. Dr. Tony Attwood guided us towards other research in the field, and Eustacia Cutler answered our questions about Temple Grandin's childhood. Finally, we thank the many spectrum elders around the world whose participation, input, and inspiration to this work have been invaluable.

NOTE ON VOCABULARY:

It is difficult to know how to identify those of us *older autistic adults*. Many of us were diagnosed [or self-identified] with *Asperger's Syndrome* and informally have called ourselves *Aspies*. However, with the newer coding of the *Diagnostic Statistical Manual 5*, *Asperger's Syndrome* is no longer listed. And many of us are disturbed by new historical research on Hans Asperger's connection with the Nazis in Austria during World War II. Knowing this, we don't want to use his name to define ourselves. The official diagnostic term now for any form of autism is *Autism Spectrum Disorder*. All people with autism are on one spectrum with different numbers designating levels of functioning. So sometimes we identify our diagnostic category as the official *Autism Spectrum Disorder or ASD*. However, that means we have a *disorder*, a concept most of us reject. In this book, we use *Aspergers* and *Asperger's Syndrome* in historical context. Otherwise, we primarily refer to ourselves as on the *autism spectrum* or *autistics* or *older autistic adults*.

TABLE OF CONTENTS

FOREWORD

Autistic children grow up as autistic adults… and then become autistic seniors. Centered on *The Nine Degrees of Autism* edited by Philip Wylie, Wenn Lawson, and Luke Beardon. *Older Autistic Adults* is a timely, researched-based, resource bringing these 9 degrees or stages to life as a sturdy framework for empowering both individuals on the autism spectrum and those seeking deeper understanding for supporting autistic persons. This resource is especially useful for people with late diagnoses or those who have yet to truly understand the full implications of what it means to be autistic – as can only be built by people having inner knowledge of autism, dedicated to having their fellow autistic gain deeper understanding of their true, authentic autistic selves.

Through surveys and interviews of 150 people on the autism spectrum at 50 years or older, the authors greatly deepen understanding of autism from an autistic point of view. Initially popularized by Leo Kanner in his 1943 paper "Autistic Disturbances of Affective Content" the term "autism" began its common use journey to describe people like us. As a result, the relatively short history of autism provides a curious moment of time where many on the spectrum, due to lack of knowledge and familiarity with autism, were not diagnosed until well into adulthood, plus individuals such as myself who were diagnosed in toddlerhood, but did not understand the full implication of what it means to be autistic until middle, or late adulthood.

Mirroring suggestions by the authors, the initial degrees were fairly easy for me. With the 1st degree *Being born on the spectrum*, all I had to do was to come into being in the early 1960s. However, my being autistic was only recognized with a diagnosis at 2½ after, like with about 30% of us, I was struck by the regressive autism bomb at 18 months. The 2nd degree, *Knowing you are different*, was simple since my parents were upfront about my being autistic as the reason for being different (yet accepted for who I was) for as long as I can remember. The 3rd degree, *Developing secondary health issues*, is where challenges began. While lacking identifiable co-morbid conditions, I was a social and academic catastrophe in grade school. Bullying was the norm and teachers did not know how to reach me. Typical employment was mostly a train wreck whereas I had much greater success when working for myself.

Glimmers of the 4th degree *Realization and diagnosis*, began to peak through during my undergraduate studies upon reading *The Empty Fortress* by Bruno Bettelheim. Thinking "That was me" I didn't draw much sense from it, which further cemented my belief that autism was something I had as a kid but was now "all done". It was only when I began to understand the implications of being autistic did I enter the 5th degree *Considering all the options*, where deep introspection led me to change my trajectory from a life-long dream of a doctorate in music to one in special education. This change, with the realization that special education was not a second best or back up plan, but just another equally valid and enriching course of action threw me straight into the 6th degree *Crises of identity*, leading to a *resolution to live with* as opposed to against *autism*.

The 7th degree *Self-acceptance*, consisted of my turning away from railing against real and perceived frailties autism engenders and towards understanding what autism means to me was the key to success – and entrance to the 8th degree *Unconditional service*, primarily in the areas of advocacy and education, including university, conferences, giving music lessons to autistic children, and embracing the community of autistic people. For me, the 9th degree *Recognition, mastery, unity* is the realization of turning away from being a poor imitation of a non autistic individual to enjoying the journey of becoming the best autistic person I can be.

I now welcome the reader to read, think, learn, and become enriched as you gain greater appreciation of what it means to be autistic for 150 middle aged and older autistics and apply these implications to your own life if you are, or know someone on the autism spectrum.

Stephen Mark Shore, Ed.D.
Internationally known educator, author, presenter, and advocate for autistic people

PREFACE

Specialists who diagnose autism are receiving an increasing rate of referrals for mature adults who recognize the characteristics of autism in their developmental history and current profile of abilities. They had always felt they were different to their peers, but in the last century, parents and teachers were not aware, as we are today, of the more subtle signs of autism in childhood. These people were unable to benefit from our current range of programmes at school and home that improve social understanding and friendships skills, as well as develop a positive sense of self. They have also been denied access to therapy specifically designed to reduce feelings of anxiety and depression in autistic children and adolescents; and they missed out on the environmental and attitude adaptations that we now apply at home, school and work to accommodate the sensory sensitivity and a different learning style associated with autism. They were a generation that also tried to cope with a sense of alienation and judgement and bullying and teasing by peers and family members. This lost generation are my heroes for their courage in facing and enduring a level of adversity we do not want the current generation of autistic children to experience.

The data and quotes in *Older Autistic Adults* are consistent with my clinical experience in diagnosing hundreds of mature adults over several decades: experience which is now validated by the results of the survey. The stories and statistics will be important to all those who have an interest in autism, both professionally and personally. The lost generation is at last being discovered and accepted.

Professor Tony Attwood

INTRODUCTION

THE BEGINNING

By Wilma

It was a gorgeous fall Saturday in Maine. I was on lunch break from the conference "Autism and Asperger's Syndrome with Dr. Jed Baker and Eustacia Cutler," a Future Horizons workshop in Portland, ME. My friend, Rob, and I were strolling along a road resplendent with golds, reds, and yellows. We talked about the speaker at our workshop, Eustacia Cutler, mother of Temple Grandin.

"I'm learning so much from her stories of raising Temple," I reflected. "Especially since Temple and I are the same age. Yet, she was diagnosed before 5, and I wasn't until age 66 – just a couple years ago. I'm just starting to figure out who I am."

"It's the story of our generation of autistics, isn't it?" Rob mused.

"Yes, and so little research has been done on our generation. How are others doing? How did their autism impact them growing up without a diagnosis?" I asked.

"I hope you hear soon about your proposal," Rob said supportively, reminding me about the conversations I had been having with Future Horizons. about doing some research and then writing a book on older high-functioning autistic adults. I had almost given up on hearing from them.

I grabbed a cup of hot tea as I walked towards my seat in the front row of the auditorium, glancing at the cellphone in my hand to check my email as I sat down. I almost couldn't believe my eyes—as I saw the latest email on the screen, my hand jerked, and I spilled tea all over my seat —and that of the people on either side of me—who were very helpful and immediately pulled out tissues to help clean up the mess.

"Oh, I'm so sorry! I got so excited about my email," I explained. "It's from Future Horizons, they're going to publish my book!"

I was both happy and scared as I sat down to focus on Eustacia's talk. I asked lots of questions and took many notes. I wanted to know what it was like raising an autistic child in the 40s and 50s.

During the next few weeks, I turned to Philip Wylie, author of *Very Late Diagnosis of Asperger Syndrome*, for help with drafting a questionnaire. To reach potential respondents, I decided to post the questionnaire on the Internet. That turned out to be an overwhelming task, so I asked my friend Rob, a computer expert and statistician, to help.

In a support group for autistic mental health professionals [at AANE in Massachusetts], I met a psychologist named Eric Endlich. He was intrigued by my book's topic and offered to help. We became a team of three adults over 50 on the spectrum, researching other high-functioning adults like ourselves. Our team combined the skills and experiences of a psychologist, a social worker, and a statistician/research consultant.

The experience of conducting this research has indelibly marked our lives. In the process, we came to know 150 people from around the world, who shared with us a life of at least 50 years on the spectrum.

In this book, we present what we learned from them.

WHO ARE WE?

Part 1:

Eric Endlich

The Aspie in the Mirror

By Eric

My journey to self-discovery started surprisingly late. I had been working as a psychotherapist for 30 years. I had raised an autistic child to adulthood. I had read enough autism books and been to enough autism conferences [along with my wife, Kris] to make me an honorary autism expert myself.

And then we heard Sarah. Sarah is a funny, informative, articulate public speaker who, after writing five books on autism, realized that she herself also had autism. Imagine that – an intelligent woman with a master's degree in autism studies and she didn't realize she was on the spectrum until she was in her forties!

Then there was me, sitting at the Asperger/Autism Network conference, age 54, as the dad of an autistic son. It all started innocently enough, sitting in the conference hall that morning, listening to Sarah's keynote address. Then about 10 or 15 minutes into the talk, a dreadful suspicion crept into my awareness. *Holy shit. I think I'm on the spectrum, too!* A few minutes later I thought: *Wait a minute – I bet Dad's autistic, too...*

As if that wasn't enough drama, Kris, sitting next to me, was having similar thoughts. *Oh. My. God. Eric is on the spectrum, too.* Later that day, Kris and I spoke and confirmed our thoughts with each other. (She was so relieved I brought it up – she didn't think I would welcome the idea if it came from her.) Wow, eighteen years of raising an autistic child, and we'd somehow missed my autism.

Sixteen years earlier, my son's diagnosis changed our future; this one would change my past.

The Unexpected Truth

Many people say that being diagnosed with autism brings a "rollercoaster of emotions," but that image implies being attached to some sort of track. For me, it was more like being adrift – at sea or in space. Disorienting. Who was I? I thought I was a normal – well, normal enough, anyhow – successful married professional. Apparently not. I was a member of what author Steve Silberman called Asperger's Lost Tribe: An Aspie [Silberman, 2015].

Now, as I looked back on the half-century-plus of my life, everything shifted and appeared different. And yet, in many ways, everything made so much more sense. Why had I been teased and bullied? Why did I feel so alone growing up, despite having siblings and friends? Why did I spend so much time by myself, daydreaming, and reading? Why did people keep getting frustrated with me, as if there was something obvious about how I should act that I just didn't understand? Why did people find my single-minded intensity so odd? Why was I such a picky eater, and bothered by so many smells? Because I'm autistic, that's why!

Initially, I felt disbelief: *This can't be true...I must be wrong about this.* Then when I could no longer deny it, I felt sad, disappointed, and alienated: I'll always be on the fringes, terminally odd, struggling with social complexities. I even felt like I'd never become a full-fledged human. Alone again, naturally, and sad.

I kept reading. I kept contemplating. But most importantly, I went to support groups at the Asperger/Autism Network [AANE] and met others on the spectrum. And I started to feel hopeful again.

We're Not Alone

"Mental Health Providers on the Spectrum," read the email announcement for an upcoming support meeting at AANE. Wait. Was that "Providers," as in plural? Does that mean I'm not the only one? "You may be surprised to find that you are not alone," the announcement continued. *You're goddamn right I'm surprised. In fact, I don't believe it. I'm going to go to this meeting just to find out.*

I only received the email a few hours before the first meeting, so I had patients to move if I wanted to attend. What was I supposed to tell them? *I'm going to meet with other autistic therapists, so we have to reschedule.* I hadn't even disclosed to my own mother, much less my patients. In the end, I just said, "something's come up and I have to reschedule."

I hate being late, so I made sure to leave enough time for the drive to the AANE office. I wasn't late. In fact, I was the only one in the room. Hmm...maybe I *am* the only therapist on the spectrum, after all. But then the co-facilitators entered, and they were on the spectrum, too. Including the leaders, there were just six of us that session. Still, having the opportunity to disclose my newfound self-awareness among peers was tremendously freeing.

What's in a Label?

So how did I know I was autistic? Did I need to see a professional to be sure? One adult Aspie quipped that since I'm a psychologist, my self-diagnosis means I'm also professionally diagnosed. [I think she was being facetious, but when one Aspie is trying to read the nonverbal cues of another Aspie, all bets are off.]

When I first suspected I was autistic, I did what many people would do in today's world: I went online and took a quiz. The Asperger Spectrum Quotient [AQ] was my first step, and the results confirmed my suspicions. But I kept waffling, so then I did what any self-respecting Aspie would do to marshal an argument: start a list. I put on my list every indicator of autism I detected in myself. The definition of Asperger's Disorder in the *Diagnostic and Statistical Manual of Mental Disorders, 4th Edition,* or *DSM-IV* [American Psychiatric Association, 1994] essentially requires three main criteria to meet the diagnosis; at this point, I have over 60 items on My Autism list of characteristics. [It's listed as a disorder in that book, not a syndrome, but no matter – it was eliminated altogether in the *DSM-5.*]

I've since learned that many autistics reject the diagnosis concept altogether. They identify as autistic through their own self-awareness and don't feel the need for a professional to diagnose or treat them. As Wenn Lawson says in *The Nine Degrees of Autism,* "I'm not sick, I don't need medicine for my autism" [Wylie, Lawson, & Beardon, 2016, p. 144]. If autism is not a disorder but merely a difference, then why insist on professional diagnosis? The fact that I am left-handed also indicates that my brain is organized differently, and I don't need a professional to confirm that either. But I'm also a psychologist, which means people come to me to be diagnosed [sometimes for autism], so I find myself arguing both sides of the controversy in my head. Just one more of my oddities.

Dad, Guess What? We're Autistic!

The next time my dad visited from Los Angeles, I took him for a walk to break the big news. If we'd had the conversation indoors, it would have been face to face, but this way I could conveniently look away as we talked.

It was Thanksgiving Day 2015. I had been cooking feverishly all morning and had reached the point where I could leave food in the oven and take a break. It should have been frigid in late November in New England, yet the sun was out, and the temperature was mercifully mild. We could walk at a leisurely pace without freezing our buns off. The trees were almost bare and there was no snow on the ground yet.

There was no point getting right to the point; I could still put this off a little longer, right?

"Dad, do you know what Occam's razor is?" I was hoping he wouldn't think I was talking about some medieval shaving device.

"I think so."

Guess I'd better explain to be sure. "It's the idea that the simplest explanation for the facts is usually the best. And I think I have an explanation for where Alex got his autism and why I have so many personality quirks."

"Okay, what's that?"

"I'm on the spectrum, too. I have Asperger's. Alex inherited his autism from me."

"What makes you think that?" No emotion from him at all. Score another point for *his* diagnosis.

I went on. "All of the things that have puzzled and frustrated me—and others—about myself can be explained by this one umbrella concept. I'm detail-oriented. I've had obsessions with numbers and words. I get hyper-focused on one interest: stamps, reptiles, astronomy. I speak in a monotone. I don't express my feelings. I don't even know what my feelings *are.*" I was on a roll now. "I never liked eye contact. I don't have many friends. I'm a picky eater. I'm bothered by fan noises."

"You're bothered by fan noises?" *Really? You just learned your son is autistic and that's the most surprising fact?*

"You know," he added, "I have some of the same issues you're describing."

This was it! Time to drop the second bomb on him, the real blockbuster. "I know. I told you I believe autism is genetic. I think I got it from you. And you probably got it from your mother's side. I recall she was very rigid, for example."

"That's true, she was." What? I've just told him *he's* autistic too, and he has no reaction to that either?

"Also, Dad, I took an online quiz just to confirm, and I scored in the Asperger-autistic range."

He seemed genuinely intrigued. "I'd like to take that, too."

And so, when we got back to the house, we did. He scored a 34 out of 50, solidly in the autism range, and higher even than me. [The last time I took the AQ I scored 33, giving support to my dad's old refrain, "The apple doesn't fall far from the tree."]

No surprise. I'd already gone through the test imagining his answers and came up with the same result. The only item I think he answered incorrectly had to do with people telling him he made inappropriate social comments. I distinctly remember him making inappropriate comments. "Wow, you're tall. You must be six and a half feet at least. How tall *are* you, exactly?" Then again, I don't remember anyone calling him on it, so maybe he's still clueless about this issue.

By this point in his life [age 84], Dad had developed dementia. The next day I asked him about our conversation—perhaps the most life-changing conversation I'd had with him since I left for college at age 17 and told him he was a crappy father and I wanted to stop all contact with him.

"Dad, do you remember our conversation yesterday before Thanksgiving dinner?"

"No. Why? Did we talk about anything important?"

"Naw, never mind. It was nothing."

Part 2

Rob Lagos

My Story

By Rob

I Knew I Was Different

I have known I was different since childhood. I was "quirky" and different from an early age. Emotionally and socially, I was years behind my peers; yet intellectually, I was years ahead. So much of what I experienced seemed unlike anything anyone else ever talked about or addressed, so to survive my childhood, I had to pretend to be someone other than me. As a result, I grew up confused, and consequently, unable to stand up for myself.

Nurtured but Abused

I was recognized for my giftedness, and my mother tried to see to it that I was educated and that my skills be developed to the fullest. I had musical talent as a piano virtuoso, which she wanted to encourage. I was also highly interested in mathematics. However, the personal problems I was experiencing were virtually ignored and denied. Even when I tried to point out that something was wrong, I was only given negative feedback and denial. I was silenced for crying. I made no friends—I had no social life. I lived in my own world.

Being bullied in school took a huge toll. My peers would utter things that I often didn't understand but that sounded hostile. I was hated for being smart—and more so for being unsociable and different. I believe that I also "bruised" emotionally much easier than most people, probably due to the sensitivities related to autism spectrum disorder [ASD].

I grew up painfully traumatized from infancy into adulthood. I believe that my father abused me as an infant and even beat me for crying too much, based on information that later leaked out through my mother. For this reason, along with the bullying in school, I grew up traumatized. But I was expected to behave and do things that were orders of magnitude outside my comfort zone. Nobody seemed to pay much attention to what was happening to me. This snowballed, and things got worse in terms of my emotional and psychological state. I had to withdraw from college; but I managed to come back after a couple of years to just finish up my last year and get my degree.

Identified – My Mother and Dr. Simmons

My mother, who had suspected for a while that I had a mild form of autism, contacted an autism support center, and we were eventually referred to the UCLA Neuropsychiatric Institute.

I was diagnosed with "autism, residual type" in 1980, at the age of 25. We were told by the nurse receptionist that most people who were diagnosed with autism were also "retarded."

Dr. Simmons, a specialist in autism, first interviewed my mother. He interviewed me next. At the end of the session, I was given the diagnosis of a developmental disability, affecting my development since prior to the age of 3 months, the closest match being autism. I was told that this was the reason I was having the problems I was having, and that it would affect me lifelong, as there was no cure.

I was also referred to the Los Angeles county regional center for the developmentally disabled. Based on the results of psychological testing and my school history, I was diagnosed by them with "early infantile autism leading to substantial handicap," along with severe clinical depression with poor prognosis. I became eligible for their services, with the goal of helping me become independent and employed. Much later I was rediagnosed with ASD, Level I, along with post-traumatic stress disorder [PTSD] and unspecified obsessive compulsive disorder [OCD].

It was all very well to be better understood. But in those days [at the time of my first diagnosis], there was very little outside support. There were no peer support groups. So, once I left the doctor's office, I was alone in a very different and non-understanding world. Most people did not believe I had autism, and the only person in my family who was involved at all was my mother. When my mother passed away, it became unbearable. I was left with a very painful and traumatic past, too painful to live with, and beyond the clinician's office, there was no support.

Rick and Ramona

Despite my lack of social skills, I managed to make two supportive friends with whom I am still close today. I met Rick when I was featured in a piano event, and he came to me wanting to be my student. He was a young psychiatrist and a patron of the arts. A few months later, he introduced me to a friend of his who was doing her internship at University of California at Irvine: Ramona. Ramona later accepted a fellowship in psychiatry at Harvard. Rick followed her a couple of years later. Rick helped me find a loft space in Cambridge, and I followed them in the move.

Unfortunately, I found that most therapists would not believe I had autism even after having been formally diagnosed by a top expert. And I did not have the self-confidence to proclaim what I believed inside all along: that Dr. Simmons' diagnosis and prognosis were correct. So, I had to go through a diagnostic wasteland once again. However, I did receive one new diagnosis, OCD, which made good sense to me even if, by itself, it did not explain a lot of things in my present and past. For example, OCD did not explain my developmental delay, my hypersensitivity and anxiety, or my lack of people sense, "cultural divide," and isolation.

Ramona, who had become an established psychiatrist in the Boston area, had attended a lecture on Asperger's given by the AANE, which was then the Asperger Association of New England. She thought that they had, in her words, "described me to a tee" in terms of outward symptoms and development. So, in 2007 she referred me to AANE, which, in turn, referred me to the support group in Portland, Maine, with which I have been affiliated since. At that time, the group was facilitated by a mother whose son was in the group.

AANE and the Asperger Adult Support Group/Supporting Others with ASD

I remember the faces when I walked in for the first time more than 10 years ago. I found that I had more things in common with those in this support group than almost any other group I had ever attended. For the first time, I found people a lot like me – and with issues like mine!

About six months later, the mother who was facilitating the group was looking for a volunteer to be co-facilitator, as the other co-facilitator had stepped down. I volunteered. A few months later, she herself stepped down, and I became the facilitator, a role I have assumed ever since. During that time, I have also given talks and presentations on Asperger's, in addition to keeping the support group going. I have also done some mentoring of other younger people with Asperger's. Other facilitators came on board, including our current ones, Nathan, and Wilma, who is co-authoring this book with Eric and me.

Aside from me giving to the support group, it has given back to me. This support group has helped my social life and experience grow, as well as helped heal a traumatic past. I am currently working as a computer programmer/analyst, as well as maintaining my piano performance. I often play for my friends at events. I still very much enjoy mathematics and have done one-on-one tutoring and mentoring in this field as well as computer science and physical science.

Part 3:

Wilma Wake

What Is Wrong with Me?

By Wilma

What is wrong with me? What...what...what? I've asked that question every day of my life since I was old enough to talk.

My mom may have been the first to pose the question. I remember being about five and standing out in the snow in front of the big apartment building where we had a third-floor rental. I yelled for Mom to come help me. She rushed out, and then got angry.

"You yelled at me to come out here, and you just needed help getting your mitten back on? *What is wrong with you? If you need help with your mitten, you come up to me." Oh. That makes sense,* I thought. *I could just take my mitten up to Mom to fix it in the apartment. She didn't need to come down. Mom never told me that. I didn't know. What is wrong with me?*

A few years later, Mom encouraged me to cross the street and play with the other neighborhood kids. They seemed to cluster at a house where there was a big yard. It looked like they were having fun. But when I walked over there, I was stumped. *What were these kids doing?* They were playing some sort of game - running and hiding. *What was the game? How did you play it?* It wasn't so bad that I didn't know the rules. What was hard is that everyone else *did.* How did they know these rules? Who taught them? Why wasn't I being taught? I couldn't figure out the game, and I was too embarrassed to ask. *What was wrong with me?* When no one noticed, I slipped back across the street, and told Mom I wanted to read a book.

I was a good student through elementary school. However, I often forgot that something was wrong with me and inadvertently blurted out questions and comments. I believed teachers literally when they said: "If you have a question, someone else probably has it, too. You'll help others with *your* questions." That made sense, and it was reassuring, since I usually had lots of questions. But I learned the hard way that that advice applied to other kids, but not to me. If I had a question, I was probably the only one who had it, and I would irritate the teacher by asking it.

My report cards always indicated excellent academic work, but with teacher comments like these: *Wilma asks too many questions. She asks before she thinks. If she would stop and think, she would realize she knows the answer.* I came to accept that I couldn't ask questions. Except, of course, for the Big Question: *WHAT is wrong with me?*

Years later, as an adult, I read Rudy Simone's book *Aspergirls.* She wrote: "It is not uncommon for us, when we're young, to ask too many questions of others, which makes them uncomfortable. If we could set the tone, we would probably be more comfortable, but we can't so we shut down" [Simone, 2010a, Kindle loc. 1194].

As I grew older, I was increasingly left out of conversations because I couldn't get the jokes or the cultural references. Other kids knew about sport teams, different musicians, and movie stars; even what things were in fashion. I could never figure out where they got their information.

As a teen, fashion drove me crazy. Mom would have to tell me things like, "you know that hem length...[or color or style] is not 'in' this year. We need to get you something else." By then, I knew better than to ask anyone what was in fashion, but I had no idea how to find out on my own. Was there some sort of guidebook about what is in fashion? Where do I find a copy? Or does some group get together and vote on it? Isn't there a record of the votes?

In college, I met a psychology student through computer dating. We dated for a long time and then started to talk about marriage. My mom asked, "Wilma, do you really love this guy?" I didn't have a clue. I went to the library and researched "love." What was it other people felt when they said they were in love? Why didn't everyone have to research this topic in the library before getting married? I could not find an answer. So, I just got married.

In later years, I read this in Simone's book "Aspergirls like myself have married because we were at a certain age; we didn't know what love was, we just thought it was the right time [Simone, 2010a, Kindle loc. 1194]."

The marriage went okay for many years. We were both starting our careers, and neither of us wanted children. Even after marriage, I couldn't stop going to school. The structure of the academic environment was the only place I felt safe. I excelled academically and had a quiet home life with my studious husband. I ended up with two doctorates and three master's degrees before I stopped going to school: MEd, MSW, PhD in Social Foundations of Education, MDiv and D. Min. I have satisfying careers that I love but have always lived in fear and monitored myself to avoid saying or doing something inappropriate.

I went into social work. Simone wrote, "Many of us will become interested in psychology and the helping professions along the way, in spite of our diagnosis or in search of it. We find we want to help and nurture others in their journeys because we know how hard it can be [Simone, 2010a, Kindle loc.1002]."

And I went into ministry. Simone's book said this:

> Some people, like author Bill Stillman [2006] believe that children with autism have a 'God connection' that their deficits are compensated by a higher spiritual awareness which give them access to Knowledge and gifts [Simone, 2010a, Kindle loc. 2151].

My husband and I eventually split up and went our separate ways. I thrived in living alone with my pets and maintaining a work life, but not a social one. I was content living alone. Until I wasn't.

My life turned upside down in my mid-sixties. I was working with a lot of children who were on the autism spectrum. I felt I needed to understand autism better, so started reading and taking workshops. One evening, I was lying on my bed reading, with my two dogs snuggled up to me. I had just picked up Rudy Simone's *Aspergirls*. It was extremely interesting and would help me understand autistic girls in my practice. Suddenly, I felt struck by lightning as I bolted out of bed. I had just read her statements about how female autistics are different from their male counterparts.

> Females are generally better at socializing in small doses. May even give the appearance of skilled, but it is a "performance." Like her male counterpart, will shut down in social situations once overloaded. Like males, she will dress comfortably, but may be thought androgynous, as she may have an aversion to makeup and complicated hair and clothing styles.

More likely to keep pets for emotional support, but not always, due to sensory issues [Simone, 2010a. kindle loc. 2123-2151]. I was in shock. That described *me* and *my life*! I *couldn't* be on the spectrum. Could I? I was flabbergasted. I didn't realize it then, but I had just fallen into a deep hole.

Since that dramatic moment when I absolutely knew that I was on the autism spectrum, I've never doubted it. But as a social worker, I felt I needed confirmation from a professional. Fortunately, I knew a few to whom I had referred clients. So, I consulted a neuropsychologist to confirm my diagnosis.

The four years since my diagnosis have shattered all my previous conceptions of myself and opened my heart to a new community of friends and, for the first time, a positive concept of myself—at least on most days. My life has evolved to where it is today at age 70. I love doing play therapy with children and expressive therapy with adults. Most of my clients are autistic or family members of autistics. I don't feel any desire to retire, and I get by happily with my house on a few acres of land with my pets.

I live a comfortable life for an Asperwoman.

WHAT WE WANTED TO KNOW

Once we got the green light on the book proposal, we began to distribute our survey to other autistic adults over 50. There was so much we wanted to know about our generational peers – those who were over 50 and knew or suspected they were on the spectrum:

1. What was it like being children, teens, and adults with minimal diagnostic information existing for autistics – especially those seen as high functioning?

2. How were they doing now – with relationships, jobs, health, and resources for autism?

3. What kind of help did they need? What wisdom did they have to share?

4. When and how did they get a diagnosis – and how did they feel about it? How did it change their lives?

That last question is particularly important to us because we have come to value a book, *The Nine Degrees of Autism*, edited by Philip Wylie, Wenn Lawson, and Luke Beardon [2016]. It explores the process by which one learns about the diagnosis, comes to terms with it, and faces the life changes that might be involved.

We put our questions into three main areas we wanted to explore:

1. The beliefs about autism that existed when we were born and as we grew up. This would involve some historical research.

2. The experiences of our generational peers through their lives. This would require us to do a worldwide survey with some follow-up interviews.

3. A framework that would allow us to integrate all that we have learned into our lives. This would involve an understanding of the "nine degrees" as well as listening to the voices of 150 of us from the "lost generation."

WHY WE CREATED THE SURVEY

We saw no way to get the answers to our questions without conducting our own research.

Autistic adults today who are over 50 grew up in a time when there was no concept of Autism Spectrum Disorder [ASD]. Rarely did anyone come across the word *Asperger's*. You would have had to read German to read the works of Hans Asperger before they were translated into English.

Those of us born before 1965 grew up in a world that did not have a diagnosis for us. We settled for *quirky, weird, slow,* and *retard*. By the time there was a diagnosis – and our generation started hearing about it – many of us were in our fifties, sixties, and older. What has it done to this generation – unique in history – to grow up when autism was becoming known as a severely debilitating disease, only to be diagnosed with it later in life? We wanted to find answers to those questions.

Nearly every paper on autism in older adults comes to the same conclusion: that there is startlingly little research on the subject. The few papers that do exist tend to be single case studies or very small samples. There seems to be wide agreement on this point.

OUR STUDY

See Appendix 4 for the survey we provided. It was posted online through Survey Gizmo, and we sent the link to autism groups around the world.

OUR RESPONDENTS

We hesitate to view our respondents as simply statistics. Many of them have become friends and colleagues. We'll not only introduce our 150 participants as survey takers, but will also share some of their stories.

OUR RESPONDENTS: THE STATISTICS

Around 300 people started filling out the questionnaire, and 150 completed it. Our results are limited to those 150 completed questionnaires. In addition to presenting our statistical findings, for each question, we will share some of the many written comments we received. Most of the quotations are from the stories of people who are included in the appendix, as indicated by an asterisk [*].

The 150 completed questionnaires became our study. We show a statistical breakdown of the 150 by gender, age, sexual orientation, country of residence and other demographic factors. A summary of those statistics follows, with additional details in Appendix 2.

Here's a quick rundown on our respondents. Please see "Who Are Our Respondents – the Statistics" under Appendix 1 which provides relevant graphs and tables.

- 56% are male, 44% female.
  It makes sense that our subjects included more males than females, since autism is widely considered to be more common in males, although it seems that the percentage of females is larger than what population surveys suggest. Recent research has shown that girls' symptoms are often "camouflaged" better than boys' [Dean, Harwood, & Casari, 2017]. Much of the early studies of autism focused on boys, and even today we probably know less about characteristics of female autistics.
- 58% are in their 50s, 36% in their 60s, and 5% in their 70s, and one respondent was over 80.
  We suspect that the higher number of participants in their fifties reflects the fact that some of the younger adults have had more exposure to information about autism, and thus may be more likely to seek diagnosis. In addition, older adults are more likely to have more health conditions that impair communication (or to have passed on), and less likely to have seen the survey online.
- 34% are Christian, 33% atheist/agnostic, 15% "general spirituality," 5% Jewish, 3% Eastern religions and 10% other religious preference.
  The 33% of those surveyed identifying as atheist or agnostic contrasts with a 7% rate for the U.S. overall [Pew Research Center, 2014] and confirms previous studies suggesting higher rates of atheism among autistics [Caldwell-Harris et al., 2012]. This difference corresponds to a p value of < .0001, which statistically is highly significant.
- 78% are heterosexual, 3% gay, 2% bisexual, 1% lesbian, 1% transgendered, 4% asexual, and 11% not sure/prefer not to answer/other sexual identity.
  The 78% of respondents describing themselves as heterosexual is markedly lower than the 97% reported in national samples [Ward, Dahlhamer, Galinsky, & Joestl, 2014]. The difference between the rate of heterosexuality in our sample and the national rate is also highly significant, corresponding to a statistical p value of < .0001. In addition, males were significantly more likely than females to be heterosexual [86% vs. 68%, with a p value of .0101]. Other researchers report similar findings [e.g., Hendrickx, 2015].
- 44% are U.S. residents, 48% U.K. residents, and the remainder [about 8%] live in other countries,

including Ireland, Canada, Germany, New Zealand, Kenya, Thailand, Morocco, Netherlands, and Australia.

- They reside in at least 26 American states, including MA, ME, TX, NE, MD, WV, DC, NH, WA, CO, ID, DE, NY, MO, RI, PA, HI, WI, AZ, TN, CA, OR, IL, GA, FL, and NJ. The U.K. residents are also widely distributed, from areas including Scotland, Wales, London, Nottinghamshire, Warwickshire, Birmingham, Essex, Hertfordshire, Yorkshire, Somerset, Dorset, Cambridge, Surrey, Sussex, Norwich, Lincolnshire, Hampshire, Norfolk, and Kent.
- Respondents reported a variety of ethnic or national group identities. The majority, 133 [88.7%], indicated being either Caucasian or of European descent. One respondent each indicated African American, Japanese, Australian, and Middle Eastern. Two respondents indicated Native American, one of our participants indicated Jewish [which may overlap with Caucasian], and six did not provide an answer. In all, it is a heavily European/Caucasian group, raising a concern about potential underrepresentation of certain ethnic groups. The survey was open to anyone on the spectrum over age 50, and efforts were made to obtain a diverse group of respondents, at least within the English-speaking world. Researchers consistently find that minorities are less likely to receive a diagnosis of autism [Travers, Tincani, & Kremien, 2011]. Perhaps future studies will make greater efforts to reach older minority autistics, a little-studied population.
- 79% were diagnosed with autism by a professional; 17% are self-diagnosed. The women had a significantly lower frequency of professional diagnosis, i.e., they were more frequently self-diagnosed, than the men.

OUR RESPONDENTS: THE STORIES

Getting to know the generous people who completed our survey has been a moving experience. Each of us is unique, yet there are so many commonalities among us. About 15% of the respondents were randomly selected to participate in a follow-up interview, and their stories are included in the appendix. A few others requested to be interviewed, and we included them as well. Finally, we present the life stories of about 10 more of our respondents who gave many extensive answers. We have changed names and identifying details except for those who gave us written permission to use their actual names.

We interviewed about 36 of the 150 who completed the questionnaire. A few of the stories we found we could not include due to permissions issues, so the appendix includes 30 of the stories. These stories can be found in Appendix 1.

Some people elected to have their first name used, and a few wanted their full names used. The others are given pseudonyms, and details of their lives are disguised, except for age and country/state of residence. For everyone we quote, we give the person's age as of 2016 [when the survey was conducted] and indicate where they lived then by the following abbreviations:

United Kingdom	UK
Australia	Aus.
New Zealand	NZ
Wales	Wales
Canada	CAN
United States:	
Northeast	NE
Southeast	SE
Midwest	MW
Southwest	SW
West	W
Other	OTH

Those whose life stories are included are marked with an asterisk [*] after the location code. Please also note that we have retained the British spellings, as appropriate.

THE NINE DEGREES: AN OVERVIEW

Our survey was based in part on the Nine Degrees of Autism model [Wylie et al., 2016]. You can find a complete copy of our survey in Appendix 3. The copy of the survey is labeled in terms of which sections cover which degrees. We didn't label them in the original survey, as we weren't as organized then as we were after completing the results.

This developmental model can help us understand the changes we go through in coming to grips with our autism.

First Degree: Being born autistic

The model assumes that every autistic person was born autistic. Hans Asperger himself raised the question of "genetic determination." Another pioneer of autism research, Leo Kanner, also concluded that autism is always present at birth and that there is no "cure" for the neurological condition. Leo Kanner wrote in his 1943 article: "We must assume that these children have come into the world with innate physical and intellectual handicaps" [p. 226]. Kanner did have a foray into "refrigerator mothers" for a while but finally recanted, absolved mothers, and returned to his conviction that autism was inborn.

Attwood proposes three distinct pathways that contribute to a child being born with autism:

1. Genetic inheritance of autism at conception

2. Genetic material that causes autism [before birth]

3. Toxins in utero that affect the child's brain development [Wylie et al., 2016].

Environmental models [refrigerator parents, vaccines; see Part I] have flourished at times, but there seems to be widespread acceptance at present that autism is present at birth.

Second Degree: Knowing you are different

Louise Page, a professional autism counselor and mentor in Australia, wrote about the second degree in this inspiring book. She says: "The individual on the autism spectrum attains the second degree of autism when becoming aware that he or she is different from others who may be considered 'neuro-typical' [NT]. The journey to uncover this, though, is different for us all" [Wylie, et al., 2016, p. 57].

Page goes on to say that children may first be aware of their difference when they find themselves watching other kids more than playing with them, or perhaps joining a group only to be ignored or bullied. As the child grows, she becomes more aware of her differences. This feeling can develop as a result of being treated with "disregard, avoidance, teasing, or alienation" [Wylie et al., 2016, p. 58].

It should come as no surprise, therefore, that one of the first grassroots autism websites was WrongPlanet.net, and a list of popular autism book titles says it all: *Be Different, Different Minds, Right Address...Wrong Planet, Pretending to Be Normal, In a Different Key*, and *Freaks, Geeks, and Asperger Syndrome*. But knowing that you're different doesn't mean knowing *why* you're different.

Most of our generation went through our entire childhood and much of our adulthood before learning of our autism. Unfortunately, this often resulted in the next degree, described below.

Third Degree: Developing secondary health issues

Laura Battles, M.Ed. is an autism specialist in the U.K. with 20 years' experience as a teacher, manager, director, and consultant. She wrote the third degree chapter in *The Nine Degrees of Autism*. She notes: "The key difference between the second and third degrees of autism is that the individual does not suffer initially at the second degree stage; but later adverse environmental factors cause suffering at the third degree stage." [Wylie et al., 2016, p. 74]. By the third degree, it may become clear that a child is not reaching developmental milestones at the same time as her peers.

A parent or teacher may notice that a child's development is behind classmates. Without understanding the reason, any intervention, no matter how well-intended, could make things worse. Without theory of mind [perceiving intentions and feelings of others], autistics are vulnerable to abuse and scapegoating. Low self-esteem can be severe in those not diagnosed. Battles says:

> Many people with autism who are undiagnosed particularly in early teenage years can develop a significant sense of self-loathing, anger, and frustration in relation to the expectations placed on them. The task of waking in the morning to face a world where your presence is abhorred because other people fail to comprehend or accept that an individual may see, feel, and experience the world differently can slowly erode like a cancer any sense of belonging and meaning. [Wylie et al., 2016, p. 76]

Undiagnosed autistics in this stage acquire a range of secondary problems, including depression and anxiety.

Battles [Wylie et al., 2016] points out that these issues will be with the autistic child at least until the sixth degree, when finding the authentic self.

Attwood [2007] describes four main coping strategies: retreat into fantasy, substance abuse, blaming others, and pretending to be normal. Our group exhibits a definite trend: These coping strategies were more common in childhood and early adulthood, but tapered off in midlife, perhaps as a result of finding the right outside support.

The definition of "late diagnosis" concerns the length of time the individual lives at the third degree of autism. This developmental stage is particularly challenging because the individual has developed a false self and is not equipped to protect himself or herself from negative environmental factors [Wylie et al., 2016, p. 78].

In fact, autistic persons typically feel some unhappiness from the third degree through the sixth degree, until they fully understand and accept their identity. Sadly, this is particularly true of the lost generation. We've grown up learning the skills of blending in, trying to look like those around us. By the time we are in our fifties, we no longer remember who we really are.

It is well established that autism is often accompanied by other comorbid conditions. Some of the more common conditions that co-occur with autism include ADHD, seizure disorders, depression, phobias, and OCD [Kats et al., 2013; Leyfer et al., 2006]. Sadly, most of us have had lifelong anxiety and stress. Over 90% of our respondents recalled having these feelings from their teens to at least age 50. A full three-quarters of our group also experienced depression during the same period. Furthermore, 87% recalled childhood bullying, and 83% of those who felt targeted reported workplace discrimination as well.

Fourth Degree: Self-identification

Dr. Debra Moore is a psychologist who has published extensively in the autism field. Her publications include *The Loving Push: How Parents and Professionals Can Help Spectrum Kids Become Successful Adults* [Moore & Grandin, 2016]. Moore points out that events prompting self-identification can include media reports, having a child diagnosed, having the question raised by a mental health professional, and experiencing a major life crisis or transition such as childbirth or retirement [Wylie et al., 2016].

It is more common today for a child to be diagnosed at a young age. We don't yet know the experience of these degrees for a child who reaches the fourth degree in childhood. This is an important topic for future research.

Fifth Degree: Considering all the options

After developing an awareness of one's autism, at some point the way forward becomes less clear: "a landscape of opportunity and a road full of pitfalls and open caverns" [Wylie et al., 2016, p. 109]. One respondent said, *finding out I've had autism late in life has been so incredibly freeing, but it also came with a lot of sadness and regret.* It is difficult to quantify how many of our survey takers have experienced the fifth degree of autism.

Stephen Shore, PhD, wrote the chapter on the fifth degree in Wylie et al. [2016]. He says:

> Having come this far and gaining a sense of self-identity one might think he or she has arrived. However, the word "commencement" may be more appropriate, as in reality this is just the beginning of your true [new] life. This is the time when you will battle with unique challenges that those of us living as autistic individuals fear and feel the most. This is because we are encountering "change" from all angles. [p. 109]

Shore has a long history of involvement with autism. He is currently assistant professor of special education at Adelphi University. He has published many books, including *Beyond the Wall: Personal Experiences with Autism and Asperger Syndrome; Ask and Tell: Self-Advocacy and Disclosure for People on the Autism Spectrum;* and *Living Along the Autism Spectrum: What It Means to Have Autism or Asperger Syndrome.*

Shore was diagnosed at a young age. It did not, however, change his need to experience the fifth degree. In fact, he had to go through it twice. He writes:

> Twice I have gone through phase 5 with the second trip being done much more mindfully. With the benefit of early diagnoses [sic] at age two and a half, coupled with my parents openly using the word "autism," since age five and a half I knew I had autism. However, it was not until I reexamined how autism affected me during my struggles toward the end of a doctoral degree in music did I begin to develop an understanding of what it meant to me to be on the autism spectrum. [Wylie et al., 2016, p. 111]

We all have life options, and degree five is an opportunity to examine them. We transition out of the fifth degree when we come to terms with our new self and are examining our options for the future. We then find ourselves in the sixth degree.

Sixth Degree: Crisis of identity/resolution to live with autism

The initial diagnosis can be very unsettling, triggering an identity crisis. "Suddenly all the confusion you've experienced throughout your life begins to make sense" [Wylie et al., 2016, p. 130]. Attwood says this about the sixth degree: "This degree is about acknowledging which parts of the self to accept, which parts to change, and which parts cannot be changed" [Wylie et al., 2016, p. 11]. Here are some other statements that shed light on the sixth degree:

- John Elder Robison recalls, "I was autistic. Everything else seemed secondary to that new facet of me. *This must be how it feels when you find you have cancer*, I thought" [Robison, 2011, p. 8].
- For single mother Heidi Kunisch, "Everything changed. I sat there thinking so many things. Will I be treated differently? Will life get better or worse?" [in Ariel & Naseef, 2006, p. 182].
- As Karla Fisher, senior technical program manager at Intel, describes it, "Now I had to replay my whole life, with this thing that was deemed a disorder by this doctor and his peers...At first, this realization made me feel very alone" [in Grandin, 2012].

Over time, the diagnosis leads to identity realignment, a new sense of self.

Seventh Degree: Self-acceptance

The 7th degree of autism in the Wiley, et.al. book is addressed by Dr. Wenn Lawson: psychologist, autism researcher, lecturer, and writer. He writes: "This development [toward acceptance] is much more than a grudging tolerance of autism, but rather believing that "our autism will be the key that unlocks our future" [Wylie et al., 2016, p. 139]. Dr. Lawson addresses this degree through a series of action steps in the chapter on the 7th degree:

1. Acceptance of our label
2. Believing in ourselves
3. Seeking I.T. support [low- or high-tech]
4. Self-acceptance
5. Environmental support
6. Exercise
7. Sensory dysphoria [accepting our sensory limitations]
8. Coping with change
9. Interests [exploring our skills and passions]

By emphasizing our strengths and interests and utilizing appropriate supports and strategies, we become energized to move forward.

Only a minority of adult autistics reach the final stages – the eighth and ninth degree.

Eighth Degree: Unconditional service

After letting go of past hurts, the focus in the eighth degree becomes "active service to help others...passionately applying your gifts with an open heart. The key to success is being aware of our gifts and finding a way to apply them for the benefit of humanity" [Wylie et al., 2016, p. 161]. Sarah Heath tells us:

> This is where self-acceptance and identity alignment combine to empower the autistic individual forward. This gives more self-confidence in his or her abilities, but still with skills to learn and practice, and many issues needing to be acknowledged. The autistic individual starts to create and later accept a place in society, where he or she can use his or her skills and receive acknowledgement for them. Eighth degree autism is more than a promise, it's now on the horizon. [Wylie et al., 2016, p. 151]

In time, we can let go of our hurts and problems of the past and explore ways we can make a difference in the world. Throughout, it is important to stay engaged in support systems, such as counseling, coaching, support groups, meditation, and treatment for issues such as depression.

Ninth Degree: Recognition, mastery, unity

Temple Grandin and Debra Moore wrote together about the final degree:

> The ninth degree of the developmental trajectory of autism continues this movement into an increasingly complex, nuanced, and personal actualization. Grounded in awareness and acceptance of one's autism, this period adds greater appreciation of all parts of oneself. Autism no longer defines our entire being – it is simply a label that helps highlight both struggles to be cognizant of, and unique gifts to be treasured. Life goes on within the awareness of our common humanity, no matter what our personal neurological wiring. [in Wylie et al., 2016, p. 164]

While some of those who have reached the ninth degree have worldwide fame [e.g., Temple Grandin], others apply their mastery in a much smaller sphere such as their local community. It is difficult to determine from people's self-reports if they have reached the ninth degree.

PART I
THE EARLY HISTORY OF AUTISM

Our research focuses on people 50 and older. We used a person's age in 2016 on the date he or she completed the questionnaire for our study. That means that in order to participate in our research, a person would have to have been born by 1966. So, our research population is largely from the Baby Boomer generation – those born between 1946 and 1964 – but some of our folks, naturally, predate the Baby Boomers, including Donald Triplett – a spectrum elder whom you'll hear about in a moment – who was born in 1933, and was 83 in 2016.

Every generation is unique in some way. In terms of autism, spectrum elders have a common bond: We grew up when there was minimal understanding of autism and no formal awareness of those who were higher functioning. Things started to change in the 1970s, but most of us grew up before anyone understood who we were. As we age, it's important for us to learn more about ourselves, and to leave a legacy for future generations to understand this worldwide transition in autism awareness. To understand the struggles that beset our spectrum elders, we need to look at what was happening in the world, and in the world of autism, when we were born and grew up.

This brief historical overview focuses on some of the people who participated in making this history.

Donald Triplett

Donald Triplett was born in Kansas City on Sept. 9, 1933, and is still doing well at age 85.

He was the first child born to Mary and Beamon Triplett. Everything about baby Donald seemed normal at first, but his parents were soon concerned that their baby wasn't interacting with them normally. As a toddler Donald became even more withdrawn, not wanting to be held or connect with others. At age 3, he still couldn't feed himself. Mary was exhausted, having to be with him every moment for his safety.

Mary and Beamon took their 3-year-old son to the family doctor, who concluded that the boy was being overstimulated by his parents. The doctor gave the usual advice for that era: *institutionalize him.* Parents were urged to put such "defective children" in an institution for life and cut off all contact. Mary and Beamon lived at a time when people believed that children with disabilities were a danger to society and were considered less than human [Donvan & Zucker, 2016].

So, with both sadness and hope, Mary and Beamon drove their son to the Preventatorium in Sanatorium, Mississippi, where children were typically sent for life. The decision was very difficult for the Tripletts, but it was the norm at that time. Parents were shamed when their children were viewed as "defective." "Defective" children included those with epilepsy, Down Syndrome and – as in the case of Donald Tripplett – autism.

The Eugenics Movement

In 1927, six years before Donald Triplett's birth, a pivotal Supreme Court case, *Buck v. Bell,* was handed down that influenced views of people with disabilities for years afterwards. The following are the highlights of *Buck v. Bell* and the eugenics movement that was burgeoning in the 1930s and 1940s.

The state of Virginia wanted to sterilize a woman named Carrie Buck who had been labeled "feeble-minded." [Eventually, it was learned that although she was poorly educated, her IQ was in the normal range]. The chief justice on the case was William Howard Taft, with Louis Brandeis signing the majority opinion. The opinion was written by Oliver Wendell Holmes, who said, referring to Carrie, her mother, and her daughter: "three generations of imbeciles are enough." [Cohen, 2016, p. 1]. Holmes wrote, in the 8-to-1 opinion: "It is better for all the world, if instead of waiting to execute degenerate offspring for crime, or to let them starve for their imbecility, society can prevent those who are manifestly unfit from continuing their kind" [Cohen, 2016, p. 2].

The Supreme Court was working out of a social construct that was spreading rapidly: society would be better off if the "defectives" were sterilized so that they could not reproduce. This ideology was taught in schools.

> Universities were quick to embrace eugenics and give it their intellectual imprimatur. Eugenics was taught at 376 universities and colleges, including Harvard, Columbia, Berkeley, and Cornell. Prominent professors were outspoken in support, including Earnest Hooton, the chairman of Harvard's anthropology department, who warned that educated Americans were selling their "biological birthright for a mess of morons," and called for a "biological purge." [Cohen, 2016, p. 4]

The primary goal of the movement was to maintain superiority of the "Nordic" race, but there was also an intent to stamp out mental illnesses and epilepsy. This movement began in the U.S. and then expanded to Europe, particularly to Hitler and Nazi Germany. The Nazis expanded the concept of "defective" to include children we consider normal today.

Mary and Beamon Triplett of Kansas in 1936 couldn't bear to keep their son in an institution, so they brought their young son home and looked for ways to have a relationship with him. Friends suggested they try that child psychiatrist in Baltimore, Leo Kanner.

Leo Kanner

Leo Kanner had been born to Jewish parents in Austria in 1894. He served in World War I, and then went to medical school, becoming a cardiologist. An American physician friend encouraged him to move to the States, given difficult postwar conditions in Europe. Kanner took that advice and was later extremely grateful that he did. Otherwise, he would have been caught up in the

Holocaust with other Jewish professionals – such as Hans Asperger, a contemporary of Kanner. Indeed, Kanner was to play an important role in helping other Jewish physicians escape the Nazis.

Kanner immigrated to the States in 1924 to take a position as assistant doctor at the South Dakota state hospital. There he got on-the-job training in the psychiatry of children. In 1930, he was offered a position at Johns Hopkins to start a children's psychiatric department. [The concept of "childhood" as being a distinct period of life needing a particular training had only been around for about 30 years.]

By 1933, the year Donald was born, Kanner had become a professor of psychiatry. Two years later he published *Child Psychiatry,* the first textbook in English about children's mental health. He rapidly became well-known in medical circles and was a champion for the needs of children with mental health issues. Kanner was especially fascinated by young children who displayed two features: They were withdrawn, and they had to have a daily routine. He was developing ways of evaluating children in his clinic with the help of psychiatrist Georg Frankl, who had come to the United States from Austria.

Kanner received a letter from Beamon and Mary Triplett about their isolated son, who had just been pulled out of the Preventatorium and was back home in Kansas. They begged Kanner to see their son. He did, and made history. Donald Triplett was the first child Kanner observed in his study. The child psychiatrist was intrigued by the young boy, who was in Kanner's study rooms for several days for rigorous observation. As Kanner considered Donald's unusual behaviors, he also began seeing other children with similar characteristics. Finally, it all came together for Kanner. He wrote a paper in 1943 about 11 children he had been observing. Donald, "Case #1," has become known in the U.S. as "autism's first child" [Donvan & Zucker, 2010].

Kanner's historic 1943 paper begins: "Since 1938, there have come to our attention a number of children whose condition differs so markedly and uniquely from anything reported so far, that each case merits— and, I hope, will eventually receive—a detailed consideration of its fascinating peculiarities" [Silberman, 2015, p. 181]. He proposed two "essential common characteristics" shared by all children with this syndrome. The first was a will to self-isolate, present from birth, that he called *extreme autistic aloneness.* The second common characteristic was a fear of change and surprise, which Kanner named *an anxiously obsessive desire for the maintenance of sameness* [Silberman, 2015].

Kanner didn't name the syndrome in his paper, although he did say that the children had autistic behaviors. A year later, he rewrote the paper for a journal, and called it "early infantile autism."

Kanner is often viewed as the first researcher to use the term "autism." That's not entirely accurate, however. Another researcher across the Atlantic was looking at the same characteristics at the same time.

Hans Asperger

Hans Asperger was also writing about autism around the same time as Kanner, but the first one to use the term *autism* was Swiss psychiatrist Eugene Bleuler. In his study of schizophrenics, Bleuler noticed that some of them – usually adolescents or adults – withdrew from their environment with an inner focus [Donvan & Zucker, 2016, p. 40]. Around 1910, he began to use the term *autistic thinking* to describe that behavior. It came from *auto* – a Greek word meaning *self.* According to Bleuler, we all have healthy periods of inner experience, but for his schizophrenics it continually came and went like hallucinations did. When Kanner started using the term, then, it was like the behavior of schizophrenic adults, but was happening to children.

Hans Asperger was born in 1906 in Austria. He grew up with many intellectual skills but was a very withdrawn child. Some say that he himself had characteristics of Asperger's Syndrome. He studied medicine at the University of Vienna and focused on working with children. He submitted his thesis in 1943: *Autistic Psychopathy in Childhood*, the same year Kanner published his study that included Donald Triplet.

Asperger was only five when a clinic/school was created at the University of Vienna Children's Hospital by radical social reformer and pediatrician Edwin Lazar. Lazar did not believe in treating a child's psychological issues in an office, but rather as part of a community. The child shouldn't be blamed, he felt. He wanted his clinic to become a healthy and nurturing society of its own. It was based on the concept of curative education: *Heilpädagogik*. Lazar wanted to move this field out of special education and into "something more like medical and holistic psychiatry" [Sheffer, 2018, p. 33]. He was able to get the support of Clemens Von Pirquet, head of the children's hospital and highly respected for his medical research. Lazar and Pirquet developed a highly esteemed program within the Vienna Children's Hospital. They received referrals from schools, courts and welfare workers and were able to be of help in treatment and recommendations. They taught courses for social workers, doctors, and teachers and were considered a model treatment setting within the Vienna welfare system. "Curative education dovetailed with the main goal of welfare efforts, which was to socialize children" [Sheffer, 2018, p. 35].

As with the rest of pre-war Vienna, there was a slow drift towards more authoritarian intrusions into child-rearing. In 1929 there was a dramatic change in the children's hospital when Pirquet and his wife were found dead in bed – a double suicide.

There was a bitter political battle over who would lead the school next with Nazi supporters playing an important role in the selection process. Franz Hamburger, a Nazi and eugenicist, was selected for his political views. The prestige of the children's hospital declined as Hamburger worked within a Nazi structure. Edwin Lazar had been allowed to stay but died in 1932. A new hire was needed for the Curative Education Unit. Hamburger hired a twenty-five-year-old young man who had just finished his medical studies on March 31, 1931: Hans Asperger.

The clinic team worked well together and included Anna Weiss, psychiatrist Georg Frankl, and a nun named Sister Viktorine Zak. The team would observe the child during the day to determine a diagnosis. Frankl was especially astute at diagnosis and became the primary diagnostician there. [Frankl ended up later as chief diagnostician at Kanner's clinic in Baltimore].

The Nazis

Questions have been raised for years about the relationship between Asperger and the Nazis in Austria during World War II. Steve Silberman's book, *Neurotribes: The Legacy of Autism and the Future of Neurodiversity* [2015], suggests that Asperger may have had some kinship with the Nazis:

> Though Maria Asperger-Felder's claims that her father never joined the Nazi party are credible, owing to his loyalty to the Wandering Scholars, it's unlikely that he would have been allowed to retain his position at the university without signing a loyalty oath to Hitler, given Pernkopf's 1938 decree. [p. 137]

At the same time, Silberman also saw Asperger as a courageous man who tried to protect children from the Nazis.

Still, Asperger apparently refused to report his young patients to the Reich Committee, which created what he described in a 1974 interview as "a truly dangerous situation" for him. Twice, the Gestapo showed up at his clinic to arrest him. Both times, however, Franz Hamburger used his power as a prominent NSDAP member to intervene in his favor. How can we dare predict the behavior of man? [pp. 137-138]

However, John Donvan and Caren Zucker [2016], whose book *In a Different Key: The Story of Autism* came out a year later than Silberman's, cite evidence that Asperger may have been closer to the Nazis than historians have believed. There was no clear evidence until May of 2010.

A symposium was held in Vienna in 2010 to honor the memory of Dr. Asperger. Everybody seemed to be there to laud Asperger's life and work, except for Herwig Czech, historian, and lecturer at the University of Vienna. He had researched the role of medicine in the Third Reich and found some interesting tidbits on Asperger. Although Asperger never joined the Nazi Party, most of his friends did, and he was treated favorably by the party. He also signed several letters with "Heil Hitler!"

But the most explosive finding was that Asperger signed a letter concerning Herta, a 2-year-old girl, who was sick with encephalitis. She was having a problem with brain development and had developed epilepsy. Herta's mother brought her to *Heilpädagogik*, Asperger's clinic within the Viennese Children's Hospital. Asperger said that the girl must be a terrible burden to her mother and would need "permanent placement at the Spiegelgrund." She was dispatched there at once and died two months later from "pneumonia." The audience at the conference was aghast. They knew what "placement at the Spiegelgrund" meant for the child.

Silberman [2016] wrote an article in response to Donovan and Zucker. He is clear that he sees Asperger as the true discoverer of the "autism spectrum" and the one who anticipated the modern neurodiversity movement. He mentions a letter that Asperger sent to his Nazi friend Hamburger in 1943: "The example of autism shows particularly well how even abnormal personalities can be capable of development and adjustment …This knowledge…gives us the right and the duty to speak out for these children with the whole force of our personality."

Some researchers have been critical of Silberman's favorable view of Asperger, including Dr. Lutz Kaelber from the University of Vermont, who specializes in the sociology of collective memory and crimes against children in Nazi Germany.

> Recent attention to the Spiegelgrund has been paid by the science author Steve Silberman in his book *Neurotribes*, which in one chapter addresses "children's euthanasia" in the context of Viennese medicine under der Nazis, with a focus on Dr. Hans Asperger. The author does not engage with some of the most recent literature [much of it in German]. This literature includes the foundational studies by Herwig Czech [2011, 2014a, 2015], who shows Dr. Asperger...to have been part of a commission as a "special education consultant" for the city of Vienna …. At the Pediatric Clinic, at least one case is known in which Dr. Asperger by way of his evaluation initiated the direct transfer of a child to the Spiegelgrund, the almost-three-year-old Herta Schreiber, in 1941. The child died less than 3 months after Dr. Asperger's evaluation, at a time when there was little question among leading medical practitioners about the role of the Spiegelgrund as a killing facility for infants and children. [Kaelber, 2015]

We now have concrete answers to Hans Asperger's relationship to the Nazis from Dr. Edith Sheffer's book *Asperger's Children: The Origins of Autism in Nazi Vienna* [2018].

Sheffer provides disturbing and definitive evidence of Asperger's role in the Third Reich:

> When it came to the child euthanasia program, Asperger does not appear as a submissive figure, working within a system beyond his influence. Nor does he appear to have been coerced, since many of his choices were elective. While knowing of the euthanasia program, Asperger publicly urged his colleagues to send children to Spiegelgrund; he participated in numerous Reich offices that sent children to Spiegelgrund; and he sent children to Spiegelgrund directly from his clinic. He met many of the youths one-on-one, talked with their parents, and studied them closely over time. Available records suggest that Asperger sent dozens of children to Spiegelgrund who perished, and sent numerous children to Spiegelgrund who risked death but survived. None of these were simple or ordinary actions. They required initiative, determination, and Improvisation. [Sheffer, 2018, p. 217]

One of the reviews of this book says this:

> Sheffer also gives a long-overdue and gripping analysis of Asperger's own writing before, during and after the Third Reich. She details his wartime denigration of the cognitively and physically disabled children in his care. She frames him as complicit in "negative eugenics" and a careerist. Jewish doctors were forbidden to practise public medicine during the Anschluss. While never a Nazi party member, Asperger did not protest about his more senior Jewish colleagues' exclusion. Aged 28, he became the head of the Curative Education Clinic within Vienna's prestigious children's hospital. [Baron, 2018, p. 1]

The release of this book has confirmed what many in autism communities were suspecting: that Hans Asperger was far more complicit with the Nazi regime than previously thought.

How important are these revelations? A reviewer of *In a Different Key* says: "Whether Asperger was a saint or a sinner should not dominate the discourse around autism, which could better concentrate on whether the concept of autism as a single entity has had its day." [Baron, 2016].

The question for our purposes is: What impact – if any – did the Kanner-Asperger influence have on the generation of autistic babies being born in the 1930s and 1940s?

Refrigerator Mothers

Life for Kanner in the U.S. was drastically different from that of Hans Asperger in Austria. Kanner's career was skyrocketing from his "discovery" of autism. He felt increasing pressure to bow to the psychoanalytic forces around him and admit that bad parenting caused autism – or "refrigerator parents," which quickly became "refrigerator mothers." In April of 1948, *Time Magazine* published a story about refrigerator moms and autism.

> The parents wanted to do the right thing by them; but their idea of the right thing was "the mechanized service of the kind which is rendered by an over-conscientious gasoline station attendant." The children, says Dr. Kanner, were "kept neatly in a refrigerator which didn't defrost." Were the cold parents freezing their children into schizophrenia? Dr. Kanner did not say yes or no; but he has found no case of infantile autism among children of "unsophisticated" parents. Said he of his pathetic patients: "Their withdrawal

seems to be an act of turning away . . . to seek comfort in solitude. ["Frosted Children,"
Time Magazine, April 26, 1948]

Kanner had crossed over from insisting that children with autism were born that way to blaming "cold" professional women for not being affectionate enough. [To be fair, Kanner also gave fathers some of the blame.]

It is unclear how much Kanner pursued "refrigerator mothers" after his 1943 paper. He did talk more about the impact of parenting, and somewhere around 1951 he made a reference to mothers as "refrigerators that didn't defrost." It was after that that *autism* as a word in conversation took off. In 1969, Kanner tried to set the record straight when addressing an audience containing many parents. He said: "'As for the refrigerator-mother myth, that was a misunderstanding. I have been misquoted often as having said that it is all the parents' fault,' he told his listeners. 'I never said that.' Then he delivered seven words, to electrifying effect: 'Herewith I acquit you people as parents,' he said" [Donvan & Zucker, 2016, p. 93].

Kanner was not alone during the years he was blaming mothers. He had a companion and supporter: Bruno Bettelheim.

Bruno Bettelheim

Bettelheim is a controversial figure who was active in the autism field during this period. Many books have been written about him from various perspectives.

Bettelheim was director of The Orthogenic School in Chicago, which had some similarities to the Children's School of Hans Asperger. There are many accounts from former students and staff about widespread cruelty. Bettelheim played a significant role in popularizing the theory that cold mothers caused autism. Kanner may have introduced that concept, but Bettelheim was often listened to by parents. Kanner wrote for academic audiences. Dr. B. wrote for the public – in *Harper's*, *Redbook*, the *New York Times Magazine*, *Life*, and others. He also had a regular column in *Ladies Home Journal*. Similarly, his books, such as *The Empty Fortress*, were geared to a general audience. In short, his ideas permeated society and were especially absorbed by mothers. There is no question, therefore, of Bettelheim's role in blaming mothers for autism. He would not even allow parents to visit his Orthogenic School for fear that they would contaminate their child's treatment.

Empowered Parents

Given the prevailing professional climate at the time, it was up to mothers and fathers themselves to correct the record on the cause of autism. Many mothers – and fathers – changed the autism landscape forever. Below is an overview of some of them.

Eustacia Cutler

Eustacia Cutler is the mother of the most famous autistic in the world, Temple Grandin. Temple was born in 1947, so she is within the age of our survey population. Eustacia was overwhelmed with the unruly behavior of her toddler, so she dragged Temple to a neurologist, Dr. Bronson Crothers, at Boston Children's Hospital, when she was two years old. Eustacia had had it with Temple's crayon scribblings on her wall and peeing on the rug. Dr. Crothers diagnosed Temple with brain damage and suggested speech therapy. Eustacia enrolled her in speech therapy and hired a nanny to work with her intensively to learn interactive skills.

Temple still wasn't talking at age four, so her parents went back to Boston Children's Hospital for more tests. This time the hospital scheduled them with a psychiatrist, who said Temple had "autism" or "infantile schizophrenia," which is what autism was generally called at that time. On the next visit, he called Eustacia a "hysteric" and recommended foster care for Temple. At home, Temple's father, Richard, was relentless in his desire to institutionalize his daughter, but Eustacia wouldn't hear of it. She was a Harvard graduate who had worked professionally in singing and acting and was certain she could help Temple. Eustacia and Richard eventually divorced.

Eustacia, with Temple and her other children, lived in a supportive Massachusetts community, and spent summers on Nantucket. Eustacia brought all her skills into Temple's upbringing – attending community theater evenings, doing projects with kids, teaching Sunday school, and getting Temple into mainstream schools.

Eustacia spoke at a conference in September of 2015. We asked her what raising Temple was like, compared to autistic children today. She said that Temple had more advantages, in many ways, than children today. She wasn't put in special classes or programs. She was fully integrated into the life of the community and treated just like everyone else. Today, although we have a lot of special services for autistic kids, we don't necessarily make them a full part of their communities.

Eustacia has devoted her life not just to Temple and her other three children, but to the understanding of all people with autism. She continues to write, travel around to talk to interested groups, and maintain a YouTube channel for conversations.

Bernie Rimland

Bernie Rimland was born in 1928 to Russian immigrants. From age 12, he lived in San Diego, where he began to learn the locksmith trade. His parents considered college an extravagance, but Bernie had a yearning to study, so he went to San Diego State University where he was drawn to study psychology. He eventually earned a Ph.D. in experimental psychology from Penn State. Rimland moved back to San Diego, married his childhood sweetheart, and took a research position with the Defense Department in its new Naval Personnel Research and Development Center. [Donvan & Zucker, 2016].

In 1956, he and his wife Gloria were thrilled at the birth of their first child, Mark. They loved parenthood, but something seemed not right. Although he walked and talked normally, Mark never interacted with anyone. The doctor had no clue what the problem was; nor did Rimland, despite his psychology doctorate. Gloria had a vague memory of something from a college psychology class, and Bernie got to work. Soon he unearthed the word "autism" from an old textbook, and his researcher self took off. What could have caused this difficulty for Mark? Rimland found a clear answer: It was Gloria! As he read Bettelheim's works, he became enraged. That was not a description of the loving wife and mother he knew.

By 1958, Rimland was reading every research article he could find on autism. The refrigerator mother theory made no sense to him. For one thing, most autistic kids had non-autistic siblings – why weren't they traumatized by the cold mother? No form of therapy seemed to help. Rimland began to wonder if autistics were born with their autism. By 1960 he started corresponding with a known expert in the field: Dr. Leo Kanner. Kanner was warm and helpful, encouraging Rimland's work. By 1964, Rimland's book *Infantile Autism: The Syndrome and Its Implications for a Neural Theory of Behavior* was published and changed autism history.

Rimland included a form in the back to assess one's child for autistic symptoms. Hundreds of parents were pulling out the questionnaire, filling it in, and sending it to him. He was also getting countless letters from parents telling of their struggles with their autistic children. He responded to each one of them in longhand.

Audrey Flack

If you google the name "Audrey Flack," you'll find a great deal of information about this 85-year-old feminist artist known for photorealism and sculpture. To learn about the other major passion in her life, try googling her name with the word *autism*.

Flack gave birth to an autistic daughter, Melissa, in 1959. (You can learn more about her struggles as a young mother in the book *In a Different Key* [Donvan & Zucker, 2016], where her story is featured in Chapter 10.) In 1964, when Melissa was four years old, Rimland's book was published, but Flack knew nothing about it. She had a BFA from Yale and had studied at the New York University Institute of Fine Arts and Cooper Union in New York City. Yet, at this point in her life, she was penniless and living in a small apartment with her two daughters and a musician husband who was often absent.

The only help she could find for Melissa was at Lenox Hill Hospital in New York, which had a program to study children three to four years of age with severe learning impairments. A lot of commitment was required from parents. They had to bring their child five days a week, and the mother had to come in weekly for therapy. They only accepted children who were dealing with "psychogenic factors" – emotional trauma. It was assumed that the mother had caused the problems through emotional distance, and Flack found herself being pushed away from involvement with her daughter's treatment. The best part of the program for Audrey was connecting with other mothers of autistic children who knew they were not the cause of their children's autism.

In the years after that, Flack became a devoted advocate for the rights of autistic children and adults. Melissa, now 58, lives in a group home that her parents helped to establish. Flack has continued to flourish in her artistic career, as well as being involved in fighting for services for autistic children.

Ruth Sullivan

In 1964, the same year Flack was taking Melissa to Lenox Hill and Rimland's book was being published, Ruth Sullivan was taking her son Joey to a psychiatrist in Albany, NY. Many mothers, stumped with a child's difficult interaction, brought their children to this psychiatrist, who was starting a group for mothers to share feelings with each other. Sullivan thought that it was a great idea for mothers to meet – not just to share feelings but to organize. A former army nurse, Sullivan had a master's degree in public health. Her husband was an English professor. She was in an advantageous position to do research. And research she did, going through medical journals to read about autism. When she came across the statement that Joey had autism because she was cold and unfeeling, she became furious – that conclusion meant that no research was needed into causes of autism, and no treatment was needed – except to defrost those cold mothers! Sullivan now had a cause – to enlist autism mothers to be part of the solution, not the problem.

A plan came together in her mind. She would accept the psychiatrist's invitation to join her group of mothers for one session. At that session, Sullivan wrote her name and phone number on a small piece of paper and surreptitiously passed it around the group of mothers. Every one of the women she contacted wanted to be part of her group. A movement had begun. Ruth gathered mothers in the Albany area to start a local support group.

By 1965, Sullivan found Bernard Rimland's book, *Infantile Autism: The Syndrome and Its Implications for a Neural Theory of Behavior* [Rimland, 1964]. Bernard Rimland was a psychologist and father of an autistic son. He had done extensive research on autism, finding that "refrigerator mothers" was the prevailing theory of causation. He knew his wife hadn't caused their son's autism! Rimland's book created considerable enthusiasm among parents of autistic children who had found a professional who didn't blame mothers for autism.

It took a while for Sullivan to hear about Rimland's book, but when she did, she contacted him and the two bonded instantly. They both had a goal of starting a parents' support group. On Nov. 15, 1965, the National Society for Autistic Children was founded at a home in Teaneck, New Jersey. History was made on that day: the parents' movement in the U.S. was born. The house was overflowing with parents who drove from all over the Northeast. Sullivan drove down from Albany. Rimland flew out from San Diego. Participants were excited and hopeful [Donovan & Zucker, 2016].

This history had already been made by autism parents in the UK, where in 1961, parents had started the Society for Psychotic Children. However, Donvan and Zucker [2016] see the research in the U.K. as significantly different from that in the U.S.:

> Yet despite their common language, American and British researchers had noticeably different priorities. Americans sought to treat – and even cure – autism. Among researchers in the United States, there was a sense of emergency, a drive to find solutions as soon as possible. In Britain, the approach was calmer, aimed more at finding an explanation for autism. Driven more by curiosity, British researchers sought to map the contours of autism and understand the autistic mind. The British approach – which they stuck with for the next five decades – produced a distinctive set of outcomes. A small group of British-trained experimental psychologists and research psychiatrists came up with insights that permanently altered how autism was perceived and understood around the world. [pp. 273-274]

Lorna Wing

In 1956, British psychiatrist Lorna Wing was riding a train with her 6-month-old daughter when she noticed that another baby about the same age was excited to see sheep out the window and was very interactive with his mom. Lorna's child, Susie, was withdrawn and uninterested. Lorna and her husband, John, were stumped. Although both were psychiatrists, they had no idea what was wrong with Susie. When she was 3, John went to a lecture on autism, where he started to make the connection.

One day soon after that, John came home excited about a lecture he had attended by psychiatrist Mildred Creak. They took Susie to Dr. Creak, who confirmed the diagnosis of autism. They felt discouraged when they found no viable treatment options. She wouldn't be allowed in school, and institutionalization was out of the question. Nor would Lorna consider psychoanalyzing her supposed "refrigerator mother" characteristics [Donovan & Zucker, 2016].

Intent on learning more, Lorna switched to child psychiatry and became a well-known researcher in autism. She, along with other autism parents in the U.K., founded the National Autistic Society.

The NAS, in turn, helped establish the Society School for Autistic Children, which became a hotbed of autistic research as well.

During her work, Wing came across the writings of Hans Asperger, and was impressed by his work with higher-functioning autistics. As a result, she came up with the term *Asperger's Syndrome* and the concept of a "spectrum" that includes many different experiences of autism [Happe & Baron-Cohen, 2014]. She was instrumental in getting Asperger's Syndrome recognized, although she always felt that all names for people on the spectrum were just "autism." She died in 2014.

Ultimately, Lorna Wing regretted how she brought Asperger's ideas to the English-speaking world and changed the face of autism. She said before her death in 2014: "I wish I hadn't done it. I would like to throw all labels away today, including Asperger's syndrome, and move towards the dimensional approach. Labels don't mean anything, because you get such a wide variety of profiles" [Sheffler, 2018, p. 243].

Uta Frith

Uta Aurnhammer, born 1941 in Germany, is Emeritus Professor of Cognitive Development at the Institute of Cognitive Neuroscience at University College in London. In 1964, after completing her degree in psychology at Saarland University in Germany, she went to England to work on her English language skills. There she met and married psychologist Chris Frith and became fascinated with the research being done in London. She received a work-study position in psychiatry and soon found herself involved in research about autism. She was one of the early researchers in the field and also became a significant writer explaining autism to the public.

As we move into the 1980s and '90s, autism history becomes more complex. There is too much happening with diagnosis, treatment, education, and support groups to adequately look at them in depth. You can find guidelines at the back of Donovan & Zucker's book or Project Autism: History of Autism online [http://projectautism.org/history-of-autism; Sole-Smith, 2014].

Why Does the History of Autism Matter to Those of Us Over 50?

Because we grew up during that era! Donald Triplett was born in 1933, so he was 83 in 2016 when we conducted this study. He was born when children such as him were sent to institutions, sometimes never to be visited by family. He came into the world at the height of the eugenics movement, when anyone significantly different was considered inferior, and efforts were made to eliminate them and, if possible, their genetic line.

What impact did these trends have on Donald and others born in the 1930s as they grew to adulthood? Donald was fortunate to have extremely attentive parents and receive an early diagnosis from Kanner. He was one of a handful of children diagnosed in the early years.

Temple Grandin was born almost 15 years later, but still there were discussions about putting her in an institution. She had an incredibly educated and involved mother, who was able to ignore the "refrigerator mother" theory. Her mother took her to Boston Children's Hospital, where they identified "autism: infantile schizophrenia" when Temple was 4, in 1951.

Was the experience of being born autistic in the 1930s and 1940s significantly different than it was for autistics born in the 1950s and 1960s? Many of us were raised by mothers who believed their "coldness" was the cause of our autism. We show some loosening of attitudes and prejudice through the decades. It was rare for a parent to get a diagnosis for an "odd" child. However, Donald

Triplett was correctly diagnosed by Kanner in 1943 and Temple Grandin at Boston Children's Hospital in 1951.

In 1975, Congress passed Public Law 94-142 that required public schools to open their doors to children with physical and mental disabilities. That included children who were denied access to public schools as well as those who had only partial access. There was minimal diagnosis and understanding of autism at that time, and services provided varied greatly. In many ways, that is still the case. However, in general, you would need to have been born by around 1969 to be covered under that federal law in public schools. Those who completed our survey were born by 1967, so the youngest were only about 8 years old when this law went into effect. However, most participants in our study were too high functioning to have been noticed or diagnosed in childhood.

Our study allowed us to explore questions about those of us born before 1967. It is a unique situation for this generation of autistics, who grew up during such tumultuous times for autism. Most of us had no diagnosis until our 50s, 60s, or later. Those of us at the higher-functioning end of the spectrum were generally not recognized until 1994 when Asperger's Syndrome was added to the *DSM-IV*. The youngest of us were 28 before our "difference" was identified.

In the next chapter, we'll look at some ways that we have been impacted by the autism-related events occurring during our early childhood.

PART II
GROWING UP QUIRKY

Degree One: Being born on the spectrum

There are two questions in the survey that pertain to being born on the spectrum:

Do you believe that you were born on the autism spectrum? [Question #2]

Were you born with any other developmental conditions or health issues? [Question #11]

<u>SURVEY QUESTION #2:</u> *Do you believe that you were born on the autism spectrum?*

Responses

Response	Count	Percent
Yes. I believe/know that I am on the autism spectrum and believe that one is born with autism.	63	43.4%
Yes. I believe/know that I am on the autism spectrum and believe that autism is in part hereditary.	76	52.4%
No. I believe/know that I am on the spectrum, but I believe that circumstances in my childhood are the cause such as...	6	4.1%
Total Responses	145	100%

As shown above, about 96% answered "yes" – they believe that they were born on the autism spectrum and that autism is totally or partly hereditary. Only about 4% felt that autism is caused by the circumstances of childhood.

43.4%: Yes. I believe/know that I am on the autism spectrum and believe that one is born with autism.

Many participants came to that conclusion through their own reading. For example, one participant did enough research to diagnose herself, and become convinced that it was hereditary by looking at her family. She began noticing family members who are probably on the spectrum. She envied her grandchildren who were diagnosed as toddlers. She had to figure out her diagnosis in adulthood by reading. In contrast, her grandchildren were diagnosed while very young – a tremendous change in the course of her lifetime, as is true of most of our generation.

Earl [57, NZ*] also came to his conclusions through reading widely in autism literature, including the book *Neurotribes*, a resource we consulted for our background research. He has very strong feelings about autism's cause, writing, "If your book focuses on non-genetic causes or cures, I withdraw my consent to participate."

Others knew it was hereditary, but seemed rather depressed. Sally [51, UK] was quite clear and concise. When asked if she was born on the spectrum, she responded, "I don't think it's something you can catch!" When asked how her life changed after diagnosis, she responded, "It didn't. It's still hell!"

Many of our folks, after realizing their diagnosis, could see it in their own families. For example, David [70, NE*] wrote: "My brother had been diagnosed with AS in his sixties, but I was not told before he passed. I am sure my father had AS as well." Pat [64, NE*] diagnosed herself by taking an online quiz. She suspected her late father was on the spectrum when she came across some things he had written: "He would calculate how many seconds were in a day, a week, a month, a year, etc., etc. (He died when I was a baby, so I never got the chance to talk to him about a lot of stuff that we have in common)."

Anita [57, SE*] wrote: "I believe autism is hereditary. After I got diagnosed at age 50 [by chance], we realized my mom was on the spectrum as well. My 30-year-old nephew also has Asperger's."

52.4% Yes. I believe/know that I am on the autism spectrum and believe that autism is in part hereditary.

These respondents agreed that autism was hereditary, but some felt that environment also played a role. One respondent wrote: "While BEING on the spectrum is genetic, the symptoms can be affected (i.e., made better or worse) by other factors."

4.1% No. I believe/know that I am on the spectrum, but I believe that circumstances in my childhood are the cause such as …

Some comments suggesting other causes included: "my mother left me when I was about two years old, I contracted chicken pox at 6 months old and almost died, and I was confined to a playpen then led a life that was curiously isolated from other children or people."

SURVEY QUESTION #11: *Were you born with any other developmental conditions or health issues?*

Response	Count	Percent
Yes	42	28.6%
No	105	71.4%
Total Responses	147	

As shown above, 71.4% responded "no" to this question. Only 28.6% responded in the affirmative. However, we will see that many comorbidities – physical, emotional, and neurological – are reported.

Participant Comments

28.6%: I was born with other developmental disabilities.

Some of our respondents identified vision problems. Wenn [64, AUS*]: "Born with astigmatism and poor sight in the left eye." Carlos [66, NE*] was born with some vision, but it was very low. William [67, NE*] wrote: "I can't even get my vision corrected in any conventional way. I can't see through plastic lenses at all. My field of vision then looks like a hallucination. I must have lenses made of glass. I see so poorly and have such slow response times that I can't play any ball game or drive a car."

Many of our participants mentioned depression and anxiety: Rob [61, NE]: "I had developmental delay, thought retention (related to OCD), and hyper-anxiety, which affected me through childhood and adulthood." Larry [69, UK*]: "I have suffered from depression most of my life." Judy [52, UK] wrote:

> I have suffered strongly seasonal depression since about age 15/16 and was diagnosed and first treated in my mid-30s. Ongoing medication for this has been successful and the condition has improved, especially since autism diagnosis. I experienced some possible symptoms of epilepsy as a child that were never investigated, and suffered a temporal lobe seizure last October, for which I am now on ongoing medication. So far, this treatment has been successful.

Some of the other responses to the developmental question include:

David [70, NE*]: "Atopic dermatitis is an immune system disease with a variety of manifestations that unlike for most people has gotten worse with age."

Pat [64, NE*]: "There's so many details that I don't know where to start with the physical disabilities/birth defects." Nancy [57, NE*]: "I have experienced gastrointestinal issues all my life."

Summary

96% answered "yes" to Survey Question #2: They believe that they were born on the autism spectrum and that autism was totally or partly hereditary. Only about 4% felt that autism was caused by the circumstances of childhood. About 29% indicated being born with another developmental disability.

In the second degree, we come to recognize we're different but don't know why.

Degree Two: Knowing we're different, but not why

The feeling of being different can develop because of being treated with "disregard, avoidance, teasing, or alienation" [Wylie et al., 2016, p. 58]. As seen in the chart below, 94.6% of our group felt "different from other children or teens."

We asked two questions about Degree Two:

Awareness: Do you believe you are on the autism spectrum? [Question #1]

Did you feel different from other children and teens? [Question #13]

() Yes

() No

Provide whatever detail you can to explain your answers above:

SURVEY QUESTION #1: *Awareness. Do you believe you are on the autism spectrum?*

Response	Don't know	Childhood	Teens, 20s	30-50	50+
I knew I was on the autism spectrum at these points in my life	7	2 (1%)	4 (3%)	56 (39%)	105 (73%)
I suspected I was on the autism spectrum at these points	16	5 (4%)	15 (11%)	68 (51%)	66 (49%)
I felt I was different from others, but didn't know why at these points	5	126 (87%)	101 (70%)	70 (48%)	37 (26%)
a. I felt that there was something wrong with me	12	88 (64%)	81 (59%)	64 (46%)	34 (25%)
b. I felt special and unique	37	63 (56%)	52 (46%)	46 (41%)	37 (33%)
c. I felt better than others	62	26 (30%)	20 (23%)	12 (14%)	13 (15%)

An overwhelming majority of the respondents indicated that they knew they were "different" during childhood without knowing why [87%, adjusting for "Don't know" responses]. This drops to about 70% during their teens and twenties, and even further with age. As they got older, participants may have learned about the autism spectrum or discovered explanations for feeling different, or they may have decided they were not so different after all.

Over half of the respondents, about 60%, felt there was something wrong with them during their youth, and about 55% felt they were special and unique. About 30% felt better than others when growing up. These figures continue dropping with age.

The table above illustrates that, with age, awareness of autism goes up *monotonically* [i.e., without decreasing], as the percentage of those who feel different without knowing why decreases nearly monotonically [almost without increasing]. A statistical test, the Cochran-Armitage trend test, confirms this, not surprisingly, with $p < .0001$, indicating a significant association between awareness of autism and feeling different and not knowing why.

Never did the reality of a painful childhood become clearer to us than when we read participants' comments, conveying years of confusion and despair. It seems that the deepest pain came from not just being out of the norm but from not even having words or concepts to express it. Most of us were adrift for years in inability to express our bewilderment. As we started to grasp some concretes – such as social awareness – we got the "how" of our uniqueness, but most of us didn't get the "why" until much later in life.

Participant Comments

"I felt I was different from others but didn't know why" at these points: 87% in childhood; 70% teens and twenties.

Lauren [51, NE*] described her "outsider" feelings as a child: "I alternate between feeling better than others and feeling like there is something terribly wrong with me. I am usually at such odds with the world around me, that I spend a lot of time blending and trying to accommodate the world around me, just so I can get by. When I was young, autism was not spoken about openly. It was something discussed in hushed tones in private, and it was a cause for shame among parents and family members. If I'd known about the full spectrum, as well as Asperger Syndrome at a younger age, it would have really 'clicked' for me."

Jack [57, UK] had similar feelings when young: He always felt that he was somehow different from other people in some way he couldn't define. He never liked group activities, never really understood why people got upset about things.

Most of the respondents noted that feeling different meant they felt inferior.

One respondent from the U.S. said she felt "Worthless. Ashamed. Broken!" Another commented that she couldn't understand the weird rules or ways that others her age seemed to make up just to harass her. As she got older, she started to realize that everyone did have rules, but no one had told her about them…"I thought everyone saw the world the same way."

Some of our folks knew they were unusual even as children but didn't mind. Anita [57, NE*] recalled: "I simply realized I wasn't like them. It didn't bother me, because nothing they did interested me."

Some of us struggled a great deal to understand others, especially in our teens. Wilma [69, NE] complained, "I hated being a teen as I couldn't ever figure out what was in fashion like the other girls could. I wondered if there was a secret guidebook on the subject that I couldn't find!" Julianne [69, AUS] also was clueless about other teen girls. She was always a loner: "I felt neither liked nor disliked…nonexistent. Sort of invisible. Didn't understand other teens, their mannerisms, popular slang language, music, etc."

Sadly, many were bullied because of their differences. Emily [70, UK*] grew up to become a psychologist who wrote a book about bullying [Lovegrove, 2013]. Regarding childhood, she wrote: "I found it hard to make friends. I just wanted one close friend. I found one eventually, but she always bullied me." Jonathan [54, UK *] also got pushed around: I felt like an outcast and was relentlessly bullied."

Some of our folks pointed out that they were misdiagnosed, which generally added to their despair and pain. Samantha [52, MW*] was diagnosed at age 8 as being mentally retarded: "I had lots of problems leading up to that, it got worse after that." Jonathan's [54, UK*] misdiagnosis was especially confusing to him:

> In 1974, my primary school/GP referred me to an educational psychologist to determine what type of schooling would suit me best. This was because I was displaying a lack of focus in my schoolwork and problems integrating and socializing with my peer group. To confirm the initial diagnosis, I was assessed by a second educational psychologist. who diagnosed significant behavioural issues. including a "dreamy personality" and the possibility of "chromosomal abnormalities." He was put into a very unstructured classroom in which he isolated even further.

Jackie [61, UK*], who had also been misdiagnosed, describes a miserable childhood with few friends. When she was an adult, her mother told her that as a baby, she processed things differently from her older brother. Less than a month after that conversation, she notes:

> I happened to watch a documentary on Asperger's, and the psychiatrist described infant and baby behaviours that literally left me with my mouth hanging open and on that

day, approximately 9 or 10 years ago, I began my own research on the autism spectrum and took a Cambridge-sponsored test online that placed both myself and my husband high in the category of high functioning autism...it changed my life.

And those are apt words to end this section: "It changed my life." We have heard similar statements from most of our "lost generation." We didn't know. Then we found out. And everything changed.

SURVEY QUESTION #13: *Did you feel different from other kids and teens?*

Response	Count	Percent
Yes	140	94.6%
No	8	5.4%
Total Responses	148	

An overwhelming 94.6% answered yes to this question.

Being different also meant being a potential target. As we'll see in more detail later, 83% of the sample reported bullying and teasing in childhood [This is referenced in the table under the "Sensory Experiences" survey question, in the "Degree 3" section, "Sensory Experiences: Which of these have you experienced and when?"]. As noted previously, this figure contrasts markedly with the nationwide bullying prevalence of 30% [Nansel et al., 2001], which shows a very high significant statistical difference [$p < .0001$]. The overwhelming response of "yes" to feeling different from other children and teens is also reflected in the volume and passionate spirit of the comments, some of which are detailed below.

Participant Comments

Some talked about having no friends.
Anya [69, NE*]: "I had no social life, friends, relationships, few common interests." Samantha [52, MW*], with a sense of humor, wrote: "The humanoid alien stuck on an alien planet." School was also hard for Carlos [66, NE], who told us: "I was very withdrawn, was bullied and always felt disliked. I hated competitive sports and avoided playing with boys my age. I related better to older adults than to kids my age."

Many were bullied.
Karen [62, W*] said that she had: "few friends, got bullied/picked on a lot; didn't understand people, why they did things I thought were stupid. Read a lot in middle school. Always thought there was something wrong with me."

Quite a few felt like outsiders.
Mathew [69, NE] told us: "felt very much an outsider and different somehow, but I can't really explain why. I did have friends as a child, but within these friendships I felt they were shallow for me and that there was little emotional attachment or intellectual rapport. Something I wanted deeply was always missing...when dating started in high school I felt left out of the socializing and very lonely."

Rob [61, NE] felt alone in his differences: "My differences were a real mystery, and not anything I was ever prepared for by any outside counseling or parental advice to deal with. My sexual, emotional, and social development were way different; I had no social life; but I did well in school and was talented musically, so the fact that I had developmental abnormalities or problems was dismissed."

As children, they couldn't understand social norms.

Lauren [51, NE*] wrote: "I always felt like I was two steps behind, like I didn't understand what was going on around me. I was socially awkward, and shy. I always felt like I was going to mess up – say something wrong or do something that would make the other kids make fun of me. I didn't care about the things they cared about. I thought a lot of them were just plain stupid, and I resented being around them." Graham Beck [65, UK] told us despondently: "Very lonely and isolated. No means of forming friendships."

Many "Just felt different."

Marilyn [65, W*] shared: "I always felt they were older than me. I was always shy. Fortunately, my family was loving and supportive and I always had a few friends. The feeling of being really different started in junior high." Wayne [58, UK*] never followed the crowd, "but did lead my own band of misfits." Rhys [52, UK*] had similar feelings: "I didn't seem to want to do what other children did, or even understand why they wanted to do these things. I tried to join in, but I just wasn't interested in being part of a group or gang, I was far happier on my own and concentrating on my interests. I felt like I was in a bubble and the "normal" world was carrying on around me without it actually being aware of me."

May [70, SW] also preferred to be alone: "I never had a desire to play with my siblings, cousins, or peers. I just wanted people to 'leave me alone' so I could play with my clothespins or later read my books or spend time inside my head trying to figure things out. I did what I felt I had to do to survive in a world I didn't understand. People were obstacles that I had to get around. It wasn't until college that I started to actually notice people as separate individuals with differing thoughts and emotions."

Different processing styles.

Some participants noted their different processing style. Pat [64, NE*], for example, wrote: "I couldn't process the same as other kids and my learning style was often met with ridicule and physical punishment/bullying."

5.4% did not feel different from other children and teens.

Tim [76, NE*] wrote: "I had no idea that I was different really. I coped by acting out and being disruptive. Many hours of writing on the blackboard after school."

Summary

The heart of the message from our peers is: "We didn't know; we didn't have a clue. We grew up with an invisible shield around us, distorting our communication. Yet we carried on, striving to go to school, to grow up, to find love and employment. Most of us met numerous snags along the way. It was clear the rest of our generation was 'normal'; each of us felt weird in a way that we could not explain – even to ourselves."

Degree Three: Developing physical and emotional problems

The key difference between the second and third degrees of autism is that the individual does not suffer initially at the second-degree stage; but later, adverse environmental factors cause suffering at the third-degree stage. Typically, the individual would be a target of abuse and he or she would struggle to cope with normal social conventions. Naturally, third degree autistics would be misunderstood often and unable to access meaningful support [Wylie et al., 2016, p. 74].

At some point, the pressure to conform takes its toll. We become depressed, or live with insomnia, anxiety, and stress. All of this takes place without understanding who we are or why we are distressed.

What impact has this had on our growing to adulthood? Let's look more closely at the stress our generation had by growing up feeling different without knowing why.

Our Degree 3 questions included these questions and categories:

Were you sent to a mainstream school or a special needs school? [Question #12]

How did you do in elementary school? [ages 6 to 11] [Question #14]

Which of these describes your experience of elementary school? [Question #15]

Were you ever given any special services in elementary school to work on social skills, behavior, academic help, or anything related to autism? [Question #16]

How did you do in middle school? [ages 12 to 14] [Question #17]

Which of these describes your experience of middle school? [Question #18]

Were you ever given any special services in middle school to work on social skills, behavior, academic help, or anything related to autism? [Question #19]

How was your relationship with your family [up to age 12]? [Question #20]

What was your living situation [up to age 12]? [Question #21]

How did you do in high school? [ages 15 to 18] [Question #22]

Which of these describes your experience of high school? [Question #23]

Were you ever given any special services in high school to work on social skills, behavior, academic help, or anything related to autism? [Question #24]

How was your relationship with your family during your teens? [Question #25]

SENSORY EXPERIENCES: Which of these have you experienced, and when? [Question #34]

COPING STRATEGIES [Question #41]

According to Dr. Tony Attwood, a psychologist who specializes in autism, autistic individuals might use any of the following strategies to cope with feeling different. Indicate which ones you used and when.

Are there other coping strategies you have used in your life to deal with being on the spectrum? (Check all that apply) [Question #42]

DRUG USE: Which of these did you use excessively during periods of your life? [Question #43]

ILLEGAL BEHAVIOR: Indicate illegal behavior during period of life. [Question #44]

MENTAL ILLNESS/PSYCHIATRIC DISORDER:
Which of these have been an issue for you at various life stages? Give details below of symptoms, any treatment, and progress. [Question #45]

MENTAL ILLNESS/PSYCHIATRIC DISORDER:
Treatment...Which of these treatments have you had? Indicate below whether they were helpful for you. [Question #46]

PHYSICAL ILLNESS:
Indicate which of these you have had at various points in your life: [Question #47]

EXPERIENCES IN SCHOOL

SURVEY QUESTION #12: *Were you sent to a mainstream school or a special needs school?*

Mainstream school	136	91.9%
Special education program (mainstream)	1	0.7%
Special needs school	4	2.7%
Other school	7	4.7%
Total Responses	148	

About 92% responded that they were sent to a mainstream school, while only about 3.5% reported being in either a special needs school or special needs program. Among "Other School," three appeared to be special needs schools, so the percentage for special needs instruction is probably around 5%, still a very low number. Of course, most of this group didn't have a diagnosis, so there was no awareness of having special needs.

Participant Comments

About 92% went to a mainstream school.

Lauren [51, NE*] was impacted by the limited knowledge and attitudes of her era: "When I was young, autism was not spoken about openly. It was something discussed in hushed tones in private, and it was a cause for shame among parents and family members. If I'd known about the full spectrum, as well as Asperger Syndrome at a younger age, it would have really 'clicked' for me."

Stan [57, NE] provided historical context: "There was no special needs school at that time. I had to survive based on my own wits. Many, many times taken advantage of."

Anya [69, NE*] said, "Mainstream school was not helpful, but there was no alternative. I struggled from third grade. Began to fail in seventh grade. Spent the rest of school years in 'study hall.'" Ann [64, NE*] had equally bitter memories: "When I was in grade school, autism was NEVER mentioned; Asperger's was unknown."

Some of our folks were brief but emphatic in discussing school: It was a nightmare...School was horrible. Samantha [52, MW]: "It was hell...I loved learning, but hated school." Pat [64, NE*] said: "Junior high school was a nightmare!" William's [67, NE*] words were especially strong: "I despise school in all forms. Never again will I enter a classroom."

Some participants wished they'd had access to the resources of today.

Emma [60, CAN*] comments: "There were no modifications/programs where I grew up (and when I grew up). Very glad of this in many ways [no ABA or other coercive therapies], but it would have been helpful if educators had known how to differentiate instruction, understood some of my sensory issues, and spent less time blaming me for my differences [see 'moral failings']."

Kenneth [51, UK] seemed to receive fewer services during his early life than did Temple Grandin, almost 20 years earlier in Boston. Kenneth was a very intelligent child, but he was considered "odd."

For a few of our younger participants, some services were available, but they were of little help. Lauren [51, NE*], a 51-year-old autistic on the East Coast, said, "I was in a mainstream school, and I attended speech therapy for speech problems, as well as being part of a gifted students program. The school was unable to help me deal with my speech problems, and I was removed from the gifted program, after I became unruly and a discipline problem. I was insubordinate to the teacher, and I caused a lot of distractions for other students. I also was not able to keep up with the work."

SPECIAL SERVICES

SURVEY QUESTION #16: *Were you ever given any special services in elementary school, middle school, or high school to work on social skills, behavior, academic help, or anything related to autism?*

Elementary School: *[ages 6 to 11]*

Response	Count	Percent
Yes	138	6.1%
No	9	93.9%
Total Responses	147	

Middle School: *[ages 12–14]*

Response	Count	Percent
Yes	141	4.1%
No	6	95.9%
Total Responses	147	

High School: *[ages 15–18]*

Response	Count	Percent
Yes	140	3.4%
No	5	96.6%
Total Responses	147	

For all three school periods, only around 5% reported ever receiving special services: 6.1% for elementary school, 4.1% for middle school, and 3.4% for high school. This is not surprising in an era when autism without intellectual disability was not recognized as a condition.

Respondents had few experiences of special services. However, speech therapy was often available:

Rob [61, NE], one of the authors, wrote: "I was put in speech therapy in middle school. I was also suspected of being 'retarded', either mentally or emotionally, in the early grades, and was given a special IQ and psychological test. Because I did well on the IQ test, I was kept in the public school system."

Lauren [51, NE*] also had speech therapy: "I was in speech therapy, because I had trouble talking. I also could not understand what people were saying to me, but I don't think they ever realized that was a problem with me."

Special education was occasionally available. One of our respondents said: "They tried putting me in speech therapy from age 6 to 15 for my stutter." But no one thought of autism in terms of higher-functioning students. Or, as Julianne [69, AUS] said: "Autism wasn't a 'thing' in those days."

PERFORMANCE

We now turn to the section where we ask about school performance. We included all schooling from age 6 to age 18. Because of our British and Australian participants, whose school systems were set up differently than in the U.S., we added an age range in the survey to differentiate the educational periods.

•

SURVEY QUESTION #14: *How did you do in elementary school [ages 6 to 11], in middle school [ages 12-14], and in high school [ages 15-18]?*

Elementary School: *[ages 6 to 11]*

Skill Area	Above Average	Average	Below Average
Reading & language	100 (67.6%)	29 (19.6%)	19 (12.8%)
Math	71 (48.0%)	37 (25.0%)	40 (27.0%)
Science	77 (53.5%)	44 (30.6%)	23 (16.0%)
Art/drama	44 (30.8%)	56 (39.2%)	43 (30.1%)
Socially with peers	0 (0.0%)	25 (17.1%)	121 (82.9%)
Team activities	5 (3.4%)	27 (18.4%)	115 (78.2%)

Middle School: *[ages 12-14]*

Skill Area	Above Average	Average	Below Average
Reading & language	89 (60.5%)	39 (26.5%)	19 (12.9%)
Math	64 (43.8%)	36 (24.7%)	46 (31.5%)
Science	68 (47.2%)	51 (35.4%)	25 (17.4%)
Art/drama	40 (28.2%)	56 (39.4%)	46 (32.4%)
Socially with peers	0 (0.0%)	24 (16.6%)	121 (83.4%)
Team activities	4 (2.7%)	24 (16.4%)	118 (80.8%)

High School: *[ages 15-18]*

Skill Area	Above Average	Average	Below Average
Reading & language	86 (60.1%)	37 (25.9%)	20 (14.0%)
Math	63 (44.1%)	32 (22.4%)	48 (33.6%)
Science	63 (45.0%)	51 (36.4%)	26 (18.6%)
Art/drama	45 (33.1%)	47 (34.6%)	44 (32.4%)
Socially with peers	1 (0.7%)	31 (21.8%)	110 (77.5%)
Team activities	7 (4.9%)	22 (15.5%)	113 (79.6%)

PERFORMANCE IN DIFFERENT SKILL AREAS

There is clearly a dramatic difference between participants' self-evaluation of their social and academic performance across all school levels. Social performance (socializing with peers and team activities) was heavily rated "below average" [average: about 80% in this category; range 77.5% - 83.4%], whereas performance in solid academic courses (reading/language, math, science) had an "above average" trend [average: about 52% in this category; range 43.8% - 67.6%]. Art/drama performance levels appear more evenly distributed between the performance ratings of "above average," "average," and "below average."

We also grouped and totaled the actual counts of responses in each skill area to create an "Academic Performance" [Reading/Writing+Math+ Science+Art/Drama] evaluation score and a "Social Performance" [Socially with Peers+Team Activities]. We then used the Cochran-Armitage statistical test to test for trends. In each case, the trend was confirmed, with p value of < .0001, indicating a "very significant" [academic vs. social] involving perceived performance. [NOTE: The word *perceived* is used to emphasize that these are self-assessments and may not accurately reflect actual performance levels.]

The tables below show the responses for academic subjects. Respondents seemed to rate themselves very high in reading and language [67.6%, 60.5%, and 60.1% above average], and high in math and science [48%/53.5%, 43.8%/47.2%, and 43.8%/45% above average].

Elementary School: *[ages 6 to 11]*

Skill Area	Above Average
Reading & language	67.6%
Math	48.0%
Science	53.5%

Middle School: *[ages 12–14]*

Skill Area	Above Average
Reading & language	60.5%
Math	43.8%
Science	47.2%

High School: *[ages 15–18]*

Skill Area	Above Average
Reading & language	60.1%
Math	44.1%
Science	45.0%

Compare these scores with above ratings in art/drama: 30.8%, 28.2%, and 33.1%. That is a big drop in "above average" scores. As illustrated below, the scores drop the most in "socially with peers" and "team activities."

Elementary School: *[ages 6 to 11]*

Socially with peers	0.0%	17.1%	82.9%
Team activities	3.4%	18.4%	78.2%

Middle School: *[ages 12-14]*

Socially with peers	0.0%	16.6%	83.4%
Team activities	2.7%	16.4%	80.8%

High School: *[ages 15-18]*

Socially with peers	0.7%	21.8%	77.5%
Team activities	4.9%	15.5%	79.6%

These figures are consistent with the general impression of high-functioning autistics as being very academic but quite challenged in socializing and team activities.

Participant Comments

SOCIAL PROBLEMS

Not surprisingly, one of the biggest school-related issues was social interactions.

Derek [53, NE*] fell behind socially "due to being clueless about the whole boy-girl thing, and cliques." Stephen K [69, NE]: "From third grade and on, it was unmitigated hell." Lauren [51, NE*] loved reading and writing, but said: "Socially, I was a wreck. Anything that had to do with people was not a good thing." Yvonne [65, SW*] kept to herself and just faked it.

INDIVIDUAL SPORTS AND ACTIVITIES

Our community tends to be best at activities we can do alone. In group situations, we often withdraw. Many of our respondents spoke of their extremely negative experiences with teams.

May [70, SW] told us "Anything that I could learn or do on my own I did well. I felt lost and confused in group situations. I was kept in Catholic schools through high school to protect me growing up. I overheard a teacher once say that she can tell who is going to be successful in life by how they play in a team sport. I did not do well in team activities, yet I felt that I was successful. I was confused and hurt by her comment." Samantha [52, MW*] echoed this sentiment, saying she has never been able to do sports teams – either in childhood or as an adult. For many of us, the most humiliating part of team sports was when the teacher asked kids to pick their teams. Many of us were picked last.

Many mentioned <u>lack of coordination</u> as a primary difficulty in sports. One of the women added: "I was...very clumsy and uncoordinated when it came to sports, or even things like jumping rope."

Emma [60, CAN*] summed up the experiences most of us had in teams: *Team activities were hell.*

OBSTACLES TO SCHOOL SUCCESS

IN OUR OWN WORLD

Many participants saw being "in their own world" as an obstacle to school performance. One 58-year-old man in the U.S. said: "I was the kid in class who was the solitary aloof walking encyclopedia on the playground, totally locked into my own inner world." Lauren [51, NE*] wrote: "I was constantly confused. I didn't know what was happening. I was scared and shy and only wanted to hide from the world." Laura [57, UK]: "tended to have one or two friends but was never part of the popular group. In the playground I tended to watch other people playing rather than joining in."

TOO MANY QUESTIONS FOR TEACHERS

Some of us found that teachers stopped answering our questions. One man from Southern U.S. noted: "I made straight A's but would often alienate the teacher by my questioning and non-conventional attitude."

LOW SELF-ESTEEM

Some felt their low self-esteem made it difficult for them to succeed.

Carlos [66, NE]: "In spite of the fact that I always underestimated my abilities, I was way better in math than the average classmate throughout elementary and high school. I could have done much better overall if I hadn't believed I was stupid."

Many participants noted that they had no support from the school for their unique learning issues. Sally [51, UK] lamented that "they did not know how to teach...or reach me."

MIDDLE SCHOOL DIFFICULTIES

A theme that surfaced throughout the survey was the shame and humiliation of being bullied, especially in middle school. A number of our participants said that bullying was especially severe in middle school, and they felt it was their fault.

Bob [54, NE] noted: "Seventh grade was the beginning of Hell. I went to the regular school with its cattle calls. I understood little of what was going on socially. I started going to an alternative school, but I didn't get along with some teachers, and classes were slow and boring. My social life, or lack thereof, began to spill over into my classes."

Nancy [57, NE*] said: "Reading/language got harder in middle school because I didn't relate to the content of the material. The only part of reading that I liked was reading time where we could select our own books."

Anya [69, NE*] experienced a number of performance challenges: "Reading literature was enjoyable but discussing it was difficult. Enjoyed social studies and history if it was interesting but could not remember dates and facts. Greatly enjoyed sciences and science theory. Could not do problems the correct way. Could not do higher math at all. Could not learn foreign languages. Music was important. Participated in structured groups such as church choir and Girl Scouts or camp. Hated sports."

LIKED THE STRUCTURE OF SCHOOL

Marilyn [65, W*] wrote: "When I was in grade school the learning environment was usually very structured which suited me well. I generally kept to myself and was an observer more than a participator. I wanted playmates to always come to my house, not for me to go to theirs. By the time I was 11 and in the 6th grade, my sister was age 5. I had the feeling that SHE had more common sense."

Summary

The majority of folks who completed our questionnaire were bright students, but had miserable experiences in school due to social inadequacies, bullying, low self-esteem, and failure to understand what the teacher was talking about. Sadly, many reported that they were also discouraged from asking questions. For many of our generation, despite being academically capable, school was hell. For many of us, these factors impacted our performance. Some of us threw ourselves into academics, bypassing social life, sports, and – when we could – we ditched the worst period of the day: lunch.

EXPERIENCES IN SCHOOL

SURVEY QUESTION #15: *Which of these describes your experience of elementary school, middle school, and high school?*

School experience:	Elementary School	Middle School	High School
Bored a lot in classes	52.4%	50.3%	47.1%
Trouble understanding what teachers were talking about	35.9%	37.9%	35.7%
Hard to follow the instructions of teachers	43.4%	40.0%	39.3%
Easier to do homework on student's own than to pay attention in class	33.1%	39.3%	39.3%
Got in trouble a lot for not following rules	34.5%	29.7%	28.6%
Got in trouble a lot for being verbally or physically aggressive	6.9%	8.3%	8.6%
Loved classes and was a good student	30.3%	23.4%	29.3%

About 50% of the respondents reported being bored a lot in classes [about 52% for elementary school, 50% for middle school, and 47% for high school].

Around 35% had trouble understanding what teachers were talking about (consistent across all three age levels); about 40% reported that it was hard to follow instructions, and about 35% reported that it was easier to do homework on their own than to pay attention in class. About 30% got in trouble for not following the rules. So, there appears to be a sizable incidence of attention difficulties in the classroom, a communication gap between student and teacher, and problems being placed according to ability and skills. However, it would be interesting and informative to compare these experiences to other populations, including a younger population on the spectrum and a population not on the spectrum, in a future study.

About 30% reported loving classes and being a good student. About 7-8% got in trouble for being verbally or physically aggressive. No dramatic differences are apparent across the different school/age levels.

Participant Comments

Most of us felt that we did not fit into the school environment.

Stan [57, NE] spoke for many of us: 'I didn't fit in; I didn't know what 'felt comfortable' or what I wanted to do. Felt very disconnected including family; still the case."

David [70, NE*] felt that school went well through grade 3, but after that it was a slow slide downhill: "I think I might have had A.D.D., but home life was so chaotic between a father on the spectrum and a mother who resorted to alcohol increasingly as a coping mechanism. By fourth grade, my handwriting deficit due to mixed dominance began to manifest though the causes weren't diagnosed for another 10 years."

TEACHERS

Some had good experiences with teachers. Others argued with teachers, like Anya [69, NE*], who wrote: "I argued with teachers and books because of things I learned on my own. I enjoyed reading and could write well. I could not do math well at all."

Karen [62, W*] was apparently traumatized by a teacher: "When I got to first grade, I could already read although I don't recall learning how. I remember sitting in a semi-circle of students reading a Dick and Jane book, the teacher having told us to read a certain part. When I was done, I sat and waited for the rest of the children to finish. The teacher asked me why I wasn't reading, and I said I was done, and she said I was lying and made me pull my chair beside her and read the material again. I felt humiliated, and I was angry that the teacher didn't believe me. That kind of set the tone for the rest of my educational career. To this day, my interactions with teachers are affected by that first experience. If I don't have a comfortable relationship with an instructor, I have a harder time engaging with the material."

Several respondents coped by bonding with teachers rather than students. Samantha [52, MW*] told us: 'Teachers I could relate to better than peers, but I was the invisible alien child. Larry [69, UK*]: "formed friendships with teachers rather than with my peers." [Rob, 61, NE] said: "got along with my teachers, but not with my peers."

ANXIETY

Anxiety was an ever-present reality for many of our respondents. Laura [57, UK] said: "I kept finding that my high levels of anxiety make it hard to concentrate on what the teachers were saying. Also, I was so frightened of inadvertently doing something wrong that I kept asking teachers to repeat instructions." Bullying added to their anxiety.

SURVIVING SCHOOL

Most of us developed coping strategies. Emma [60, CAN*] looked out the windows a lot, as did Anita [57, NE*]: "I'd daydream a lot...gazing out windows imagining I was on a big white horse galloping across lush green pastures!" Pat [64, NE*] said: "Once I started to read, I spent most of my time in class secretly reading a book in my lap (this was possible with the old-fashioned wooden desks) rather than paying attention in class." David [70, NE*] recalled: "By middle school, I was just lost. Between large crowds, aggressive middle school students, and a fragmented home life, I think I was just shut down most of the time. I was interested in math and science and studied quite advanced electronics, building radios and things, but I was flunking and didn't know why."

Some survived by being diligent students. Nancy [57, NE*] said: "I was mostly always one of the teacher's 'pets' because I was so well behaved and such a smart student. I had a positive self-image based on my academic success."

Lucy [61, NE*]: "Since I was dealing with abuse and violence in my home as well as substandard heating and other unhealthy conditions, school was like an escape for me by comparison. I am not sure how I got along; I had my routines and I just followed my script as best I could, one day after the next."

Jackie [61, UK*] said: "No one knew, and I was 'the girl with the laugh'...I used all my strength to appear normal and to be liked."

MIDDLE SCHOOL

Many of our folks managed well in elementary school, but less well in middle school. Katrine-Estella Basso [53, UK] told us that: "My experiences were quite good when I went to school from the age of 6 to 7 because I got support from my cousin. When I moved to London at the age of 7, it got a lot worse because of bullying and being left out."

Rhys [52, UK*] also had a rough time. He wrote: "Elementary school (what I knew as "junior school") was OK. I'd have preferred not to have had to go, but I did OK & was well liked by the teachers & I had some nice friends. High school was where it all started to fall apart badly. I hated every second I was there. There were one or two teachers that were kind to me & helped me, but most of the teachers just either ignored me or bullied me. I had some friends, but I found the whole teenage social thing very difficult & I slowly began to withdraw."

Lillian [55, UK] is another person who enjoyed primary school – finding it quite creative. But then: "Things started to close in after age 10." Willie [67, UK] wrote: "I enjoyed elementary school pretty well but found secondary school increasingly difficult and was distracted by the need to survive socially. Many peers and teachers were scary to me." Marilyn [65, W*] told us: "There is a sharp contrast of how I felt between elementary and junior high/high school. Starting in about the sixth grade, my level of fear and anxiety accelerated."

Some experienced improvement in middle and high school. Larry [69, UK] realized by age 13 that he had some clear gifts. One U.S. male participant wrote: "Elementary was horrible; teachers and kids thought I was stupid. Middle school was tolerable; teachers and kids thought I was odd, but okay."

Summary of School Experience

Many of our participants were diligent students, whose academic work helped them tolerate socially awkward times. Others were bored, bullied, and anxious, never feeling they reached their potential as students. Although some enjoyed school, others were miserable because of teachers, other students, and/or a chaotic home life.

William [67, NE*] was blunt: "Nightmare! Keep me away from the classroom! Many of our needs were not noticed or addressed." But, as Julianne [61, AUS] said: "Autism wasn't a 'thing' in those days."

FAMILY EXPERIENCES GROWING UP

SURVEY QUESTION #21: *What was your living situation up to age 12?*

	Percent	Count
Lived with parents and sibs	89.2%	132
Lived with one parent	10.8%	16
Parents separated	5.4%	8
One or both parents dead	4.1%	6
Living with a relative	4.1%	6
Living in foster care	0.7%	1
Adopted	2.7%	4
Orphanage	1.4%	2
Total Responses		148

Almost 90% of respondents spent their early childhood with their family. One lived in foster care, two lived in an orphanage, and four were adopted. About 11% lived with one parent.

Participant Comments

Lived with parents and sibs: 89.2%.
Most of our participants described life at home with family. Yvonne [65, SW*] commented: "I had a regular family. My brother was gone and married by the time I was 10."

Lived with one parent: 10.8%.
Pat [64, NE*] "I lived with a sib and womb-donor. I can't call her a mother because she was NEVER a mother. After she had my sibling, she made it crystal-clear that she never wanted to give birth to me. My having multiple birth defects added to her hostility toward me because my being 'a defect' made her look bad, and she had this overwhelming need to have everything focused on her at all costs."

Parents separated: 5.4%.
Sally [51, UK]: "Parents were separated but lived in the same house."

One or both parents dead: 4.1%.
Anya's [69, NE*]: "Father died at age 12."

Living with a relative: 4.1%.
Wenn [64, AUS*]: "My parents gave me to my paternal aunt at the age of 12 because they found me difficult to understand."

Living in foster care: 0.7%.

Adopted: 2.7%.
William [67, NE*] was adopted at 2 months of age; Tim [76, NE*] was adopted within a week of birth.

Orphanage: 1.4%.
Edward [77, W]: "Was in an orphanage for about a year after my mother disappeared when I turned 2... I do not remember her at all, and the only recollection I have of the orphanage is a recurring dream I had until I was a teenager."
Feeling alone within the family was common, as Lauren [51, NE*] related: "I didn't see much of my parents. [They] both worked, and I was in childcare a lot. By the end of the day, my resources were so depleted, I wasn't even fully aware of what was going on around me." Ritamarie's [50, NE*] story was similar: "My best friend was our dog! I did most everything for myself at a very young age. Did lots of housework and learned to do domestic arts like cooking, baking, sewing, and needlework."

SURVEY QUESTION #20: *How was your relationship with your family up to age 12?*

	Percent	Count
My family was largely nurturing and supportive	41.0%	59
My family largely ignored me	25.7%	37
I was bullied and put down by other children in the family	23.6%	34
I was bullied and put down by adults in the family	29.2%	42
I was verbally abused	36.1%	52
I was physically abused	22.9%	33
I was sexually abused	9.7%	14
Other [explain below]	17.4%	25
Total Responses		144

41% say their families were nurturing and supportive. Over 25% responded that they were ignored by their family. Almost as many – 23.6% – reported being bullied or put down by other children in the family. Over 29% were bullied and put down by adults. 36% percent were verbally abused, and almost 23% were physically abused. National data suggest that 15 children per *thousand* have been abused or neglected, a far lower figure [Child Trends, 1994] than that found among our respondents. Here are some of their comments:

Participant Comments

41% Said family was nurturing and supportive.

Emma [60, CAN*] realized it's somewhat unusual to have been loved and supported: "Thankfully. When I talk to other autistic adults who were not so lucky, I am very grateful." Many others also reported happy family experiences. Doris [55, AUS*]: "A great upbringing. No regrets. At 55, I still have my parents although Mum is not well. I have been more than lucky in my childhood."

Some mentioned "grandparents" such as Anya [69, NE*]: "My grandmother was a big part of my life, and I sometimes went to visit her in the city where we would go to museums and zoos and eat out and meet interesting people."

Some noted that parents appreciated their autistic traits. Anita [57, SE]: "My mom was my best friend. She devoted her entire life to raising me." Marilyn [65, W*]: "I would say my parents were extremely nurturing and supportive. In fact, I never wanted to leave home."

EXPERIENCES OF ABUSE IN FAMILY

I was verbally abused   **36.1%**

Derek [53, NE*]: "Nurtured by mom, verbally abused by dad, but he didn't live with me."

I was physically abused   **22.9%**

Lauren [51, NE*]: "The physical abuse I experienced was due to my sensitivities. I had the experience of being beaten daily, because my mother is hyposensitive and very rough, and I was hypersensitive to even the slightest touch. It felt like I was being hit all the time when I was touched. I thought there was something wrong with me because I was being "punished" so much. My father used to call me names and treat me like crap."

Bullying added to their anxiety. One woman in the North East U.S. told us: "OMG, I was horribly bullied and beaten up by my peers, my teachers blamed me for being too 'weird' to get along with others and said I needed to quit acting 'that way.' I never understood what was going on socially. It was truly awful. Kids I didn't even know would go out of their way to punch me or push me."

I was sexually abused   **9.7%**

Many participants detailed their abuse experiences. Rob [61, NE] recounted: "I grew up traumatized by my father extending from infancy, possibly beaten. I could never figure out why I was so angry at him. My family was in huge denial about my differences, problems, and developmental delay – I would be shut up if I cried or complained. My talents were praised, but that was only one half of me. My problems were taken as "quirkiness" instead of something deeper."

Karen [62, W*] told us: "My stepfather was abusive, and he and my mother argued a lot (he directed his attacks mostly at my mother, hurting her physically and emotionally)." Yvonne [65, SW*] had a different experience with her father: "My father was my hero and I followed him and his advice. He did not harm me. My mother, brother (11 yrs. older than me) sister (4 yrs. older than me) abused me."

Some said there was emotional, but not physical, abuse. Sally [51, UK] felt blamed for everything. Jonathan's [54, UK*] father would put him down and say he could not do anything right.

Mathew [69, NE] also suffered emotionally: "I feel I was emotionally abused, but not physically or sexually (at least overtly). I sensed a distinct lack of emotional and intellectual rapport between me and my parents. I withdrew because I felt I was not understood. It seems now that I was emotionally neglected – a kind of abuse."

One participant recalled his mother saying: "She wished she could hide under a rock due to the shame of me. She also told me that I wasn't the sort of son my dad had hoped for."

BOTH SUPPORT AND ABUSE

Others reported experiences that were both supportive and abusive.

Samantha [52, MW*] articulated this dichotomy well: "My mom was very supportive and understanding, my father violent, hate-filled, dangerous, angry." Derek [53, NE*] had a similar experience, saying he was: "Nurtured by mom, verbally abused by dad." Rob [61, NE] wrote: "Mother was supportive and involved. Father was a shadow figure and was very uncomfortable with me."

I was bullied and put down by other children in the family: 23.6%.

One of our autistics wrote that an older sister bullied her by making her do the sister's chores as well as her own. She reported that her sister loved to cause her to have a meltdown.

Many of us may have been raised by undiagnosed spectrum parents.

Laura [57, UK] wrote: "My parents loved me, but they found it hard to deal with me because I was so anxious and shy, particularly in middle school." Nancy [57, NE*] wrote: "My father (who is on the spectrum) understood and appreciated my personality, but my mother did not. It is hard to answer this as my mother couldn't understand me and I knew I'd been a disappointment to her. I'm sure she was not autistic." Carlos [66, NE*] said: "My father was also on the spectrum, so he didn't know how to relate to me, and he was extremely overprotective. I would usually go to my mother when I had a problem."

SURVEY QUESTION #25: *How was your relationship with family during your teens?*

	Percent	Count
My family was largely nurturing and supportive	38.7%	55
My family largely ignored me	31.0%	44
I was bullied and put down by other children in the family	20.4%	29
I was bullied and put down by adults in the family	31.7%	45
I was verbally abused	31.7%	45
I was physically abused	14.8%	21
I was sexually abused	7.0%	10
Other	15.5%	22
Total Responses		142

This question parallels the one about childhood. The responses look similar, although the instances of *supportiveness and nurturing* are slightly fewer and *being ignored* slightly more frequent. In the following, we compare the comments to those about childhood, examining family relationships that were better, worse, and about the same.

Participant Comments

SITUATION GOT WORSE

Natalie [57, UK] said: "I had a lot of problems with depression and anger – partly over what I saw as abandonment by my natural mother and father – and self-harmed (cutting); my adoptive family despaired and mainly left me alone as they had no resources to deal with my state of mind." Pat [64, NE*] had a similar experience: "The home situation got worse, and there was no way out. The social services that people take for granted today did not exist." Mathew [69, NE] says that his problem in middle school: "Continued in spades during high school."

Doris [55, AUS*] wrote: "had major problems as a teen at school, but I didn't tell my parents, let alone anyone else. I internalized everything and kept it all a secret, because I thought that every problem I experienced was my fault. I've since told mum a few things, and she says she had no idea of my difficulties. I believe her, because I successfully pretended to be OK. But God, it was hard work at the time!" Nancy [57, NE*] described deterioration during her teens: "My relationship with my mother was extremely strained during my high school years. My mother is highly social, and we just couldn't relate to each other." Linda [56, W] said: "I was given away by my parents at age 16 – another family (that we barely knew) agreed to take me in." Pat [64, NE*]: "The home situation got worse, and there was no way out. The social services that people take for granted today did not exist."

GOT BETTER

David [70, NE*]: "Once I was in private school I was out of the clutches of my family except summers when I would mostly keep to myself."

STAYED THE SAME

Derek [53, NE*] recalled: "Same as middle school." Sally [51, UK] also said: "Same as before." Anita [57 NE*] was positive about her mother's support staying constant: "My mom always gave me 100% support."

Carlos added this about his teens: "It was complicated. My family was always supportive, but they didn't understand me very well."

The next question continues our exploration of Degree Three. We asked a number of "lifespan" questions, including one on ways of coping. The questionnaire included columns for "don't know," "childhood," "teens and 20s," "30s and 40s," and "50 and up." In this section, we're just looking at the pre-adult years, or the "childhood" and "teens and 20s" questions.

SURVEY QUESTION #34: *Sensory Experiences: Which of these have you experienced and when?*

Sensory experiences cover many common experiences that often add to feeling different throughout childhood, even though some might argue that they are not all strictly sensory, such as social and communication issues, which might be an expression of underlying sensory issues.

As reflected in the following chart, an alarming number of respondents, about 83%, reported bullying and teasing in pre-adolescent childhood. That figure went down to about 74% for adolescence/young adulthood, but that is still a high percentage. In general, bullying tended to decrease as participants aged out of school. However, "being taken advantage of" increased from 56% in childhood to almost 75% in teens and young adulthood. Perhaps as one leaves school and enters the larger community, there are fewer oversights to help protect the vulnerable.

Childhood communications issues also seemed to worsen as respondents grew into their teens and twenties. For example, communication and other social difficulties went from about 85% to 91%; being misunderstood rose from 81% to 90%. Finding it hard to understand others went up from 76% to 82%. This may be a result of our generation growing up without any specific help in relating to neurotypicals. Most of the sensory experiences stayed about the same through these years (articulating clearly, rigid routines, and noise and smells). The need to be alone also went up, from 72% to 78% after childhood. Perhaps as we leave school, we are better able to obtain alone time. There was a particularly big jump in reporting anxiety and stress: from 65% in childhood to about 84% during the teen years.

Sensory Experiences: "Which of these have you experienced and when?"

	Don't know	Childhood		Teens and 20s	
Experience	Count	Count	%	Count	%
Bullying and teasing	9	117	83.0%	104	73.8%
Being taken advantage of	8	80	56.3%	106	74.6%
Communication and social difficulties	1	126	84.6%	136	91.3%
Being misunderstood	3	119	81.0%	132	89.8%
Finding it hard to understand others	6	110	76.4%	118	81.9%
Difficulty articulating clearly	16	86	64.2%	88	65.7%
Need for rigid routines	18	76	57.6%	80	60.6%
Sensory issues (e.g., bothered by noise, smells)	7	95	66.4%	102	71.3%
Need for a lot of time alone	4	105	71.9%	114	78.1%
Anxiety and stress	2	96	64.9%	124	83.8%
Other (specify below)	5	15	10.3%	16	11.0%

Participant Comments

ANXIETY AND STRESS

Childhood: 64.9% vs. teens & 20s: 83.8%

William [67, NE*] noted that: "I probably have obsessive compulsive disorder and possibly some post-traumatic stress disorder from early family tensions." Mathew [69, NE] said: "I definitely have felt misunderstood and unable to understand others much of my life. I spend a lot of time alone, but not by choice. It is one adaptation to stress." Pat [64, NE*], Rhys [52, UK*], and Willie [67, UK] are among those who added "depression." Janet [61, UK*] reported: "Nervous breakdowns (psychotic episodes in 1984 when I was 29 and in 2004 when I was 49)."

SENSORY ISSUES: NOISE, SMELLS, ETC.

Childhood: 66.4% vs. teens & 20s: 71.3%

Emily [70, UK*] didn't get jokes and was sensitive to the feel of things.

COPING STRATEGIES

SURVEY QUESTION #41: *COPING STRATEGIES: According to Dr. Tony Attwood, a psychologist who specializes in autism, autistic individuals might use any of the following strategies to cope with feeling different. Indicate which ones you used and when.*

Strategy	Don't know Count	Childhood Count	%	Teens and 20s Count	%
Escape into imagination [e.g., imaginary world]	17	101	75.9%	85	63.9%
Denial and rigidity – blaming others	27	41	33.3%	62	50.4%
Imitating neurotypical peers or acting "normal"	9	67	47.5%	98	69.5%
Depression	7	59	41.3%	101	70.6%

Depression

Over 40% of our participants noted depression in childhood, increasing to more than 70% in their teens and 20s.

Escape into Imagination

In our group, about 76% reported using fantasy and imagination to escape in childhood, about 64% in the teen years. We assume that as we grow, we can ground ourselves more firmly in the real world.

Denial and Rigidity

Living with denial – and blaming others for their difficulties – was acknowledged by over 33% in childhood, increasing to over 50% in teens and young adulthood. Perhaps we live in more denial as we age, because we become better at maintaining a façade.

Imitation

Learning to imitate peers and "act normal" seems to be the coping skill of choice for our generation. That is, 47.5% of participants imitated others during childhood, and close to 70% used this strategy in their teens and twenties.

After asking about the four common coping mechanisms above, we listed other ways to cope and asked respondents to note which ones they had used.

SURVEY QUESTION #42: *Are there other coping strategies you have used in your life to deal with being on the spectrum? Indicate all that apply.*

	Percent	Count
Spending more time with younger children/adults than of your own age	35.0%	50
Spending more time with older children/adults than your own age	53.2%	76
Video games, TV	39.9%	57
Immersed in hobby (explain below)	56.6%	81
Immersed in academics rather than social life	60.1%	86
Second-guessing things you had said/didn't say	58.7%	84
Alcohol or drugs	36.4%	52
Other	20.3%	29
Total Responses		143

Autistic children often prefer the company of individuals older or younger than themselves. For example, 53% reported spending time with older children and adults; 35% of us spent time with younger children.

The most popular escape from our difficulties was to immerse ourselves in academics rather than social activities. 60% of us chose that approach.

The next most popular way to survive was through hobbies. Almost 57% of us used hobbies to avoid a social life. (In another question, we look in some detail at our hobbies.) Less than 40% of us used video games or television. (Keep in mind that all participants are at least 50 and grew up in a time when video games were less prevalent.) About 36% of us turned to alcohol or drugs. Several respondents commented on addictions. David [70, NE*] said: "I abused alcohol and pot from ages 18-40." Others mentioned gambling and overeating to cope with anxiety.

Almost 59% of us second-guess what we said or didn't say.

Those who selected "Other" were invited to provide more information about their personal coping strategies. Many of our community reached out for help, relying on the judgment of people in their lives that they trust.

Expansion on hobbies

We asked those who had picked "hobby" as a coping mechanism to write more about their experience.

Music was the core of many leisure-time activities. Rob [61, NE] mentioned math and piano playing. Earl [57, NZ*] mentioned music. Pat [64, NE*] likes playing musical instruments as well as doing genealogy research and writing *Star Trek* stories.

Some mentioned the autistic tendency to get immersed into whatever hobby was preferred at a given time. Natalie [57, UK] loves writing fantasy and: "becoming totally immersed in the story." Anita [57, NE*]: "I've had a lifelong passion for horses. In 1995 I got hooked on military aviation after seeing Top Gun. I eventually got a flight in an F-15 fighter jet as part of being an internationally published military aviation photojournalist. I also got hooked on making handmade soaps. Now I'm hooked on being an autism advocate!!"

Respondents frequently mentioned intellectual games, autism advocacy, and solitary hobbies such as writing and painting. Other solitary activities included being alone by the sea, prayer, meditation, and reclusiveness.

Marilyn [65, W*] said: "I make miniature dioramas based on actual historical places, I write books about history and my family, and I create art. All of these things reflect my love of sorting and organizing. Janet [61, UK*] collects postcards and sorts them by British counties. Doris [55, AUS*] expressed her creativity by spending "a whole year reading and fantasizing about Lord of the Rings to escape relationship problems. It helped."

DRUG USE BEFORE 30

SURVEY QUESTION #43: *DRUG USE: Which of these did you use excessively during periods of your life?*

Drug Source	Childhood		Teens and 20s	
	Count	%	Count	%
Over-the-counter medication	4	2.7%	8	5.3%
Prescription medication	1	0.7%	10	6.7%
Alcohol	4	2.7%	54	36.0%
Cigarettes	2	1.3%	42	28.0%
Illegal marijuana	0	0.0%	22	14.7%
Legal marijuana and/or medical marijuana	0	0.0%	0	0.0%
Heroin or other opiates	0	0.0%	0	0.0%
Amphetamines	0	0.0%	6	4.0%
Barbiturates	1	0.7%	2	1.3%
Ecstasy	0	0.0%	1	0.7%
"Bath salt" drugs	0	0.0%	0	0.0%
Other (please give details below)	1	0.7%	4	2.7%

A previous question asked about drug use as a way of coping with being different, but here we wanted to get more in-depth information on the abuse of substances throughout the lifespan. Not surprisingly, there was very little drug use indicated in childhood. However, the figures go up dramatically moving into teens and twenties.

Alcohol seems to be the substance of choice for this generation, with 36% admitting to excessive use in teens and young adulthood; 28% reported smoking cigarettes. After that, the most popular drug was marijuana, which attracted almost 15% of our folks.

Participant Comments

We didn't ask participants to specify age so, except for those who specify an age, the behaviors mentioned below may have occurred at any age.

Anya [69, NE*] and several others expressed doubts that we would get honest answers on this topic: "You actually think people will fill this out??? Personally, I tried both marijuana and psychedelic drugs way back in the 1960s. Generally speaking, I think both were helpful."

LITTLE DRUG USE

For assorted reasons, many of our respondents do not and have not used recreational drugs. Laura [57, UK] has never taken illegal drugs: "I take antidepressants and medication for anxiety, but I always stick to the prescribed dose." May [70, SW] said: "My focus has been on natural substances and supplements to ease the stresses of life." Mathew [69, NE] managed to avoid drugs and alcohol: "Don't drink at all. I think I could become an alcohol user or depressant user if I tried, and would have trouble controlling use, so I stay far away. With no history, occasional cravings are within my ability to control with little struggle." Karen [62, W*] expressed a common attitude among our respondents: "I've occasionally self-medicated with a glass of wine, but rarely to excess, except after my divorce I was in a sorry state and drank more than I should have for a bit."

Some have used drugs occasionally, as noted below.

ALCOHOL

2.7% of respondents checked the box for alcohol use in childhood, indicating that they used alcohol excessively as children. In the column for teens and '20's, 36% checked it. We will look at the adult figures in the next section.

A few talked about alcohol as a social lubricant or a way to treat anxiety.

OTHER DRUGS

0.7% indicated "other" as children and 2.7% did so as adults. [We asked for clarification.]

Rhys [52, UK*] took other drugs – "LSD, magic mushrooms, speed, cocaine – at various points between the ages of 20-30 but only very occasionally." My drug of choice was always alcohol, and I was probably drunk more days than not between the ages of 18-33. I am amazed that I never developed an alcohol dependency." Jackie [61, UK*] said: "As with many of us, my brain was always on the go so I preferred 'downers.' My drug of choice was pot, but I did THC, Quaalude, I did LSD a few times. I have used cocaine, heroin-laced pot a couple of times, and in the old days, doctors would give me black beauties –speed – which I gave away. I went through years of binge drinking. I have finally come full circle and am able to drink a few times a year with no issues."

ILLEGAL BEHAVIOR BEFORE 30

SURVEY QUESTION #44: *ILLEGAL BEHAVIOR [Indicate illegal behavior during period of life]:*

Behavior	Childhood			Teens and 20s	
	Count	%		Count	%
Using illegal drugs	0	0.0%		32	21.3%
Selling illegal drugs	0	0.0%		1	0.7%
Robbery	4	2.7%		5	3.3%
Assault	2	1.3%		5	3.3%
Domestic Violence	1	0.7%		1	0.7%
Smuggling	0	0.0%		0	0.0%
Embezzling	0	0.0%		4	2.7%
Arrests	0	0.0%		10	6.7%
Conviction	0	0.0%		3	2.0%
Served time	0	0.0%		3	2.0%
Other	0	0.0%		0	0.0%

Not surprisingly, virtually no illegal behavior was reported in childhood, but some is reported in teens and early twenties.

21.3% used illegal drugs in their teens and/or 20s.
This figure is comparable to a national rate of illegal drug use of 22.6% for adults ages 18-20 [National Institute on Drug Abuse, 2015].

Almost 7% of our group cited "arrests."
This included embezzling, conviction, and serving time.

Participant Comments

We received many comments. Of interest are several responses stating that we won't get any honest replies and that autistics rarely break laws.

Anya [69, NE*]: "I think it is unlikely people will answer these questions honestly. And you probably should [not] be asking people to incriminate themselves. You seem to forget that although you are using this information for research, nothing online is secure." Earl [57, NZ*] made a similar comment: "Someone would have to be stupid to answer any of your questions about illegal behavior. Good luck with that!"

Many the of the comments were about the boring lives many autistics have lived: Karen [62, W*] wrote: "Damn. I've had a boring life, except for stealing money from my mom, bootlegging TV, and skipping school for two weeks in second grade." Many of our folks felt that they are too honest to engage in illegal activities. Some told us that they hated to do illegal things, because they were not good at lying.

Some emphasized the autistic penchant for <u>following the rules</u>. Carlos [66, NE*] could not imagine himself doing anything illegal: "I have a very conventional morality and have never engaged in illegal behavior. I am also not a violent person; if anything, I am too gentle and kind." Mathew [69, NE] confessed to concealing snowballs: "grew up in Canada – much less socialization into, and opportunities for, crime there than here [United States]. The big bad act of my teen years, the most delinquent behavior in my community, was standing looking innocent on the sidewalk, hands concealed, then when a bus drove by, throwing a hidden snowball at the windows. Real tough-guy stuff. If you're not into crime by 21, you're pretty proof against it thereafter." Kenneth [51, UK] avoids illegal behavior. He is honest and "public spirited." Derek [53, NE*] served two days in jail for DUI ["Driving Under the Influence"] 25 years ago and pointed out that he was: "not exactly a hardened criminal."

Rhys [52, UK*] responded with candor: "Apart from the use of illegal drugs (mainly cannabis), I have never been involved in any illegal behaviour. I was arrested for shoplifting when I was about 14, but I hadn't actually stolen anything and the charges were eventually dropped due to lack of evidence."

MENTAL ILLNESS BEFORE 30

SURVEY QUESTION #45: *MENTAL ILLNESS/PSYCHIATRIC DISORDER: Which of these have been an issue for you at various life stages?*

Condition	Childhood		Teens and 20s	
	Count	%	Count	%
Anxiety	80	53.3%	109	72.7%
Depression	49	32.7%	92	61.3%
Obsessive compulsive disorder	13	8.7%	29	19.3%
Post-traumatic stress disorder	22	14.7%	34	22.7%
Personality disorder	7	4.7%	8	5.3%
Bipolar	2	1.3%	5	3.3%
Dissociative disorder	7	4.7%	7	4.7%
ADHD or ADD	18	12.0%	17	11.3%
Suicide attempt	9	6.0%	27	18.0%
Suicidal thoughts	27	18.0%	66	44.0%
Hospitalization	5	3.3%	16	10.7%
Insomnia or other sleep disorders	31	20.7%	52	34.7%
Mental hospital	0	0.0%	12	8.0%
On psychiatric medication	1	0.7%	24	16.0%
Low self-esteem	81	54.0%	107	71.3%
Other	2	1.3%	3	2.0%

Participant Comments

ANXIETY

53.3% reported anxiety in childhood, and 72.7% said they suffered with it in young adulthood.
Julianne [69, AUS] recounted that she had to spend time as an inpatient in psychiatric centers. She poignantly described her experiences: "acute anxiety disorder and PTSD...childhood trauma... nightmares...still wake up screaming sometimes in the night." Emma [60, CAN*] remembered: "probably always had anxiety, I just didn't know that other people didn't experience what I did."

DEPRESSION

32.7% of children and 61.3% of young adults experienced depression.
We looked earlier at depression as a coping mechanism in childhood. The current question asked participants to react to a list of mental issues in childhood. Here is what our group said about their encounters with depression:

Bob [54, NE] stated: "believe that I was depressed when I was 10. I was friendless and bored. I stayed up late trying to imagine death but was not suicidal nor have I ever been. "Ritamarie [50, NE*] wrote: "was diagnosed with severe depression and ADHD in my mid-20s. I believe I had depression from a very early age. I also believe, had it been a diagnosis in the 90s, I would have been diagnosed with Asperger's. Throughout my life I've struggled with low self-esteem and a variety of other problems. Had the diagnosis been available at any point in my life, I would have been considered autistic."

SUICIDAL THOUGHTS

Suicidal thoughts were the next more commonly reported concern in childhood and youth. As illustrated, 18% had suicidal thoughts in childhood, but only 6% reported actually making an attempt. However, by the teens and twenties, 44% contemplated suicide and 18% actually made an attempt. For comparison, U.S. data in 2013 suggest that 17% of high school students considered suicide and 8% made an attempt [Centers for Disease Control and Prevention, 2015]. Our study participants, frequently bullied and misunderstood, seem to have been at substantial risk.

SUICIDE ATTEMPTS

6% of children and 18% of young adults attempted suicide.

LOW SELF-ESTEEM

In childhood 54% of us were self-critical; this increased to over 71% by the teen years.
One respondent said with despair: "Always have had self-hatred. I seemed to be cursed. Wanting to be something I am not. In almost every way. Poor at things I desperately desired, good at things I did not like!"

PTSD

PTSD was reported by 14.7% in childhood years, and 22.7% by teens and twenties.
Based on comments already shared, the most common childhood traumas appear to have been bullying and abuse. There were occasionally other causes, as with Louise [52, UK], who described: "Depression from a trauma episode in her 20s."

MULTIPLE ISSUES

Carlos [66, NE*] has had anxiety and depression throughout his life: "Am very sensitive to stress, and even mild stressors or anxiety can disrupt my ability to sleep. Hypersensitivity in general." Lauren [51, NE*] noted: "I have not been officially diagnosed with psychiatric disorders, partly because I am very leery of psych folks and don't trust them to make a good determination on me. I have had suicidal thoughts for most of my life, starting in my teen years, but I know myself well enough to realize that no sooner would I do something about it, then I'd change my mind. I've had low self-esteem most of my life, but I recently decided to stop listening to that internal voice, because, well, she's so wrong about so many other things, what makes her right about me being such a lousy piece of crap? Constructive disregard...I believe I developed PTSD as a direct result of autism and living in an indifferent and hostile neurotypical world. It's like being beaten up daily, and having to constantly stay vigilant and wary is a direct contributor. I was also bullied in grade school and stalked in college, so those shaped me in ways that are sources of continual stress for me."

Childhood for most of our participants was undeniably hard. There was no diagnosis of Asperger's and no concept of autism without intellectual disability. Many suffered in childhood and young adulthood with depression, anxiety, shame, and low self-esteem. Many still struggle with the same issues.

PSYCHOTHERAPY

An array of mental illnesses was reported. The following chart illustrates how treatment has worked for us.

SURVEY QUESTION #46: *MENTAL ILLNESS/PSYCHIATRIC DISORDER: Treatment…* *Which of these treatments have you had? Indicate below whether they were helpful for you.*

Treatment	Childhood		Teens and 20s	
	Count	%	Count	%
Psychotherapy/ counseling	10	6.7%	53	35.3%
Coaching/mentoring	2	1.3%	6	4.0%
Friends	9	6.0%	25	16.7%
Family	16	10.7%	23	15.3%
Intensive outpatient hospital	0	0.0%	3	2.0%
In-patient psychiatric ward	0	0.0%	8	5.3%
Psychiatric hospital	0	0.0%	10	6.7%
Art therapy	3	2.0%	8	5.3%
Dance therapy	0	0.0%	2	1.3%
Medication	4	2.7%	27	18.0%
Exercise	19	12.7%	42	28.0%
Improving diet	7	4.7%	20	13.3%
Social skills training	0	0.0%	5	3.3%
Over-the-counter meds	2	1.3%	10	6.7%
Other	0	0.0%	1	0.7%

The most commonly cited treatment was psychotherapy, at least in adolescence and early adulthood. In childhood over 33% reported depression, but only 6.7% received therapy. One factor may have been less cultural acceptance of psychotherapy when our participants were children. Thirty-five percent received psychotherapy in their teens and twenties. By comparison, 61% reported being depressed in those years.

Many of our survey takers told us that therapy was not of much help due to inadequately trained therapists. Rhys [52, UK*] told us: "I had some counselling in 1997 when a relationship I was in ended. I didn't find it much use, if I'm honest. Talking to, and the support of, my partner and friends have proven to be more useful than the counselling I had." Stephen K [69, NE] said: "Behaviorist strategies and medication are doing severe damage to many."

Another noteworthy "treatment": 28% of us used exercise before our thirties to improve our mental health. In childhood, 19% were exercising.

Participant Comments

MEDICATION

18% ended up on medication before age 30, but fewer than 3% did so before the teen years.

[Rob] – one of our authors – told us: "Psychiatric and medication therapy was usually not very effective for me. The Asperger peer group has been the most helpful."

DANCE/ART THERAPY

	Childhood		Teens and 20s	
Art therapy	3	2.0%	8	5.3%
Dance therapy	0	0.0%	2	1.3%

In childhood, 2% said they had some art therapy. In young adulthood, 5.3% had art therapy and 1.3% received dance therapy.

DIET

Over 13% changed to a healthier diet before 30, whereas only 5% did so in childhood.

Of course, children often have little control over what is served at the family table. Carlos [66, NE*] wrote: "Improving diet has helped, especially since I am sugar sensitive. Psychotherapy has been helpful only up to a point. Spirituality helps me more than psychology."

FRIENDS/FAMILY

In childhood, 6% turned to friends and almost 11% turned to their families. Over the next 20 years, almost 17% turned to friends, and over 15% turned to family.

	Childhood		Teens and 20s	
Friends	9	6.0%	25	16.7%
Family	16	10.7%	23	15.3%

MULTIPLE STRATEGIES

Lauren [51, NE*] used many resources. She wrote: "Psychotherapy has been a pain in my neck. I have been pressured to go into therapy since I was in my 20s. I gave it a try, but the therapist was abusive…I have been involved in neuropsych rehab since 2008, working on executive function and communication skills. That has helped me immensely. Exercise and watching my diet are big parts of my strategy also. For art therapy, art is something I do, myself, when I need it, not provided by anyone else."

Sadly, most of our generation did not have a diagnosis, making treatment difficult.

PHYSICAL ILLNESSES

The final life-stages question in this section was about physical ailments in childhood, teens, and twenties. "Difficulty sleeping" was our most common choice, with almost 27% of us tossing and turning at night during childhood, and 37% of us in teens and early twenties. The rates of reported insomnia and other sleep disorders in the "Mental Illness" section are consistent with this. Many of us have allergies as well as frequent colds and flu. Five percent checked "other" for childhood and young adulthood, and many of them elaborated on these responses – samples follow below.

PHYSICAL ILLNESS BEFORE 30

SURVEY QUESTION #47: *PHYSICAL ILLNESS: Indicate which of these you have had at various points in your life:*

Condition	Childhood		Teens and 20s	
	Count	%	Count	%
Epilepsy	7	4.7%	5	3.3%
Inner ear imbalance	7	4.7%	11	7.3%
Difficulty hearing	12	8.0%	15	10.0%
Chronic fatigue syndrome	2	1.3%	12	8.0%
Allergies	39	26.0%	53	35.3%
Ulcers	6	4.0%	7	4.7%
Cancer	0	0.0%	0	0.0%
Frequent flu/colds	15	10.0%	20	13.3%
Pneumonia	6	4.0%	5	3.3%
Bad back	5	3.3%	26	17.3%
Surgery	17	11.3%	17	11.3%
Difficulty sleeping	40	26.7%	55	36.7%
Other	8	5.3%	8	5.3%

Participant Comments

Difficulty sleeping was reported by 26.7% of children and 36.7% of young adults. Epilepsy was reported by 4.7% in childhood and 3.3% of young adults.

Other ailments

Alan [62, NE*] has had chronic asthma.
Willie [67, UK] has arthritic complaints.

HEARING/SOUND

"Difficulty hearing" *was reported by 8% in childhood and 10% in youth.*

Quite a few respondents commented on issues with hearing. Lauren [51, NE*] wrote: "When I was a kid, I had a lot of trouble hearing. I could not distinguish between different sounds. "b" and "v" sounded the same to me. Also, "th" and "f" and "s" all sounded the same to me, but "s" was very painful to my ears when I said it, so I used "th" instead of "s" when I talked, which gave me a lisp. I have continued to have trouble distinguishing sounds, and unless I am listening carefully, words sound garbled to me against the background noise around me." Mathew [69, NE] says: "I am a bit hard of hearing and have slight balance problems from lack of exercise and a case of vestibulitis in my mid-50s."

OVERALL SUMMARY

We've endured substantial physical and emotional challenges in our years of growing up. Perhaps the worst part was that we knew we were different, but didn't know why.

PART III

ADULTHOOD: LIVING A QUIRKY LIFE

DEGREE FOUR: REALIZATION/DIAGNOSIS

The fourth degree of autism comes when a person realizes that he/she is on the spectrum – whether through a formal diagnosis by a professional or an informal realization of one's true neurobiology ("self-diagnosis"). The vast majority of our participants were not diagnosed until well into their adulthood. That meant that they were living through the first three degrees until their forties or later. The realization is usually a shock, introducing a concept that they had not applied to themselves through most of their lives.

We hope that later research will examine the impact of children being diagnosed in their early years. If a child is diagnosed today at age five, then they are entering "degree four" and have lived degrees one, two, and three in their first few years. They have had relatively little time to contemplate their differences from other kids or to process what the diagnosis means.

So, will the nine degrees of autism have the same usefulness in the years ahead for autistics and their researchers? Only time will tell. The model grew out of the work of a late-diagnosed older adult, and only future research will show how useful it is to other generations.

SURVEY QUESTION #3: *Have you been diagnosed with autism?*

	Percent	Count
Yes, at this age:	78.5%	117
Yes, diagnosed by a professional. What kind of professional?	79.2%	118
Yes; because of comments by friend or family member:	12.8%	19
No, but I have diagnosed myself and believe I am on the spectrum	16.8%	25
No	2.0%	3
Total Responses		149

As you can see, almost 80% of our community were diagnosed by a mental health professional. About 13% realized they were on the spectrum based on comments made from others. For example, Yvonne [65, SW*] said: "A friend online told me I remind her of her son who was just diagnosed with Asperger's syndrome."

Around 17% said they had diagnosed themselves, which is becoming more common in autism communities of adults because of negative experiences in finding good diagnosticians for autism. Of the 118 diagnosed by a professional, 68 identified a psychologist as the professional they consulted. Another 15 said a psychiatrist, and a few specified "doctor." A smattering of other professional types was also indicated (therapist, counselor, etc.). A total of 116 respondents indicated the age at which they were diagnosed. Below is a chart depicting diagnosis by age decade.

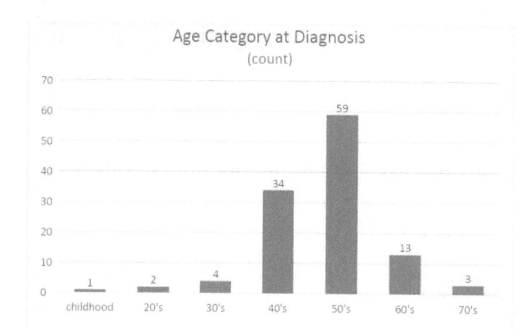

Of these, 59 members reported that they were diagnosed in their 50s, 13 in their 60s, 3 in their 70s, 34 in their 40s, 4 in their 30s, and just 2 in their 20s. Only one person was diagnosed in childhood, to be diagnosed again at 59. So, the vast majority were in their 50s and older before figuring out their true identity. This information affirms what we had suspected: Most of us who found our way to identification on the spectrum did so after age 50. This raises one of the key questions that we are looking at in this study: *What are the effects of learning so late in life that one is on the autism spectrum?*

Participant Comments

79.2% were diagnosed by a professional.

Some were struck by the questions that "hit home" during an evaluation. For example, William [67, NE*] noted that: "Certain clues loom large in this assessment. I jump and scream with sudden loud noises. I prefer solitude to the vast 'dreck' of humanity. I dread meeting new people, but sometimes get a delightful surprise when I force myself to do it. I conceptualize everything visually in my mind as Temple Grandin does."

Many have had the experience of trying to explain problems in therapy and being misunderstood. David Borey [62, NE] wrote about this memory: "About eight years ago a coworker had a son with autism. One day she was talking about her outfit for the day. Then I told her how I got dressed, and afterwards she said, 'You sound like my son!' I didn't know what that meant at the time. About 20 years ago I was in therapy and I told my therapist that I could not see people's faces. I think I meant to say I couldn't 'read' people's faces, but didn't even really know what I was saying, or even how I knew I couldn't read faces? Back then my therapist didn't know about the spectrum, and she proceeded to give me a sheet of paper with little cartoon sketches of faces smiling, crying, etc."

Some participants had to see several professionals before finding one who could accurately diagnose. It took Herman [54, OTH] a while to go through this process. He explained: "got the diagnosis after visiting my fifth psychiatrist because I kept complaining about burnout-related problems. He concluded this after my second visit and invited my mother for the next consultation. I was informed [of the diagnosis] after this third consultation." Jackie [61, UK*] recalled: "I was taken to a psychiatrist at age 5 and have been in and out of counseling...my choice...throughout my life. I have had many diagnoses, and yet I know that along with the side mental health issues I deal with, being on the autism spectrum sums it up in great part."

For some of the women in the study, realization was delayed by autism research being male-oriented. When books about women autistics came out, some women felt they finally heard a message that spoke to them.

Laura [57, UK] told us: "I had a bad experience in that my diagnostic forays fared poorly. I was met with resistance and disbelief at every turn, and I was actively discouraged from pursuing an official diagnosis. I was denied diagnosis, in fact, by a neuropsychologist I really trusted, and that was crushing. He insisted that I was too empathetic, I was too social, I made eye contact, and I didn't fit the 'theory of mind' criteria. Of course not! I'm a grown woman with a lifetime of life experience and learning, not a 7-year-old white male from an upper-middle-class family."

12.8% were influenced by comments from friends or family.

For some, the realization hit like a lightning bolt. Anita's [57, NE*] story is dramatic: "A coworker's son had just been diagnosed with Asperger's. She was very upset and started telling me of his diagnosis. I'd never heard of Asperger's. She handed me papers with info about it. That was the moment, as I read it, that my life suddenly changed, that moment I learned why I'm so different and never fit in."

For some, the realization occurred when someone they knew got a diagnosis. Bob [54, NE] thought about it when others in his family got diagnosed and saw relationships in his life breaking down.

There are still a lot of barriers to obtaining a professional diagnosis. For example, here is Jonathan's [54, UK*] perspective: "I was referred by a consultant psychiatrist. However, it was not his inference, but rather it was my girlfriend who suggested I was on the autistic spectrum, and the psychiatrist thought there was something in this. I am afraid this exposes a much deeper problem and that is a worrisome level of ASD understanding amongst a significant number of health professionals providing clinical care for individuals on the autism spectrum." Janet [61, UK] had a similar experience: "This was after over a decade of suspecting I was on the spectrum, but psychiatrists, doctors insisting that I was not autistic. I was told by a psychiatrist in 2002, 'Children with autism grow up to be adults with autism. You were not diagnosed as a child; therefore you do not have autism.' Problem was, no one knew about autism and Asperger syndrome when I was a child in the late 1950s and early 1960s. This was why I wasn't diagnosed."

Martha [57, SW*] also had a bad experience with professionals: "had an initial diagnosis of Asperger's in my late 30s by a therapist I was seeing. He was part of a group practice, and he and his colleagues did research to figure out what my diagnosis was, and that is what they came up with. At the time they told me, I asked what could be done about it, and they said 'nothing' (as I presume that was the extent of their knowledge). Since nothing could be done about it, it seemed like useless information to me so I just discarded the notion. I did not have Internet access at the time and put it out of my mind. Later on, I heard Temple Grandin interviewed on NPR and when I looked up 'Asperger's' and 'autism' on the Internet, I realized clearly that this is what fit me the best of anything else I had ever read or heard about. So, one could say I was self-diagnosed in the end, and subsequent psychiatrists and therapists have agreed that this is my diagnosis."

Some of our participants presented initially with a different complaint.

One participant told us: "I became depressed clinically at about 30... Basically, I had been juggling all my life to be normal and fit in. It became too difficult and I was exhausted, my batteries wore out."

16.8% diagnosed themselves.

Some came to realize on their own that they lived on the spectrum. For example, Emma [60, CAN*] wrote: "I have vacillated about whether I should pursue a diagnosis. It's difficult where I live, and expensive, but I could do this. However, the more time that has passed, the less need I have for 'official' diagnosis. I also know that so few professionals understand the way women show up, and the developmental nature of autism. I am very involved with other adults in the neurodiversity movement and feel less and less need for outside validation. My friends and my partner do that for me.[1]"

Some of us have had the unhelpful experience of being told that, given our age, there's no point in diagnosis: Ritamarie [50, NE*] had this experience: "When I found out I had autism, I talked with my doctor (psychiatrist) about it. He didn't think it was pertinent at "my stage of life" to have an official diagnosis. I think he's wrong. I know another doctor would diagnose me as autistic for certain. So, I identify as autistic."

These stories poignantly illustrate that for many older autistics – especially women – the road to a diagnosis has been long and arduous.

---

[1]   A few mentioned taking an online quiz. One of the more popular versions is the AQ, which may be found online at http://aspergerstest.net/aq-test/. The test's reliability and validity have been supported by published research [Baron-Cohen et al., 2001]. While it can help establish a diagnosis, it is only one piece of information and should be considered in context. Pat [64, NE*] said: "I took an online quiz that indicated that I am strongly on the spectrum. Lauren [51, NE*] related: "I have repeatedly assessed myself via a number of tests [online and in print] since 2/1998, and I always score well in the range of the spectrum." Katrine-Estella [53, UK] wrote: "I did an online Asperger's/Autism test and contacted the National Autism Society."

SURVEY QUESTION #4: *When you started thinking you might have autism, what resources did you use to explore it?*

	Percent	Count
Friend	10.7%	16
Family	18.1%	27
Spouse	22.1%	33
Social Media	14.1%	21
Internet	76.5%	114
Print media	45.6%	68
Workshop or Conference	13.4%	20
Health Professional	26.2%	39
Mental Health Professional	42.3%	63
Autism Support Groups	37.6%	56
Other	15.4%	23
Total Responses		149

Asperger's came into broader awareness in the 1980s and 1990s, and the impact increased over time. To understand these findings better, we looked at differences in how our older vs. younger respondents experienced their diagnosis. So we created two age groups by establishing a cutoff line at being born before or after January 1, 1960.

Among those born before 1960, only about 4% turned to friends for help compared to 20% for those born in 1960 or later. About 22% of the younger respondents turned to social media for help vs. 10% of their elders. Consulting mental health professionals went from 35% of the older autistics to 50% of the younger ones.

Because of the small sample sizes [$N = 54$ for the younger group and $N = 95$ for the older], these are not statistically significant figures, but they indicate that as "Asperger's" became better known in the culture, a larger percentage turned to friends, social media, and mental health professionals for help.

"Younger Group: When you started thinking you might have autism; what resources did you use to explore it?"

	Percent	Count
Friend	20.4%	11
Family	20.4%	11
Partner or spouse	18.5%	10
Social media	22.2%	12
Internet	77.8%	42
Print media	42.6%	23
Workshop or conference	11.1%	6
Health professional	35.2%	19
Mental health professional	50.0%	27
Autism support groups	38.9%	21
Other	9.3%	5
Total Responses		54

"Older group: When you started thinking you might have autism, what resources did you use to explore it? "

	Percent	Count
Friend	4.2%	4
Family	16.8%	16
Partner or spouse	23.2%	22
Social media	9.5%	9
Internet	72.6%	69
Print media	42.1%	40
Workshop or conference	11.6%	11
Health professional	20.0%	19
Mental health professional	34.7%	33
Autism support groups	34.7%	33
Other	16.8%	16
Total Responses		95

Participant Comments

76.5% used the Internet and 14.1% used social media.

45.6% used print media.

For many of us – especially those of us who are older – books are generally the first place to turn for information. Anita [57, NE*] remembered the day she realized she was on the spectrum: "That night...I stopped at the bookstore and purchased every book they had about Asperger's. I stayed up all night reading Tony Attwood's book, *The Complete Guide to Asperger's Syndrome*." Samantha [52, MW] just wrote one word: "*Books!*"

Organizations and movements.

Emma [60, CAN*] told us: "I have always been connected with other autistic people because I have been on the speaker's circuit in disability/inclusive education/human services for decades. I would not characterize my contact with Asperger's Autism support groups - more like disability rights groups. Some mentioned local support groups." A respondent [58, NE] related: "After my official diagnosis at age 47, I connected first with other autistics online via the Internet and then via local autism support organizations like the *Asperger/Autism Network*, and the *Autistic Self Advocacy Network*."

Research

Lucy [61, NE*] wrote: "knew something was 'wrong' when I was in college, back in the 70s before there was the Internet, so I sought out anything I could find in psychology textbooks and journals at the library. I finally gave up, and just started thinking about myself as having a brain that "short-circuited every now and then" as well as having what I called "no filters" so everything got into my brain and stayed there."

10.7% indicated getter help from a friend, 18% from family and 22% from partner or spouse.

Karen [62, W*] recalled: "The woman who made me aware I might have Asperger's was in an early childhood education class...All of a sudden, the pieces fell into place; I'd read about autism before but didn't know about colors and textures...Like a typical Aspie, I blurted out 'That's me, too!' "

Little support

Some participants found little support after diagnosis.

William [67, NE*] related: "I once tried to get a disability designation by visiting a doctor. The doctor told me that no one my age gets an Asperger's diagnosis and that I have absolutely no physical, mental, or developmental disability. 'Get a job' were his final words."

Lauren [51, NE*] found no support from professionals: "Except in the case of AS support groups, as well as AS-specific online resources [social media, forums, etc.], my diagnostic forays fared poorly. I was met with resistance and disbelief at every turn, and I was actively discouraged from pursuing an official diagnosis. I was denied diagnosis, in fact, by a neuropsychologist I really trusted, and that was pretty crushing. He insisted that I was too empathetic, I was too social, I made eye contact, and I didn't fit the "theory of mind" criteria. Of course not! I'm a grown woman with a lifetime of life experience and learning, not a 7-year-old white male from an upper-middle-class family."

SURVEY QUESTION #5: *When you were diagnosed (or realized you were on the spectrum), which of the following did you feel?*

One's reaction to realizing one is on the spectrum is a crucial element of the fourth degree. Debra Moore points out that an "identity crisis is often part of the fourth degree as one is moving towards the self-acceptance of the seventh degree. Without needed information and support, such an experience can be overwhelming." [Wylie et al., 2016].

	Percent	Count
Relief	78.8%	115
Disbelief	13.0%	19
Fear	11.6%	17
Rage	5.5%	8
Disappointment	10.3%	15
Excitement	29.5%	43
Other	41.8%	61
Total Responses		146

Learning in your fifties (or later) that you are on the autism spectrum can be a shock, but it can also be an enormous relief. In fact, the most cited reaction, reported by almost 79% of the group, was a sense of relief. Almost 30% were excited. Only about 10% were disappointed, and about 6% felt rage. In addition, 43% experienced other feelings, including joy, wonder, clarity, grief, sadness, and for several individuals, "nothing."

Participant Comments

78.8% felt relief.

Kenneth [51, UK] wrote: "I felt I didn't have to blame myself any more for being me...at least not so much." Laura [57, UK]: "felt some relief, but I also wasn't sure other people would believe it." Rhys [52, UK*] told us: "When I was diagnosed, it was a massive relief for me as it made my whole life finally make sense. I did, however, have trouble believing that I am on the spectrum, and at times still do, though these thoughts seem to be getting less as time goes on." Lucy [61, NE*] commented: "It was so nice to have a name for it! And it allowed me to join a support group and start learning more about myself, as well as being clearer about which aspects of being on the spectrum I could work on and which I would just have to live with."

Derek [53, NE*]: "I realized that the final pieces of the puzzle as to why I am the way I am fell into place, and that others feel the same way. OTHERS FEEL THE SAME WAY. That is why I attend support group. Because others can relate to what I feel." Karen [62, W*] was quite excited: "It took about six weeks to internalize/accept the label; I could see how well it explained my entire life [epiphany is too small a word, but enlightenment and having one's entire life illuminated, is pretty close]." Kenneth [51, UK] felt that by having a name for his challenges, he no longer needed to feel that these issues were his fault.

13% felt disbelief.

A much smaller number of folks experienced a sense of disbelief.

11.6% felt fear.

An even smaller percentage of folks were afraid after diagnosis. Karen [62, W*] was one of them, describing "apprehension and uncertainty." Graham [65, UK] felt anxious. Doris [55, AUS*] wrote: "It was a relief to be diagnosed, but I felt some fear for the future. It takes a while to get used to the 'new normal.'"

5.5% felt rage.

This was the least common response. Most of the rage described stemmed from not knowing earlier. Martha's [57, SW*] anger seems to be directed at God: "I was relieved at first to finally understand myself. Later on, I have been rageful about the sense of being robbed of so many aspects of life that other people enjoy. Especially the ability to live comfortably in my own body without sensory torments and to have normal sexual relations and family life. I struggle with my relationship with God because I cannot understand why he did this to me."

10.3% felt disappointment.

29.5% felt excited.

David [70, NE*] just wrote: "Wonder. He was on cloud 9 for weeks." Nancy [57, NE*] was amazed. Carlos [66, NE*] was: "Happy I had something objective to blame for my differences, something I was born with and not responsible for." Marilyn [65, W*]: "Joy, I finally understood that there was something different about me."

41.8% checked "Other."

Grieving

Some grieved. Yvonne [65, SW*] wrote: "Felt I lost my lifelong identity and went through a year of mourning the loss of knowing who I was before and there is a new identity." Ann [64, NE*] had similar feelings: "It's hard to verbalize right now about the grief."

Lillian [55, UK]: "Grief – for the time I spent so misunderstood and isolated, for the impact of having to act for a lifetime to appear normal, for the self I am just beginning to know."

Sadness

Emily [70, UK*]: "Huge sadness that no one had understood me and had laughed at me for years."

Identification

Others found a community to identify with. One of our respondents commented: "It explained my living in my own inner world all the time. Inability to make and keep friendships." Derek [53, NE*]: "I realized that the final pieces of the puzzle as to why I am the way I am fell into place, and that others feel the same way. OTHERS FEEL THE SAME WAY. That is why I attend a support group. Because others can relate to what I feel." Anita [57, SE*] had thought: "I was the only person in the world like me! I was TOTALLY relieved!!!!!!!"

Isolation

Jonathan [54, UK*] wrote: "For a couple of weeks after my diagnosis I felt relief, but this was quickly followed by despair as the signposting for support that was promised quickly evaporated and I am left completely on my own in having to deal with my diagnosis of Asperger's."

Regret

One of our respondents said disclosing his diagnosis caused him trouble at work and with his health.

Mixed reaction

Lauren [51, NE*] remembered: "I felt a number of things in a variety of ways. I was relieved that there was a way to understand myself. I also had some disbelief, at first, because I never thought of myself as being autistic. I was fearful of being exploited and/or mistreated. And I was also disappointed at the reactions of others who were incredulous. I was so excited, at times, to have found a way to understand myself, but that feeling was not shared by anyone I knew – least of all my healthcare providers."

Martha [57, SW*] was relieved at first to understand who she was. But: "Later on, I have been rageful about the sense of being robbed of so many aspects of life that other people enjoy...to live comfortably in my own body without sensory torments...I struggle with my relationship with God because I cannot understand why he did this to me."

Jack [57, UK] noted that he felt some relief following diagnosis but he is still confused about who he is.

Seeing family connection.

Jackie [61, UK*] shared: "One of the most amazing parts has been quickly coming to also understand that my husband is also on the spectrum...my grandfather was born in London but left for America as a child...but I met my husband while researching on the Internet, and we have always said that something far beyond us drew us together...and I know the autism is a big part of it."

As noted, almost 79% felt relief about the diagnosis, and close to 30% felt excitement. These comments show some of the depth of feeling behind those numbers, as well as range of reactions.

SURVEY QUESTION #6: *In the year after diagnosis/realization, how did your life change?*

	Percent	Count
My life did not change	22.2%	32
I felt better about myself	66.7%	96
I felt worse about myself	20.1%	29
I became depressed	21.5%	31
I was more withdrawn	23.6%	34
I was more outgoing	14.6%	21
I developed mental health problems	6.3%	9
I developed health issues	6.3%	9
Total Responses		144

Almost 67% of us – the overwhelming majority of our participants – felt better about ourselves in the year after a diagnosis. Only 20% of us felt worse. Almost 24% were more withdrawn, and over 21% were less depressed.

Participant Comments

22.2% said their life didn't change.

William [67, NE*]: "My life did not change substantially. I remained poor, isolated, alienated. Big deal." Sally [51, UK] says the same, quite dramatically: "It's still hell!"

66.7% felt better about themselves.

Some started to understand themselves better after the diagnosis. Wenn [64, AUS*] wrote: "I was finally able to make sense of who I was." Bob [54, NE] told us: "My depression lifted without medication. I was better able to plan work since I understood my limitations." Alan [62, NE*] pointed out: "Knowing I'm Aspie helped me to decide when to interact and when to be alone." For Anita [57, NE*], life changed in amazing ways: "First I wrote a memoir that I self-published. That led to me meeting Dr. Temple Grandin. She included me in a book she had just started, *Different...Not Less.* I'm Chapter 7 in there, 'Nurse Anesthetist/Aviation Writer.' Then I got placed in contact with Dr. Tony Attwood, who asked me to help write a book with him and Craig Evans, *Been There. Done That. Try This!: The Aspie's Guide to Life on Earth.* I've also become an autism advocate, national speaker, blogger, regular contributing author for Autism Asperger's Digest, and recently founded the Global Autism Consulting Organization. Also, back in September 2015 my husband and I opened our ALL-AUTISTIC WEDDING to the public and attracted international media attention!"

Many of our respondents reported being able to let go of blaming themselves for life problems. Janet [61, UK] found it helpful to have a written diagnosis. For one thing, it has helped her open doors to work accommodations: "finally realised it wasn't all in my head." Martha [57, SW*] wrote: "For a while, I felt better about myself because I no longer felt I was as much to blame for the fact that my life did not turn out as well as I expected."

Many felt able to restructure their lives around their strengths. For example, Louise [52, UK] told us: "I've always been a loner but no longer feel I have to 'remedy' that. It's fine to prefer my own company. Diagnosis also gave me permission to focus on the things I'm good at and seek to excel at those."

Some found additional support communities. For example, Nancy [57, NE*] said: "I felt better about myself and was more outgoing with people who identified as AS to me, mainly because I felt my success in academics, career, and relationships, gave me skills to help other adults on the [autism] spectrum. I started a women's AS support group and found strength from other women." Derek [53, NE*] said: "I was still the same person. I don't need to label myself. But knowing the problem helped me as I reached out to Rob [Lagos] and the support group and did research on it."

There were many stories of how the diagnosis had helped. Yvonne [65, SW*] told us: "I had many questions answered about me. I felt good." Lillian [55, UK] wrote: "When I got my autism diagnosis I was experiencing high levels of stress and got very depressed/suicidal, my autism diagnosis got me support and enabled me to keep hold of my job."

Emma [60, CAN*] wrote: "I am proud of being Autistic. And, like so many, reconfiguring my life experiences in the context of this understanding transformed many of the issues I've faced from 'moral failings' to differences. Liberating!" Carlos [66, NE*] found help in support groups and confirmation that he was not alone, that it wasn't just me who was defective and hateful, but a condition people have that they didn't ask for and had no control over. "It made sense out of so many things in my life, most especially the repeated rejection I have experienced throughout and that has devastated my self-image."

Tim [76, NE*] said "I felt better and my wife felt better because we had found the name of the cause of much of our marital problems." Another respondent told us: "Well, to use the cliché, 'Knowledge is power.'"

Graham [65, UK] gained confidence "from knowing who I was personally and professionally." Wayne [58, UK*] said it "helped me understand myself better and also my son." Penny [58, SW] became more compassionate towards herself.

20.1% felt worse about themselves.

Unlike those who felt welcomed into autism support communities, Ritamarie [50, NE*] struggled with feelings of not being accepted. "Some in the autistic community have questioned my diagnosis because I have achieved so much in my lifetime. That really hurts when the people you are now identifying with won't accept you!! In regular life, I still struggle with telling people I just meet that I am autistic. I don't usually reveal it unless absolutely necessary." Katrine-Estella [53, UK] had a similar experience: "My life did not get better in regard to getting support to help me understand my autism and receive the support for my poor social skills and coping with sensory problems."

Some respondents, especially those who were in the mental health field, felt worse because they hadn't figured it out earlier. For example, Emily [70, UK*] wrote: "Wish I'd known sooner. Or didn't have it so I could understand others better. Also, as a psychologist, I feel stupid for not guessing earlier."

Rhys [52, UK*] also had a difficult time. "have been diagnosed for less than a year, and my diagnosis came at a time when there was quite a lot of upheaval in my life. I had had a meltdown at work and had walked out and was on long-term sick leave with stress and depression. I finally retired on ill health grounds after four months and have been unemployed since. As my diagnosis happened during all this, it was difficult for me to know how I felt about it as I was so preoccupied with the work situation. I have suffered with depression for years so this was not caused by receiving the diagnosis, but it did make it harder for me to deal with what the diagnosis meant for me."

21.5% became depressed.

Some became depressed for a while and then pulled out of it. David [62, NE] said: "About a year or so after finding out, I became somewhat depressed. Not sure if this was because I knew I had AS and it was never going to get better for me, but now those feelings are becoming less and less."

23.6% became withdrawn.

14.6% became more outgoing.

Karen [62, W*] said: "At this point in time, it's less than a year from when I discovered I have Asperger's. I only learned eight months ago. I consider Asperger's my 'superpower,' given that since I've embraced who I am and what it is, a lot of things seem better in part because of being able to let go of the self-blame. I also feel more creative and more intelligent (I guess because a lot of the social anxiety due to being on the spectrum has diminished.) Ironically, having PTSD from my abusive ex-husband's treatment of me (19 years of emotional abuse) and researching that gave me insights on Asperger's, as has the book *Uniquely Human [Prizant, 2015]*, with regard to autism-related anxiety."

6.3% developed mental health problems.

[69, NE]: "My wife is trying to divorce me, and is extremely hostile, and our income declined to the point where I am worried. I think these factors rather than the diagnosis caused the increased depression. The health issues, if they are not just random or age-related, are probably more from the divorce issue than the diagnosis issue."

SURVEY QUESTION #7: *In the year after diagnosis/realization, which support resources did you use?*

	Percent	Count
Family	34.8%	49
Friends	27.7%	39
School	0.0%	0
Therapy	37.6%	53
Coaching	5.7%	8
Mentoring	4.3%	6
I was in psychiatric day treatment	4.3%	6
I was in a psychiatric hospital	0.0%	0
Support groups [incl. for autism]	41.1%	58
Other:	44.0%	62
Total Responses		141

Support groups, therapists, family, and friends were the primary support resources in the year after diagnosis, but the most frequently cited was "Other" [44%], followed by support group [41%] and therapy [37.6%]. Finally, family at 34.8% and friends at 27.7%.

Given that we are dealing with a complicated neurological difference between those on the spectrum and neurotypicals, one might expect there to be more outreach to therapists. Yet, the HFA/Asperger's community tends to hold the professionals at arm's length and to learn from each other in support groups. The reason for this is reflected in the stories of our participants. Many of us have had to teach our therapists how to recognize and support autism. We have had therapists who misdiagnosed us, often with labels such as "schizophrenia," "retarded," and "personality disorder." Remember that therapists were first learning about Asperger's in the 1980s and 1990s. "Asperger's Syndrome" wasn't a diagnosis until 1994 when it entered the *DSM*. It was many years after that before therapists understood it or had any training about it. The following puts this in perspective:

When Asperger was translated into English:

Wilma was 34.

Rob was 27.

Eric was 21.

When "Asperger's Syndrome" was included in the *DSM*:

Wilma was 47.

Rob was 40.

Eric was 34.

We researched this book in 2016 and wrote it in 2017, yet we still struggle to find competent therapists to diagnose and work with our fellow autistics. It is not surprising that older spectrum folks have never fully trusted the professional mental health community. Much of the energy for understanding the range of autism has come from the autism community. When people in our community get diagnosed – by a professional or themselves – they turn to support groups in greater numbers than they turn to therapists.

Participant Comments

41.1% turned to support groups.

Rhys [52, UK*] wrote: "I am very lucky in that there is an excellent autism support service not far from where I live. I registered with them when I got my private diagnosis and they have been invaluable. My partner has also been incredibly supportive, and is in fact thinking of undertaking a pre-diagnostic assessment for Asperger's Syndrome herself." A number of folks (including Earl [57, NZ*]) found The Artist's Way groups very helpful. These are groups that came from Julie Cameron's book, *The Artist's Way* [Cameron, 1992].

Many of our folks used online support resources. Carlos [66, NE*] said: "The GRASP groups [https://grasp.org/] were extremely helpful in making this adjustment to my identity. I learned a lot about the condition. Also, watching the movie about Temple Grandin helped me make sense of my life and experiences." A few specifically cited "wrongplanet.net." Anita [57, NE *] started an autism support group in her community. Emma [60, CAN*] told us: "I'm really involved in online autism communities, but again, I would not characterize them as support groups, more as friends." Lillian [55, UK] mentioned social media/autism support at work. In addition, Janet [61, UK] included meditation. Yvonne [65, SW*] showed true initiative. She wrote: "I could not find much information on females, so I started the first and largest Internet group worldwide for women on the autism spectrum for education and support."[https://www.facebook.com/autisticwomen-sassociation/ and https://autisticwomensassociationworldwide.wordpress.com/]

Natalie [57, UK] had a unique perspective: "have joined a couple of online groups for women with autism, but am not sure if they are supportive for me; I do not think I know how to be supported." Her observation is probably true for many of us.

37.6% turned to therapy.

Many found that therapy did not help. One of our discouraged respondents told us "Therapy and psychiatric treatment has done nothing other than to try to force acceptance of one's poor situation and to point out how fruitless life-enriching pursuits, college, etc., will be." Lauren [51, NE*] had a similar reaction to her therapy. "My friends and family were useless to me. Therapy, I thought would help, but it turned out to be a terrible idea. The therapist I was seeing refused to believe I was on the spectrum until I terminated with her and she was looking through her notes about me and found the documentation I'd put together. Then she said, "There may be something to that after all. A lot of good it did me...I'm still bitter over it, because she did such a terrible job of 'therapizing' me, which was more like gaslighting. She was a nice lady, but an awfully under-informed therapist. I mostly went online and read what books I could find."

34.8% turned to family.

27.7% got support from friends.

Emma [60, CAN*]: "I'm really involved in online autism communities, but again, I would not characterize them as support groups, more as friends." William [67, NE*] added: "and a very few friends at that!"

44.0% checked "Other."

Adam [56, OTH] wrote books. Wenn [64, AUS*] read books and journal articles on autism. Mathew [69, NE] tried to read some of the professional literature on ASD and Asperger's: "That gave me more information than my therapists did." Linda [56, W] added: "Online sites *Wrongplanet. net* and books."

Some respondents noted disappointment in resources.

APPROACH TO DIAGNOSIS

SURVEY QUESTION #8: *This is one approach to diagnosis. Check any of these that you feel are true of you:*

Observation	Percent	Count
Difficulty in ordinary social interactions	88.7%	133
Difficulty in understanding and expressing emotions	79.3%	119
Difficulty understanding non-verbal social interactions, such as body language, eye contact, gestures, and facial expressions	74.0%	111
Difficulty in initiating and maintaining regular social relationships, such as making friends and adjusting to different social contexts	86.0%	129
Repetitive use of the same gestures or words or objects (e.g., lining up objects)	45.3%	68
Insisting on routine and being upset by small changes	65.3%	98
Getting fixated on particular interests or objects	80.7%	121
Overreacting or underreacting to stimuli such as noise, lights, smells, textures, touch, temperatures	77.3%	116
These behaviors have always been part of your life in some way. However, they may not have been clear early on, and have may have improved over time	66.0%	99
These symptoms have caused significant problems in your social life, work life, or other aspects of living	75.3%	113
These symptoms aren't totally explained by something else, like intellectual impairment	57.3%	86

This question was designed to include the basic criteria for high-functioning autism in the *DSM-5* [APA, 2013]. Our participants identified strongly with most of the criteria. Specifically, almost 90% identified with "Difficulty in ordinary social interactions" and 86% endorsed "Difficulty in initiating and maintaining regular social relationships, such as making friends and adjusting to different social contexts." This was of particular interest since the *DSM-5* eliminated the category of Asperger's Syndrome and put many of its characteristics under High-Functioning Autism, a change that prompted vociferous protest from the Asperger' community claiming that the new criteria would leave out many of us. The smallest number of our participants who related to a criterion was 45.3%. Our folks related to the rest of the criteria in a range from 57.3% to 88.7%.

Participant Comments

88.7% reported difficulty in ordinary social interactions.

Jim [53, NE*] was reflective about these criteria in his life: "I am 'high-functioning,' but I had no friends in high school, no girlfriends in college, became depressed about my social situation and let my grades slide, drank too much alcohol, and was angry. Things got better, I got married at 28. But I still have melt-downs, which are basically minor spaz attacks of frustration." Lucy [61, NE*] had some interesting observations on the criteria in her life: "Periodically these symptoms have caused significant problems, but currently they are not, and there have been long periods of time where they have not. Depends on the people in the work or other situation. Good people, I do OK. Mean, manipulative, deceitful, angry, or mentally ill people, I don't do OK."

79.3% indicated difficulty in understanding and expressing emotions.

One woman in the U.S. said: "I take people literally and at face value, not realizing underlying meaning or intent of someone's words or actions."

86.0% have difficulty in initiating and maintaining regular social relationships, such as making friends and adjusting to different social contexts.

80.7% get fixated on particular interests or objects.

Pat [64, NE*] explained how this is for her: "Get me started on talking about a particular interest, and I'll keep going until the other person's eyes start to glaze over!"

77.3% said they overreact or underreact to stimuli such as noise, lights, smells, textures, touch, temperatures.

Emma [60, CAN*] commented: "I'm a combination of sensory seeking and sensory avoiding. Looking at this list, some of these things were more prominent when I was younger." Carlos [66, NE*] told us: "You just summarized my life story. I also have hyperacusis and extreme sensitivity to glare. I cannot leave the house without my sunglasses and hearing protectors."

William [67, NE*] elaborated on his challenges: "NOISE! NOISE! NOISE! I jump and scream when my neighbors knock on my door...and it takes me a long, LONG time to recover." Anita [57, NE*] said that her sensory issues: "have always been BIG issues at my job. Prior to being diagnosed, bosses and coworkers were extremely harsh to me."

66.0% said that these behaviors have always been part of their life in some way. However, they may not have been clear early on and may have improved over time.

Rhys [52, UK*] commented on the value of his diagnosis: "Having got to the age of 50 without a diagnosis, I have of course learnt numerous coping strategies to get through life. But the effort of having to do this has taken quite a toll on me over the years, and many of my symptoms are now worse than they have ever been because I just don't have the strength to keep up the facade anymore. The great thing about being diagnosed is that I now feel comfortable being who I actually am and don't feel the need to put on an act anymore."

57.3% agreed that these symptoms aren't totally explained by something else, like intellectual impairment.

Lauren [51, NE*] noted that: "Although I may not appear to have issues in many of these areas, my internal experience is extremely challenging. I don't instinctively know how to do a lot of things others take for granted. I have to do them deliberately, and in ways that I have practice more times than I can count. Unfortunately, one's lived experience isn't always quantifiable on a doctor's chart."

Not everyone agreed with the way the diagnostic criteria are used, but overall they identified with the issues described. To probe further, we added a question related to other approaches to diagnosis, outside of the *DSM-5*, which is based on pathology.

SURVEY QUESTION #9: *Not everyone agrees with a symptom and deficit-based approach to autism. Check any of these statements that you agree with:*

Statement	Percent	Count
Autism isn't an illness. It's a different way of being human...to help them, we don't need to change them or fix them. We need to work to understand them, and then change what we do. [1]	78.7%	118
Instead of classifying legitimate, functional behavior as a sign of pathology, we'll examine it as part of a range of strategies to cope, to adapt, to communicate, and deal with a world that feels overwhelming and frightening. [2]	62.7%	94
Diagnosis with...the...*DSM-5* is not precise like a diagnosis for bacterial infections where precise lab tests can be used. Psychiatric diagnostic labels were determined by both scientific studies and the opinion of committees sitting around conference room tables in hotels. Nobody debates the results of lab tests for a strep throat. Over the years, many psychiatric diagnoses have changed. [3]	59.3%	89
When individuals on the milder end of the autism spectrum are labeled, you must remember that the following words all mean the same thing: *Asperger, Aspie, geek, nerd, mild autism, social communication disorder*, or *socially awkward*. The science clearly shows that the social problems on the autism spectrum are a true continuum. [4]	57.3%	86

The above statements were gathered from several recent sources. The first two are from *Uniquely Human: A Different Way of Seeing Autism* [Prizant, 2015].

78.7 % agreed with the first statement: "Autism isn't an illness. It's a different way of being human...to help them, we don't need to change them or fix them. We need to work to understand them, and then change what we do." [Prizant, 2015, p. 4]

Yvonne [65, SW*] said: "do not believe it's a disorder. Autism is just a different brain operating system." Pat [64, NE*] paraphrased one of her favorite characters from Star Trek: "I'm an Aspie, not an amoeba!" Lauren [51, NE*] told us: Autism is only a problem in situations that cannot or will not accommodate us...Pathologizing difference seems to be a specialty of neurotypical people ...The *DSM-5* is a travesty by the standards of people who have worked on former versions. It's a work in progress, and it is not THE LAST WORD on What Is What. Kenneth [51, UK] told us that he doesn't mind a symptom/deficit approach to autism. He does consider himself to have a disability, and he is comfortable with that.

62.7% agreed with the second statement, also from Prizant: "Instead of classifying legitimate, functional behavior as a sign of pathology, we'll examine it as part of a range of strategies to cope, to adapt, to communicate, and deal with a world that feels overwhelming and frightening [Prizant, 2015, p. 6]."

Karen [62, W*] was exuberant: *Yay! for quoting* Uniquely Human*!!!!* Martha [57, SW*] had a practical thought: "The first two points listed here don't make much sense to me because I cannot expect the world to change to accommodate me. I have to find ways to cope with the world the way it is now."

59.3% agreed with the third comment, which was from Temple Grandin's website: "Diagnosis with...the...*DSM-5* is not precise like a diagnosis for bacterial infections where precise lab tests can be used. Psychiatric diagnostic labels were determined by both scientific studies and the opinion of committees sitting around conference room tables in hotels. Nobody debates the results of lab tests for a strep throat. Over the years, many psychiatric diagnoses have changed" *[Grandin, website] [http://templegrandin.com/].*

57.3% of responders agreed with the fourth statement, also from Grandin's website: "When individuals on the milder end of the autism spectrum are labeled, you must remember that the following words all mean the same thing: Asperger, Aspie, geek, nerd, mild autism, social communication disorder, or socially awkward. The science clearly shows that the social problems on the autism spectrum are a true continuum" *[Grandin, website] [http://templegrandin.com/].*

Earl [57, NZ*] gave us his reaction to this statement: "don't agree that Asperger's can be clustered in with the other terms. I still believe it may not be the same as HFA. Perhaps there are shared genetics between some types of autism, but likely some remain discrete and less related." Bob [54, NE] only partially accepts this quote: "One can be a 'geek' or 'nerd' without being autistic." Jackie [61, UK*] also had strong reactions: "can only say that the me inside silently screams out to the world about all of the above...but it will take a few more generations to adapt to us as we are forced to adapt to them..."

David [70, NE*] had a practical approach: "I am confused by these statements. I am going to leave the science to others and concentrate on learning new coping skills for both internal and external behaviors."

Emma [60, CAN*] had mixed feelings: "I dislike the distinctions caused by labelling people 'high- or low-functioning' and, therefore, reject them. I'm also increasingly uncomfortable with the idea of a spectrum. In many respects, it's likely that life would improve for many people without the *DSM*, except, of course, that it is the basis for people being eligible for supports."

Some respondents had strong reactions to the quotation: Lucy [61, NE*] told us: "don't believe autism is either a disease or a disorder; I believe it is a delay that can be caused by a variety of reasons. So, I don't believe I need to be fixed and I don't believe others can change me, but I DO believe I need to change if I can by maturing as much as possible even if I'm 50 years behind others." One impassioned response claimed: "I am not broken! I am not diseased! I have autism! If you have a problem with it, 'So what?'"

Sally [51, UK] quotes ASAN [the Autistic Self-Advocacy Network] in writing: "Nothing about us – without us." This is a powerful statement for our closing to Degree Four.

DEGREES 5, 6, AND 7: INTEGRATION, COMING TO TERMS

We have heard the stories from the earlier stages: the experience of having a diagnosis or realizing you are on the spectrum. For our population, this is primarily in one's fifties or later. According to Wylie et al.'s model, the next phases of adjusting to the awareness and making it part of one's life are Degrees 5, 6, and 7. Wylie et al. cover them as three separate phases, but we have combined them. We see most of our participants somewhere in these three phases.

Degree Five: Considering all the options. After developing awareness of one's autism, at some point the way forward becomes less clear: "a landscape of opportunity and a road full of pitfalls and open caverns" [Wylie et al., 2016, p. 109].

Degree Six: Crisis of identity/resolution to live with autism. "Suddenly all the confusion you've experienced throughout your life begins to make sense" [Wylie et al., 2016, p. 130].

The initial diagnosis can be very unsettling, triggering an identity crisis. John Elder Robison recalled, "I was autistic. Everything else seemed secondary to that new facet of me. "This must be how it feels when you find you have cancer, I thought" [Robison, 2011, p. 8]. For single mother Heidi Kunisch, "Everything changed. I sat there thinking so many things. Will I be treated differently? Will life get better or worse?" [Kunisch, in Ariel & Naseef, 2006, p. 182]. As Karla Fisher, senior technical program manager at Intel, described it, "Now I had to replay my whole life, with this thing that was deemed a disorder by this doctor and his peers...At first, this realization made me feel very alone" [in Grandin, 2012, ch. 4, "Accepting..." Kindle Para. #1].

Over time, the diagnosis leads to identity realignment, a new sense of self. As one respondent commented: "The final pieces of the puzzle as to why I am the way I am fell into place...my life suddenly made sense...it was so nice to have a name for it!...the diagnosis explained quite a bit about my previous life...I had many questions answered about me." Respondents described a crisis of identity as well: "I felt like I had lost my lifelong identity and went through a year of mourning... GRASP [https://grasp.org/] groups were very helpful in making this adjustment to my identity...I was finally able to make sense of who I was." And finally, on the resolution to live with autism: "I was better able to plan work since I understood my limitations better...I felt less compelled to work at appearing NT." At least 40% of our survey participants made statements such as these, suggesting they have reached this stage.

The most common feeling survey takers experienced after diagnosis (by 77% of the group) was relief, and the second most common feeling cited (by 28%) was excitement. Many other autistic adults describe similar experiences. For example, peer support specialist Anna Magdalena Christianson notes, "Now that I know I have Asperger's syndrome, it actually feels liberating" [in Grandin, 2012, Ch. 3, "Awakening"].

Degree Seven: Self-acceptance/owning we are not typical. This development is much more than a half-hearted tolerance of autism, but rather believing that "our autism will be the key that unlocks our future" [Wylie et al., 2016, p. 139]. By emphasizing our strengths and interests and utilizing appropriate supports and strategies, we become energized to move forward. This was a common theme, as evidenced by statements such as these: "I began to explore who I was and what made me happy...I consider my Asperger's my 'superpower,' given that since I've embraced who I am and what it is, a lot of things seem better...I also feel more creative...I am proud of being autistic...Since coming to terms with my diagnosis over the past year, I feel happier and at peace with myself...I was better able to plan work since I understood my limitations better...I am now at peace and optimistic."

By age 50, 46% of our group agrees with the statement, "I celebrated my differences," 44% with the statement, "I am proud of my autism," and 61% with the statement, "I accepted who I am." Most also agreed with these statements: "autism is a positive part of my life" [58%] and "I have been content since knowing about my autism" [55%]. Sixty-nine percent are comfortable with their autism and consider it a positive part of their lives. More than a third spontaneously made autism-positive comments such as, "autism can be empowering...we have our own special gifts... we are brilliant in our own right." Similarly, tour guide Charli Devnet said, "I have never become exactly like the other guides here, but in my eyes I've managed to become something even more meaningful. I've finally become myself" [in Grandin, 2012, Kindle. Ch. 1, final para.].

DISCRIMINATION

After coming to terms with the diagnosis, we look differently at our lives, and may become aware of discrimination we hadn't noticed before.

SURVEY QUESTION #10: *Do you believe you have been discriminated against due to being on the autism spectrum?*

	Percent	Count
Yes	64.2%	95
No	35.8%	53
Total		148

Nearly two thirds of the respondents indicated they have been discriminated against in some way. For those who answered "yes" to this question [N = 95], the next question was: "How have you been discriminated against?"

SURVEY QUESTION #11: *How have you been discriminated against [check all that apply]?*

	Percent	Count
School	58.5%	55
Job	83.0%	78
Relationships	61.7%	58
Housing	9.6%	9
Other	24.5%	23
Total Responses		94

As illustrated, the most common area of discrimination was related to employment, selected by 83%. Almost 62% selected "relationships." Over 58% picked "school" and 24.5% checked "other." Only 9.6% indicated "housing."

Participant Comments

58.5% identified discrimination at school.

Lucy [61, NE*]: "have periodic mutism as one of my symptoms. In school I have been graded down because of that, even when I have gotten A's on all assignments. Teachers have assumed it was deliberate, or that I was being cavalier, etc. I got diagnosed at age 54 because I was experiencing harassment in my workplace and I could not understand what was going on enough to defend and protect myself."

Some of our respondents indicated that they had two primary discrimination problems: at school and in the workplace.

83.0% complained of job discrimination.

Carlos [66, NE*] pointed out: "As an adult, I was not considered for jobs for which I was qualified." Tim [76, NE*] encountered discrimination on job interviews after college. He complained: "The recruiters might not have known about Asperger's, but they didn't like the manifestations that I had." Mary [68, UK] discovered that after disclosing her diagnosis, her "job assessment went from 'Very good' to 'unsatisfactory' in one step. Martha [57, SW*] had a number of discouraging experiences: "Once people find out you have a weakness of being bothered by certain sensory stimuli, they have the power over you to cause that stimulus just to torment you. Or else they complain to the boss who directs me that I cannot ask people not to produce the stimulus. This happened at some of my workplaces."

61.7% cited discrimination in relationships.

Wenn [64, AUS*] tells us: "In day-to-day interactions with ordinary folk...I am sometimes treated disrespectfully or like an unwanted added extra." Lauren [51, NE*] also has had some rough times. She told us: "In relationships, I tend to be taken advantage of and sometimes ridiculed." Wayne [58, UK*] found his marriage on the rocks. "Got divorced as my ex-wife blamed me for all our difficulties and those of my son."

24.5% indicated experiencing other forms of discrimination.

SURVEY QUESTION #26: *Educational experiences after high school [check all that apply]:*

	Percent	Count
I attended a community college	24.4%	31
I graduated from a community college - degree:	16.5%	21
I attended a 4-year college	40.2%	51
I graduated with a degree from year college - degree:	52.8%	67
I was in a program for a master's and/or doctorate degree	21.3%	27
I graduated with a master's and/or doctorate degree:	37.0%	47
Other post high-school degree(s):	18.1%	23
Total Responses		127

Clearly, most of us have had considerable education after high school. Almost 53% of us graduated from a four-year college; 21% were in a program for a master's or a doctorate degree; 37% of us graduated with a master's or a doctorate. About 24% attended a community college and 16% graduated. Finally, 18% achieved some other post high school degree, including certificate in computer science, law degree, art classes, master's in educational psychology, musical theater degree, and others.

This is an ambitious group striving to better themselves and their lives through education. But although most of our community is quite intelligent, there are enormous barriers to advanced study, including depression, anxiety, low self-esteem, and low processing speed. We grew up before we could go to a college/university disability rights center and ask for accommodations in our studies. Most of us still don't know enough about what we need to advocate for ourselves. Some report that many educational institutions are not prepared to help aging autistics who are just figuring out what that means.

Participant Comments

24.4% attended a community college.
David [70, NE*]: "I have attended many schools from community colleges (4), four-year colleges (2), trade schools (2), but graduated from none [the sum of my credits would probably equal a BA] although I tested at the post-graduate level in vocabulary when I was 28." Some participants found classrooms too filled with sensory overload, so they took online classes.

40.2% attended a four-year college.
One of our respondents is working on a B.A. in education, and another is studying medical technology.

52.8% graduated with a degree from a four-year college.

21.3% were in a program for a master's or doctoral degree.
Jackie [61, UK*] did a year of architectural drawing, started first-year nursing school, was trained as an EMT (emergency medical tech), but learning disabilities made it impossible, along with her lifestyle, addictions, and low self-esteem.

37.0% graduated with a master's and/or doctorate.
Lucy [61, NE*] has a BA, MA, MS, and JD.

Derek [53, NE*] got a master's in statistics when he was in his 40s.

18.1% have another post high school degree.
Here are some of the post high school degrees mentioned by our participants.
Wayne [58, UK*] has DIP WSOH (degree in Homoeopathy) and Dip WSM (diploma in metaphysics). Rob [61, NE]: Certificate in Computer Science.
Carlos [66, NE*] has a Certificate in Psychoanalytic Coursework.
Doris [55, AUS*] told us: "I obtained an Associate Diploma in animal husbandry from an agricultural college. I liked working with animals."

Some had discouraging experiences with schooling after high school.
Anya [69, NE*] told us: "I was not able to go to any kind of college due to poor grades, learning disabilities, social immaturity."

Some were unable to meet their educational goals due to issues related to autism.
Rhys [52, UK*]: "The terminology used in these questions seems to be aimed at Americans ("Community College" etc.), but I will try and answer as best I can. After leaving school I started work as an apprentice bookbinder, which included having to study at a technical college. Later on, when I was in my thirties, I started to take evening classes in computing and gained a degree in computing. As a result of the work I did on this course, I was offered a place on a master's degree course, but I had to turn it down as I could not afford to fund myself as I was about to be made redundant from my job."

The educational accomplishments of this group are especially noteworthy given that this group did not receive early intervention or special programs in childhood.

SURVEY QUESTION #27: *EMPLOYMENT: Indicate all that apply.*

	Percent	Count
I am currently employed full time	25.2%	36
I am currently employed part time	11.9%	17
I am retired	30.8%	44
I am looking for work	11.9%	17
I am self-employed	14.7%	21
My autism has made employment difficult for me	58.0%	83
My autism has helped me in my work life	25.9%	37
Total Responses		143

Despite the rich variety of educational backgrounds, 58% of the respondents found that autism makes employment difficult. Over 30% are unemployed, which is not a surprise, given that the group is both older and autistic. Even though 58.0% feel that autism has made work difficult, almost 26% have found that autism helped in their work life. A number of our folks said that both are true: It makes it harder in some ways and easier in other ways. Almost 15% [14.7%] of the group are self-employed, with 11.9% looking for work and 11.9% employed part-time.

Participant Comments

11.9% are currently employed full-time.
Lauren [51, NE*] wrote: "I am working full-time, and I have been since 1988. I have nearly 30 years of uninterrupted employment...I have always had a job, because I need to support myself and have a decent life. I have always made do, taking whatever work that I could find, gradually teaching myself new skills and working my way up to be a...manager at...a tech company. I hate it. It is constantly stressful...as my success depends on my ability to socialize...I am looking for other work that suits me better." Anita [57, NE*] has been working full-time as a certified registered nurse anesthetist for the past 27 years. "Only having been diagnosed 6 years ago at age 50, those first 21 years were spent not knowing I have it! Lots of trouble over the years!"

22.9% are currently employed part-time.

Yvonne [65, SW*] told us she does "art lectures and gets paid occasionally or it's volunteer."

30.8% are retired.

Rhys [52, UK*] said: "I have been employed for most of the time since I was 18. I was lucky in that the job I had for 23 years was, purely by coincidence, very well suited to somebody with Asperger's [I worked with books]...My employment problems really started after I was made redundant from this job and had to work in more traditional office-type environments. I quickly came to find that the amount of noise and the constant interaction with people in these circumstances was completely overwhelming and began to suffer badly with stress."

Julianne [69, AUS]: "I'm retired but doing unpaid work for an autism-related institution writing documents, co-writing, and commenting on documents, courses, etc., related to autism research and Inclusion. I speak at conferences...pay my own way despite being on an aged pension. When I taught, I was always drawn to helping the children with learning difficulties, social and/or behavioural difficulties, cultural differences. I now can see that this attitude and my ability to relate and help these students would have most likely been due to my being autistic...despite not being aware of 'autistic'....was autistic but not diagnosed."

11.9% are looking for work.

14.7% are self-employed.

Wenn [64, AUS*] told us: "My work is casual and within time limits that I can manage. My work centers on writing and delivering educational workshops about autism. Being autistic is a plus for this work."

Emma [60, CAN*] "has always worked in disability-related fields. For the last 30 years, my partner (who has a physical disability) and I have provided in-service training to universities, school districts, human service agencies, parent groups, and advocacy/activist groups internationally. It's where I've fit in best, and where I could make a passionate contribution. Currently, my partner and I operate a successful online training program for workers in disability-related fields called Conversations That Matter, and are working on a series of books. I have always done best as self-employed and understand my privilege and the luxury of this. Many of my disabled friends have not been as lucky or as well understood. People usually assume the best about me, which makes my professional life a lot easier!"

Jackie [61, UK*]: "I have developed a business that I hope to expand in the next year or two."

David [70, NE*] says: "Until I was 28, I was consistently under-employed, seldom working more than 18 months in a job. I just couldn't get along with anyone and find anything that didn't bore me in three months. This all changed in 1975 when I discovered computer programming. Despite a lack of formal education attainment, I can program in at least a dozen languages. Most of my programming is designing and developing small business websites and related applications."

Peter Cox [67, UK] told us: "Doing a bit of this, a bit of that, but also not getting the big picture, immersed in the details of a job, not aware of goals – where am I going – until recently as I am now making progress as writer and poet aiming at writing books about my life with autism, insights into things like my dreams. A special interest in ghosts and spiritualism is driven by a fear that there may be no life after death or not a nice life after death and fear of living forever!"

58.0% indicated that autism has made employment difficult.

Samantha [52, MW] told us she had a work life that she valued, but she burned out and had to quit. Many of our folks said they found their autism a barrier to jobs – in part, because of difficulty relating to both coworkers and managers.

Earl [57, NZ*] also had problems with employment: "Serial job loss due to a series of bosses who could not handle a thinker." Peter Cox [67, UK] described his experiences: "It was April 12, 2007. Just made redundant from a job as an accounts clerk handling money and currency I had held for 22 years, a former employee of the firm, a lady, took me to tea. She felt I, like a relative of hers, showed signs of Asperger's Syndrome because I'd spoken of my inability to teach due to a lack of the right interpersonal skills. She was right. Diagnosed by a NHS [National Health Service] psychiatrist in Nov 2007, by Institute of Psychiatry psychologists in 2009 when patient participant on a project, and then in May 2013 when 64 years old, diagnosed by an autism specialist after a two-hour meeting."

Carlos [66, NE*] has become a volunteer due to negative work experiences: "Because of my autism, my work history is dismal. I was never paid what I was worth and never made a living wage. I do excellent work now as a volunteer certified nursing home resident advocate."

Derek [53, NE*] noted: "I feel I am lousy in interviews." Sally [51, UK] has a lifetime of abuse and no support, which makes life hell for her. She says: "I barely function."

25.9% indicated that autism has helped in their work life.

Nancy [57, NE*] has found autism an asset in the workplace: "My career in finance and information technology has been a very good fit for my AS traits. I currently work for a global IT company as a project manager. I have worked here for over 16 years, most of that time I worked remotely from my home. I have managed people located across the globe [North America, South America, India] on cross-functional projects. Many people in the company know of me and reach out to me for my expertise ..."

James Hunt [74, NE] said: "Autism made for difficulties in work interactions, but also gave me intense focus and persistence."

Many are underemployed.

Pat [64, NE*] says: "I've tried to explain to Voc Rehab how Asperger's has made employment difficult for an older adult like me, and they just can't understand why I can't just accept any job that a high school kid can do while ignoring the fact that I'm a 64-year-old senior citizen with a master's degree and have encountered age-ism and able-ism repeatedly! Employers don't want to hire someone who has more education than they do and who is old enough to be their grandmother! I've hit that brick wall over and over again!"

Martha [57, SW*]: "Work has been difficult due primarily to my sensory issues and also to social issues. I am 'underemployed'...with an IQ of 150. I have done clerical work all my life."

Summary

Meaningful employment has eluded many of those on the spectrum. Rudy Simone started her book *Asperger's On the Job* [2010] because "the majority of adults with Asperger's I spoke to had great difficulty earning a living. Most were on unemployment, welfare, or disability" [Simone, 2010, p. xiii]. Howlin [1997] reported that "even amongst those who are most able, only around 20-25% are likely to be employed" [p. 187]. Even when autistic adults manage to find work, they encounter numerous challenges, including communication difficulties, resistance to change in routine, inability to work independently, and mistreatment by others [Howlin, 1997]. Luckily, as we saw above, some of our study participants report that autism is an asset at work.

While many autistic adults face an uphill battle in the workplace, a few pioneering companies actively recruit autistic employees. German software company SAP, through its Autism at Work program, has a corporate goal of having autistic employees comprise 1% of its workforce by 2020 [SAP.com]. The British/German IT firm Auticon proudly calls itself "the first enterprise that exclusively employs autistic adults as IT consultants" and extols the advantages of autistic employees, including "sustained concentration and perseverance even when tasks are repetitive," "conscientiousness, loyalty and sincerity," and "an exceptional eye for details, deviations and potential errors" [Auticon.com]. Simone [2010, pp 2-3] addresses the question of "Why should you employ someone with AS?" with a list of nine "gifts," including independent, unique thinking and visual, three-dimensional thinking.

Lest you think that this hiring trend is restricted to tech-savvy autistics, the Society for Human Resource Management reports that a number of companies have autism-positive hiring initiatives, including Kohls, CVS Caremark, Walgreens, and Home Depot [SHRM.org, 6/1/10].

SURVEY QUESTION #28: *INCOME: What have been your primary source/s of income in your adult life?*

	Percent	Count
Job or jobs	80.4%	119
Self-employment	25.7%	38
I am retired	16.2%	24
Disability benefits	29.7%	44
Retirement benefits	11.5%	17
Spouse or partner	18.9%	28
Family support	8.8%	13
Savings and/or investments	18.2%	27
Illegal endeavors	0.7%	1
Gambling	0.7%	1
Other:	9.5%	14
Total Responses		148

This question was designed to understand how participants are managing financially. Over 80% of the group have had one or more jobs. 26% have been self-employed. Almost 30% are receiving disability benefits, and over 11% have retirement benefits. Over 18% have savings or investments to live on. However, many describe a rather grim financial situation and worry about the future.

Participant Comments

80.4% said that jobs have been their primary source of income.

For example, Tim [76, NE*] was in "the Navy [active duty] for 20 yrs. And then in the Navy Reserve." Jackie [61, UK*]: "I was a sole supporting woman from age 17 until moving here at age 48...I had three short-term relationships, but in two of them I was the breadwinner...I lived alone all but 4-1/2 years. "Yvonne [65, SW*] told us: "I worked all my adult life...worked full-time and paid for my own college and put my husband through law school and I paid for my way in law school as well...Never had a student loan and was never given anything." Lauren [51, NE*]: "I have a good job, which keeps us afloat, and we don't pinch pennies, but I constantly worry about money and my future, because it could all evaporate so quickly."

25.7% are self-employed.

Emma [60, CAN*]: "Lucky me, but like many of us who are self-employed, it can be tenuous at times."

29.7% live on disability benefits.

Rhys [52, UK*] has concerns about the future: "I have been in employment for the vast majority of my adult life so far and have never needed to claim benefits of any kind. I am now retired from my last job on health grounds and am living off my savings. I am about to submit a claim for disability benefit with the help of my support worker at the autism centre I am registered with, but I have my doubts as to whether this will be successful." Julianne [69, AUS] is retired but doing unpaid work for an autism-related institution writing documents, co-writing, and commenting on documents, courses, etc., related to autism research and inclusion. "I speak at conferences...pay my own way despite being on an aged pension."

11.5% live on retirement benefits.

Pat [64, NE*] wrote: "I'm trying to make do on a small retirement pension but have recently been hit with medical bills that have made everything worse. With the small pension that I have, plus mounting medical bills, I find that there's often more months than money and wonder how to cope." Larry [69, UK] was doing well on a pension: "I was very lucky to be born when pensions were so good and disability benefits were paid to people like me. I would have been crucified by the present system." David [70, NE*] is still working about 50-75% of the time but also receiving Social Security.

18.9% rely on spouse or partner.

Laura [57, UK], for example, says: "My husband worked full-time." Emily [70, UK*] told us: "Before my degrees, I taught piano. But my partner has always been the main source of income."

8.8% have family support.

18.2% have savings and/or investments.

An example is Carlos [66, NE*] who told us "I'm OK right now given my wife has a good job and I have some savings. I don't really need to worry (at least for now), but that doesn't mean that I never do."

0.7% illegal endeavors.
Karen [62, W*] commented on this as follows: "Hmmmm...too bad I had my 'crime spree' in second grade and got it out of my system. Illegal endeavors might have been an interesting field of employment ..."

0.7% Gambling.
Derek [53, NE*] joked: "Gambling – primary source of income? Ha ha."

9.5% Other.

SURVEY QUESTION #29: *INCOME: Check whichever statements are true for you now.*

	Percent	Count
I am quite comfortable financially	39.3%	59
I rarely worry about money	27.3%	41
I have to "pinch pennies" to get by; I barely manage	37.3%	56
I am homeless	2.0%	3
I go hungry many days for lack of food	2.7%	4

Below is a sample of responses to the above question. A common theme in the answers was worry and fear about managing financially as one ages. About 39% checked "quite comfortable financially," but some responses show financial insecurity.

39.3% are quite comfortable financially.
Yvonne [65, SW*] said: "I worry always about money, but we are doing well."

27.3% rarely worry about money.
Earl [57, NZ*] wrote: "The future is hit or miss financially. I have a few years to make money, but it hasn't been my focus." Jackie [61, UK*] is happy about her situation. "We are blessed, and we are able to afford things like computers or things for my husband's autistic endeavors – he is building his self-designed 3D printer at the moment – but we do not have money for vacations and have moderate debts we know we can pay off."

37.3% have to "pinch pennies" to get by.
Anita [57, NE*] cared for both her parents until they died. She says: "I ended up with medical bills over $150,000 that I'm paying back. It isn't easy but manageable." Pat [64, NE*] tells us: "With the small pension that I have, plus mounting medical bills, I find that there's often more months than money and wonder how to cope." Linda [56, W] is always stressed about money and works 14 hours a day.

2.0% are homeless.
Stan [57, NE]: "I was homeless many times and lived in unhealthy environments."

2.7% go hungry many days for lack of food.

LIVING SITUATION

SURVEY QUESTION #30: *LIVING SITUATIONS IN YOUR PAST AND PRESENT ADULT LIFE: Indicate all that apply.*

Living situation	Percent	Count
Apartment	54.7%	81
Renting home	46.0%	68
Own home	77.0%	114
Landlord	15.5%	23
Living on a boat	2.7%	4
Boarding house	7.4%	11
Homeless	9.5%	14
Living with friends	14.9%	22
Living with children	12.8%	19
Living with partner	43.2%	64
Living alone	46.6%	69
Other:	16.9%	25
Total		148

Participant Comments

Respondents' answers to this question reveal a range of living situations. Lucy [61, NE*] did communal living (back in the 70s). Lauren [51, NE*] had to return to living with her parents after leaving home. David [70, NE*] says: "I have been living in the house with my wife for the last 21 years. Prior to that I moved every two to three years."

Yvonne [65, SW*]: "have owned a home since I was married 41 yrs. ago." Emma [60, CAN*] has lived in a variety of places in her adult life, "mostly in homes we/I owned. Now we are in an apartment now that our children are grown."

Pat [64, NE*] has tried living with roommates, but "that situation became too stressful, especially when they would go through my belongings and take stuff without asking." Derek [53, NE*] tells us he "lived alone for maybe a year and a half of my life and that includes two different times – sheesh." Lauren [51, NE*] says: "I have mostly lived in apartments in my adult life. I have also been homeless (briefly)…and I lived on my own for a while, and then when I met my partner we moved in together in an apartment…Up until 2002, I had a fairly mobile life, moving around every couple of years, and shifting in and out of different situations. I think it's been fun and exciting. I have no children who would be traumatized by this, so I've been free to come and go as I please, as the situation demands."

Wayne [58, UK*] told us: "When I got divorced, my three sons chose to live with me; two still do." Rhys [52, UK*] "lived at home with my parents until I was 25. I then moved out to live with my (then) girlfriend. When we split up, I continued to live in a rented apartment for the next 13 years or so until I moved into my current partner's house, where I have been for over 12 years now." Marilyn [65, W*] has never made enough money to live independently. Jackie [61, UK*] moved 24 times between age 5 and age 48, "that includes some short-term motel stays as a kid when my family moved to a new city two times and I moved back to central Florida from Fort Lauderdale… but yes, a weird moving life."

Jack [57, UK] told us that he rented houses at various points in his life, but he has had ups and downs with depression. He has been homeless at times, but right now he is renting a room. It seems that his autism has impacted his life in profound ways. Nancy [57, NE*]: "Lived in an apartment with my family until I went to college. Then lived in a college dorm during the school year and boarded a room during summer so I could work a good summer job. In my junior year, I moved from campus to an apartment with three friends. In my senior year, I moved into an apartment by myself (to get away from a roommate situation). Lived in this same apartment until I graduated college, then my future husband moved in. We bought our first house 1.5 years after we were married. We bought [built] our second house 4 years later and have been living in this same house for over 25 years, where we have raised our two sons."

SURVEY QUESTION #31: *CURRENT LIVING SITUATION: Indicate all that apply.*

Living Situation	Percent	Count
Apartment	18.9%	28
Renting home	10.1%	15
Own home	64.2%	95
Landlord	2.7%	4
Living on a boat	0.7%	1
Boarding house	0.7%	1
Homeless	2.0%	3
In assisted living	1.4%	2
In nursing home	0.0%	0
Living with children	10.1%	15
Living alone	18.9%	28
Living with friend/s	0.7%	1
Living with partner	28.4%	42
Other:	12.8%	19
Total Responses		148

Participant Comments

Mary [68, UK] has an independent living apartment in a seniors' development. She said: "I own the flat but pay ground rent and service charges."

64.2% own a home.
Yvonne [65, SW*]: "I live in my own home with my husband."
Lauren [51, NE*]: "My partner and I jointly own our home, and we live here together. We are both homebodies, and we intend to stay in our home till the end of our days (it's a great house in a great town, on a quiet street, with a beautiful view). My house is the one thing I have going for me with regard to my long-term self-support plan."

10.1% are renting a home.
Emma [60, CAN*]: "We moved to the very expensive lower mainland of Vancouver, where renting is the best option." Rhys [52, UK*] has been "living with my partner in her house for the past 12+ years."

RELATIONSHIPS AFTER AGE 30

SURVEY QUESTION #32: *RELATIONSHIPS: Indicate all that apply.*

	Percent	Count
I'm in a close relationship	23.1%	34
I have a committed partner	27.9%	41
I am married	44.2%	65
I know my partner/relationship is on spectrum	6.1%	9
I think my partner/relationship is on spectrum	8.8%	13
I have been married but now divorced or widowed	25.9%	38
I have been married more than once	26.5%	39
I'm happy with my relationship/partner	35.4%	52
I have had a number of intimate relationships	22.5%	33
I've never really been close to anyone	25.9%	38
Other	12.2%	18
Total Responses		147

As illustrated, 23% of our participants are in a "close relationship." Almost 28% have a committed partner, and 44% are married. However, these are undoubtedly overlapping categories. A number of respondents said they were married or in a committed relationship but were miserable, primarily because of problems with communication. Almost 26% report never having been close to anyone – even some who have been/are married.

Participant Comments

44.2% are married.

Tim [76, NE*] has a hopeful view of his marriage: "My wife and I originally [before diagnosis] were in couples therapy because our long marriage was falling apart, particularly after my retirement. After the diagnosis, we now have couples' therapy with a LCSW who knows Asperger's, and my wife is in a group with spouses of Aspies."

6.1% know their partner is on the spectrum.

8.8% think their partner is on the spectrum.

25.9% have been married but now are divorced or widowed.

26.5% have been married more than once.

35.4% are happy with relationship or partner.

Yvonne [65, SW*]: "I had one intimate relationship with a boyfriend before I met my husband. We have been married 41 yrs. this year." Emma [60, CAN*]: "I have been married twice before to neurotypical men. My current partner is not autistic (he has CP) but is definitely neurodivergent. Our relationship works exceptionally well and has lasted 25 years. Natalie [57, UK] has a middle-of-the-road view: "Sort of happy, anyway."

22.5% have had a number of intimate relationships.

Adam [56, OTH*]: "I have been alone/ single for four years, but I have had many relationships over my life." Helen [50, UK]: "I've had several relationships, but they've never worked out."

25.9% have never been really close to anyone.

12.2% marked "Other."

Anya [69, NE*] is currently single. Katrine-Estella [53, UK] says: "I am single, and I am happy to be single."

Some described relationships with neurotypicals that didn't work out. Pat [64, NE*] wrote: "The last one knew about the autism spectrum but just didn't 'get it.' Eventually, he left, too." Several found that diagnosis improved the marriage. Tim [76, NE*] related: "My wife and I originally [before diagnosis] were in couples therapy because our long marriage was falling apart, particularly after my retirement. After the diagnosis we now have couples' therapy with a LCSW who knows Asperger's, and my wife is in a group with spouses of Aspies."

Many participants described a happy and stable long-term relationship. For some of them, it has lasted through the years and is still loving and stable. Many of these relationships have required some therapy along the way. Others have never had a satisfying relationship, and some have had a series of close relationships.

SURVEY QUESTION #33: *FAMILY IN ADULT LIFE: Indicate all that apply.*
Note: Percentages in parentheses indicate percentages of relevant subcategory – see detail.

	Percent	Count
1. Mother still living	35.3%	53
If "yes," I'm close to her	18.0% (50.9% of #1)	27
2. Father still living	19.3%	29
If "yes," I'm close to him	6.7% (34.5% of #2)	10
3. I think my partner/relationship is on the spectrum	12.0%	18
4. I have children up to age 18	14.0%	21
5. I have children over age 18	45.3%	68
6. Children in either of the above two categories not in graph)	50.7%	76
I'm close to my children	30.7% (60.5% of #6)	46

I'm not close to one or more of my children	16.0% (31.6% of #6)	24
I think/know one or more of my children are on the spectrum	33.3% (65.8% of #6)	50
TOTAL		150

Only about half feel close to their living mother and only about a third feel close to their living father. More than half [61%], however, feel close to their children. Notably, 66% of those with children believe at least one of their children is on the spectrum.

Yvonne [65, SW*] has lost her parents: "My parents are both deceased. I was close to my father, not my mother." Emma [60, CAN*] has a similar situation of loss: "Both parents are deceased. My children are grown and are wonderful and supportive [they are both children from previous relationships]."

Eric [55, NE]: "My 18-year-old son is on the spectrum; my 16-year-old daughter is not. I believe my father is on the spectrum as well."

44% reported that they are currently married.
May [70, SW]: "I have no other close relationships besides my husband although I have connected to a few close friends along the way, but they died."

26% have been married but are widowed/divorced.

26% have never really been close to anyone.
Janet [61, UK]: "I never had children as I didn't know what was wrong with me and did not want to pass it (whatever 'it' was) on to any offspring. I did not want them to suffer as I did at school and at work."

Most report current difficulty with communication, such as being misunderstood, finding it hard to understand others, and needing a lot of time alone. Of those who have felt discriminated against [close to two thirds of the respondents], 62% have felt discriminated against in relationships.

In terms of sexual orientation, here is how the respondents categorized themselves: 77.9% heterosexual, 3.4% gay, 2.1% bisexual, 1.4% lesbian, 0.7% transgendered, 3.4% asexual, and 11.0% not sure/prefer not to answer/other. In contrast, U.S. national surveys of sexual orientation find that 97% of the general population identify as straight, and only 2% as LGBT [Ward et al., 2014]. Our study appears to be one of the few that have studied this difference. Significantly more males than females considered themselves heterosexual [85% vs. 68%]. This finding is consistent with what other researchers report [Gilmour, Schalomon, & Smith, 2012; Hendrickx, 2015].

Participant Comments

Nancy [57, NE*]: "My relationship with my father changed after I came to understand that he was on the spectrum. He always seemed to understand me, but I struggled to understand him... My relationships with my sons are close because my husband and I were committed to valuing their strengths and getting them support for their 'weaknesses.'...They are both growing into confident young men with critical thinking skills. We have very open and safe relationships with them."

Note: Questions #34 and #41-49 are lifespan questions that have columns for "Childhood," "Teens and '20's," "30-50," and "50." Some of the results were looked at with only "childhood" included in earlier sections. Now, in the adult section, we'll consider all columns.

SURVEY QUESTION #34: *SENSORY EXPERIENCES: Which of these have you experienced, and when? [30 YEARS UP]*

$N = 150$	Don't know	Childhood		Teens and 20s		30-50		50+	
	Count	Count	%	Count	%	Count	%	Count	%
Bullying and teasing	9	117	83.0%	104	73.8%	58	41.1%	36	25.5%
Being taken advantage of	8	80	56.3%	106	74.6%	96	67.6%	57	40.1%
Communication and social difficulties	1	126	84.6%	136	91.3%	129	86.6%	109	73.2%
Being misunderstood	3	119	81.0%	132	89.8%	128	87.1%	116	78.9%
Finding it hard to understand others	6	110	76.4%	118	81.9%	112	77.8%	96	66.7%
Difficulty articulating clearly	16	86	64.2%	88	65.7%	73	54.5%	64	47.8%
Need for rigid routines	18	76	57.6%	80	60.6%	81	61.4%	72	54.5%
Sensory issues (e.g., bothered by noise, smells)	7	95	66.4%	102	71.3%	107	74.8%	103	72.0%
Need for a lot of time alone	4	105	71.9%	114	78.1%	124	84.9%	112	76.7%
Anxiety and stress	2	96	64.9%	124	83.8%	130	87.8%	117	79.1%
Other	5	15	10.3%	16	11.0%	17	11.7%	15	10.3%

The most notable change from childhood is *bullying and teasing*: **41% during 30s and 40s, and about 25% during 50s and beyond, down from 74% during adolescence.** This decrease is to be expected since such behaviors tend to peak in early- to mid-adolescence.

All of these negative experiences show a marked decrease from the 30-50 age range to the over-50 age category, particularly bullying and being taken advantage of. Except for sensory, these differences are of statistical significance, as seen in Appendix 2. The difference for being taken advantage of between childhood and adulthood, while also being significant, is not quite as dramatic as for bullying, and it shows a different kind of progression. That is, it peaks from adolescence to mid-life, then drops off after age 50. This makes sense if one thinks of *bullying and teasing*, especially the *teasing* part, as something that tends to occur during a more immature stage of life, but *being taken advantage of* as something that tends to happen during a more adult stage of life, or at least is evenly distributed across age periods. [Note: Being bullied may be thought of as being taken advantage of, so the wording may have affected the choice of response.]

For the areas of communication, being understood and understanding others, and articulation, rates of reported problems are close among adolescence, young and middle-age adulthood, with small drops during the 30-50-year-old period, and more dramatic drops after 50. This makes sense, as the respondents gained experience in these areas or developed coping skills. Anxiety and stress go up a little into adulthood, which also makes sense, as the respondents gained more responsibilities. Need for rigid routines, alone time, and sensory issues do not change very much (or go up a little), as these are attributes that are generally more innately characteristic of the person's needs (and of being on the autism spectrum) and, therefore, are less likely to change with life experience.

SURVEY QUESTION #41: *ATTWOOD'S COPING STRATEGIES: After 30*

N = 150	Don't know	Childhood		Teens and 20s		30-50		50+	
	Count	Count	%	Count	%	Count	%	Count	%
Escape into imagination (e.g., imaginary world)	17	101	75.9%	85	63.9%	65	48.9%	52	39.1%
Denial and rigidity – blaming others	27	41	33.3%	62	50.4%	43	35.0%	31	25.2%
Imitating neurotypical peers or acting "normal"	9	67	47.5%	98	69.5%	104	73.8%	79	56.0%
Depression	7	59	41.3%	101	70.6%	108	75.5%	91	63.6%

The coping strategy of escape into imagination, in particular, decreases with age – again, consistent with the idea of development and maturity continuing well into adulthood. The need to act "normal" as a coping strategy plateaus from adolescence up to age 50, and then decreases. As noted earlier, these coping strategies were more common in childhood and early adulthood, but tapered off in midlife, perhaps as a result of finding the right support. Depression seems to peak and plateau from adolescence all the way through mid-life, then drops off after 50. Denial and rigidity peak during adolescence and the 20s. For most of us, this was long before we were aware of Asperger's and the autism spectrum, in terms of our identity.

Participant Comments

David [70, NE*] said: "I abused alcohol and pot from ages 18-40."
Martha [57, SW*] said: "Overeating. Immersed in own fantasy life until menopause."
Nancy [57, NE*] becomes immersed in her work.

DRUG USE AFTER 30

SURVEY QUESTION #43: *DRUG USE: Which of these did you use excessively during periods of your life?*

N = 150	Don't know Count	Childhood Count	%	Teens and 20s Count	%	30-50 Count	%	50+ Count	%
Over-the-counter medication	16	4	3.0%	8	6.0%	15	11.2%	12	9.0%
Prescription medication	12	1	0.7%	10	7.2%	30	21.7%	24	17.4%
Alcohol	7	4	2.8%	54	37.8%	46	32.2%	23	16.1%
Cigarettes	8	2	1.4%	42	29.6%	24	16.9%	12	8.5%
Illegal marijuana	8	0	0.0%	22	15.5%	13	9.2%	7	4.9%
Legal marijuana and/or medical marijuana	9	0	0.0%	0	0.0%	0	0.0%	2	1.4%
Heroin or other opiates	9	0	0.0%	0	0.0%	1	0.7%	0	0.0%
Amphetamines	9	0	0.0%	6	4.3%	5	3.5%	0	0.0%
Barbiturates	8	1	0.7%	2	1.4%	1	0.7%	0	0.0%
Ecstasy	8	0	0.0%	1	0.7%	1	0.7%	0	0.0%
"Bath salt" drugs	8	0	0.0%	0	0.0%	0	0.0%	0	0.0%
Other	5	1	0.7%	4	2.8%	6	4.1%	5	3.4%

Compared to adolescence and early childhood, the most marked difference is a decrease in excessive drug use after age 50. The consumption of alcohol, cigarettes, and illegal marijuana peaked at adolescence and the 20s but was less after 30, and down further after 50. *Excessive* over-the-counter and prescription medication peaked during the 30-50 age range. It could be that alcohol, cigarettes, illegal marijuana, and excessive medication could all be ways of trying to cope with a life on the spectrum [Note: Reported rates of consumption of other substance types are too low across the board to make a comparison].

Participant Comments

The top three substances used excessively during the different lifespan periods were prescription drugs, alcohol, and cigarettes.

Prescription Medication
30-50   *21.7%*
50+   *17.4%*

Yvonne [65, SW*]: "I just used over-the-counter meds for sleep until I got a psychiatrist, who now prescribes medication, as well as my endocrinologist."

Alcohol
30-50   *32.2%*
50+   *16.1%*

Pat [64, NE*] tells us: "I hit bottom on March 16, 1985, and nearly died. I've been in recovery ever since."

Cigarettes
30-50   *16.9%*
50+   *8.5%*

Other Comments

One of our respondents said: "As an OT I focused on sensory integration to help my hypersensitivities." Martha [57, SW*] uses food, primarily sweets.

Mathew [69, NE] managed to avoid drugs and alcohol: "Don't drink at all. I think I could become an alcohol user or depressant user if I tried and would have trouble controlling use, so I stay far away. With no history, occasional cravings are within my ability to control with little struggle." Anya [69, NE*] asked us: "You actually think people will fill this out??? Personally, I tried both marijuana and psychedelic drugs way back in the 1960s. Generally speaking, I think both were helpful." Helen [50, UK]: "I used to smoke pot all day every day during my 20s and most of my 30s. I have gone through phases with alcohol. Right now I smoke pot on weekends, but only one or two. Alcohol is a regular thing right now."

Rhys [52, UK*]: "I did take other drugs – LSD, magic mushrooms, speed, cocaine – at various points between the ages of 20-30 but only very occasionally. My drug of choice was always alcohol, and I was probably drunk more days than not between the ages of 18-33. I am amazed that I never developed an alcohol dependency."

Others pointed out that autistics need to follow rules. A 52-year-old woman in the U.S. said: "My thing is following the rules. The rules say you shouldn't use drugs, so I don't."

Some of our community use substances to survive social situations. Nancy [57, NE*] commented: "My 'drug' of choice is CHOCOLATE!"

ILLEGAL BEHAVIOR After 30

[Indicate illegal behavior at specified life period.]

N = 150	Don't Know	Childhood		Teens and 20s		30-50		50+	
	Count	Count	%	Count	%	Count	%	Count	%
Using illegal drugs	3	0	0.0%	32	21.8%	14	9.5%	7	4.8%
Selling illegal drugs	4	0	0.0%	1	0.7%	0	0.0%	0	0.0%
Robbery	5	4	2.8%	5	3.4%	1	0.7%	0	0.0%
Assault	5	2	1.4%	5	3.4%	2	1.4%	0	0.0%
Domestic violence	4	1	0.7%	1	0.7%	0	0.0%	0	0.0%
Smuggling	5	0	0.0%	0	0.0%	1	0.7%	0	0.0%
Embezzling	4	0	0.0%	4	2.7%	1	0.7%	0	0.0%
Arrests	3	0	0.0%	10	6.8%	3	2.0%	3	2.0%
Conviction	3	0	0.0%	3	2.0%	3	2.0%	1	0.7%
Served time	4	0	0.0%	3	2.1%	1	0.7%	0	0.0%
Other	1	0	0.0%	0	0.0%	1	0.7%	1	0.7%

Compared to adolescence and the 20s, illegal behavior (particularly, illegal drug use and arrests) decreased after 30, and even more so after 50. This question brought out a law-abiding nature of our participants.

Participant Comments

Larry [69, UK] is clear: "Never done anything like this!" Similarly, Laura [57, UK] says: "I've never done anything illegal." Carlos [66, NE*]: "I have a very conventional morality and have never engaged in illegal behavior. I am also not a violent person; if anything, I am too gentle and kind."

Here is one of the few comments about drug abuse. Pat [64, NE*]: "Before I became clean and sober on March 16, 1985, at the age of 33, I smoked illegal marijuana. I was terrified of the other street drugs because I saw what they did to my sibling. The rest of my addiction history involved abusing benzodiazepines and alcohol."

MENTAL ILLNESS AFTER 30

SURVEY QUESTION #45: *MENTAL ILLNESS/PSYCHIATRIC DISORDER: Which of these have been an issue for you at various life stages?*

N = 150	Don't Know	Childhood		Teens and 20s		30-50		50+	
	Count	Count	%	Count	%	Count	%	Count	%
Anxiety	1	80	53.7%	109	73.2%	118	79.2%	110	73.8%
Depression	4	49	33.6%	92	63.0%	106	72.6%	85	58.2%
Obsessive compulsive disorder	23	13	10.2%	29	22.8%	28	22.0%	22	17.3%
Post-traumatic stress disorder	13	22	16.1%	34	24.8%	46	33.6%	45	32.8%
Personality disorder	18	7	5.3%	8	6.1%	16	12.1%	11	8.3%
Bipolar	18	2	1.5%	5	3.8%	7	5.3%	6	4.5%
Dissociative disorder	19	7	5.3%	7	5.3%	6	4.6%	4	3.1%
ADHD or ADD	18	18	13.6%	17	12.9%	15	11.4%	17	12.9%
Suicide attempt	5	9	6.2%	27	18.6%	23	15.9%	6	4.1%
Suicidal thoughts	4	27	18.5%	66	45.2%	62	42.5%	56	38.4%
Hospitalization	4	5	3.4%	16	11.0%	16	11.0%	8	5.5%
Insomnia or other sleep disorders	2	31	20.9%	52	35.1%	70	47.3%	71	48.0%
Mental hospital	5	0	0.0%	12	8.3%	12	8.3%	6	4.1%
On psychiatric medication	2	1	0.7%	24	16.2%	54	36.5%	41	27.7%
Low self-esteem	2	81	54.7%	107	72.3%	101	68.2%	77	52.0%
Other	1	2	1.3%	3	2.0%	3	2.0%	4	2.7%

Overall, responses revealed a moderate to significant improvement in most respondents' quality of life after 50, presumably in part as a result of receiving a diagnosis. [This is also visible in Appendix 2, as most of the differences seen above show marked statistical significance.] A couple of things that support the idea of the improvements being due, in large part, to having been diagnosed, as well as increased awareness of autism, is that 77% reported having a feeling of relief after diagnosis. Further evidence is also found in respondents' comments.

There is no general improvement between the adolescence/20s period and the period between 30 and 50. Indeed, certain disorders, such as anxiety, depression, and PTSD, are more frequently reported. It makes sense that these disorders would surface more for some people as adulthood progresses.

On the other hand, the prevalence of depression and low self-esteem significantly decreased after age 50, along with hospitalization. One striking difference is the reduced frequency of suicide attempts: 4.1% after age 50 compared to 15.9% in the 30s and 40s and 18.6% during adolescence and 20s. Finally, the prevalence of insomnia and sleep disorders seems to have worsened – either gradually or moderately – as respondents aged. However, this finding is not surprising, since sleep disorders are common in older adults in the general population as well.

Participant Comments

Anxiety
30-50	79.2%
50+	73.8%

Emma [60, CAN*] probably always had anxiety: *I just didn't know that other people didn't experience what I did.* Lauren [51, NE*] wrote: "I believe I developed PTSD as a direct result of autism and living in an indifferent and hostile neurotypical world. It's like being beaten up on a daily basis, and having to constantly stay vigilant and wary is a direct contributor. I was also bullied in grade school and stalked in college, so those shaped me in ways that are sources of continual stress for me."

Depression
30-50	72.6%
50+	58.2%

Low self-esteem
30-50	68.2%
50+	52.0%

On psychotropic medication
30-50	36.5%
50+	27.7%

Martha [57, SW*]: "I have used talk therapy all my adult life and also meds for the anxiety and depression." Lillian [55, UK] "will not take medication—have had bad reactions—have always been wary of the mental health system, though have used it at certain points in my life."

Insomnia or other sleep disorders
30-50	47.3%
50+	48.0%

Kenneth [51, UK] has had lifelong insomnia. Julianne [69, AUS] wrote: "Psychiatric centres inpatient...acute anxiety disorder and PTSD...childhood trauma...nightmares, still wake up screaming sometimes in the night...can't remember the nightmare. Sometimes I have flashbacks to what seems to indicate sexual abuse at very young age. Fear has ruled my life and I can still feel intimidated... usually associated with fear rejection /admonition/unjust criticism, etc."

Other

David [70, NE*] spent three months at Menninger Clinic [psychiatric clinic] when he was 20. "My mother (the alcoholic) wanted me institutionalized to learn to 'deal' with my anger issues. My father didn't believe in mental illness and, fortunately, got me out before too much psychic damage occurred. Of course, that's when I began abusing pot."

TREATMENT FOR MENTAL HEALTH ISSUES AFTER 30

<u>**SURVEY QUESTION #46:**</u> *MENTAL ILLNESS/PSYCHIATRIC DISORDER: Treatment... Which of these treatments have you had?*

N = 150	Don't know	Childhood		Teens and 20s		30-50		50+	
	Count	Count	%	Count	%	Count	%	Count	%
Psychotherapy/counseling	1	10	6.7%	53	35.6%	101	67.8%	66	44.3%
Coaching/mentoring	8	2	1.4%	6	4.2%	12	8.5%	13	9.2%
Friends	6	9	6.3%	25	17.4%	36	25.0%	40	27.8%
Family	6	16	11.1%	23	16.0%	31	21.5%	36	25.0%
Intensive outpatient hospital	6	0	0.0%	3	2.1%	10	6.9%	5	3.5%
In-patient psychiatric ward	5	0	0.0%	8	5.5%	9	6.2%	5	3.4%
Psychiatric hospital	5	0	0.0%	10	6.9%	11	7.6%	6	4.1%
Art therapy	4	3	2.1%	8	5.5%	12	8.2%	12	8.2%
Dance therapy	6	0	0.0%	2	1.4%	2	1.4%	1	0.7%
Medication	2	4	2.7%	27	18.2%	52	35.1%	47	31.8%
Exercise	3	19	12.9%	42	28.6%	63	42.9%	60	40.8%
Improving diet	7	7	4.9%	20	14.0%	56	39.2%	59	41.3%
Social skills training	6	0	0.0%	5	3.5%	7	4.9%	11	7.6%
Over-the-counter meds	4	2	1.4%	10	6.8%	17	11.6%	16	11.0%
Other	0	0	0.0%	1	0.7%	5	3.3%	5	3.3%

Not surprisingly for our generation, many tried counseling before there was a diagnosis for a higher functioning autism, or before therapists could diagnose it in adults. It seems that during their 30s and 40s, participants reached out to more sources of help, then somewhat less often after age 50, possibly as they were diagnosed or became aware of their autism. After age 30 they made more efforts to exercise and improve diet, along with getting medication and psychotherapy. This is also true of aging neurotypicals, but perhaps pursued with deeper intensity by those aging on the spectrum.

Friends
30-50   *25%*
50+   *27.8%*

Family
30-50   *21.5%*
50+   *25%*

Psychotherapy/Counseling
30-50   *67.8%*
50+   *44.3%*

Most of the comments were about bad therapy experiences. For example, Lauren [51, NE*] was in therapy in her 40s "but again, it was a waste of time, and the therapists just made things worse, because they were treating me for what they thought was going on with me and treating my Aspie qualities like they were pathological conditions to be fixed rather than understood and managed. I have been involved in neuropsych rehab since 2008, working on executive function and communication skills. That has helped me immensely. Exercise and watching my diet are big parts of my strategy, also. For art therapy, art is something I do, myself, when I need it – not provided by anyone else. My family has provided very spotty support, but I have to list them, because they have been helpful from time to time. I don't have a lot of friends, but the ones I have do occasionally help me work things out. Coaching and mentoring comes from more experienced people who share their life experiences."

Stephen K [69, NE] was disappointed in therapy: "Most interventions were only marginally effective; PTSD (flashing light) therapy highly effective; Aspie diagnosis was life changing."

Tim [76, NE*] and his wife experienced "couples' therapy." Tim said it was "not helpful because we had not had my diagnosis yet. Couples therapy after diagnosis was helpful because we were with a LCSW who understood Asperger's medication – sertraline prescribed by my primary care physician for anxiety – night-and-day difference."

These experiences are echoed by the findings of a recent Asperger/Autism Network couples-focused survey of 461 adults in which 90% felt that seeing a couples' therapist experienced with neurodiverse couples was "important" or "very important" [Grace Myhill/AANE, personal communication, 2018].

Medication
30-50   *35.1%*
50+   *31.8%*

Rob [61, NE]: "Psychiatric and medication therapy was usually not very effective. The Asperger peer group has been the most helpful."

Exercise
30–50   *42.9%*
50+   *40.8%*

Diet
30–50   *39.2%*
50+   *41.3%*

Carlos [66, NE*]: "Improving diet certainly has helped, especially since I am sugar sensitive. Psychotherapy is helpful only up to a point. Spirituality helps me more than psychology."

May [70, SW] also felt good about dietary changes. "Going on the specific carbohydrate diet and taking natural supplements recommended by naturopathic and homeopathic doctors have helped the most. Exercising and discovering friends in later life are outcomes rather than assists in dealing with the stresses in life." Emma [60, CAN*] added: "Improving diet does NOT include wacky therapies designed to 'cure' people. Just a good diet with lots of veggies." Natalie [57, UK] shared: "I've never received any formal help; there were two follow-up sessions with a psychologist after diagnosis, but this was mainly discussing the diagnosis. I have myself found yoga helpful and follow a healthy diet."

12-Step Program

A number of our respondents indicated that they attended 12-step programs and found them very helpful.

"Other"

Karen [62, W*] shared that getting educated about ASD had improved her mental health considerably; "I was able to let go of a ton of self-recrimination and blame for things that weren't my fault." Natalie [57, UK] is helped by a healthy diet and yoga. Lucy [61, NE*] found dance and art to be very therapeutic.

Marilyn [65, W*] kept her art hidden from the time of her divorce in 1992 until 2009 "when I was given my first art show. In retrospect, I realize I was trying to visually describe an unknown, which I later learned had a name, Asperger's Syndrome. That was my own devised therapy. Also, I'm taking ballet, and that exercise is helpful. I think the thing that saved me was my perseverance and willingness to try different things. I kept searching to find out why I wasn't succeeding."

May [70, SW] found other helpful resources: "Social skills training is not disability-related; I became interested in conflict processes as a young adult and I believe this is how I taught myself to read other people."

Some had negative experiences with a number of resources. Kenneth [51, UK] seems discouraged in that he is not sure whether anything has really helped him.

PHYSICAL ILLNESS AFTER 30

SURVEY QUESTION #47: *PHYSICAL ILLNESS: Indicate which of these you have had at various points in your life.*

N = 150	Don't know	Childhood		Teens and 20s		30-50		50+	
	Count	Count	%	Count	%	Count	%	Count	%
Epilepsy	5	7	4.8%	5	3.4%	5	3.4%	5	3.4%
Inner ear imbalance	6	7	4.9%	11	7.6%	13	9.0%	15	10.4%
Difficulty hearing	5	12	8.3%	15	10.3%	22	15.2%	37	25.5%
Chronic fatigue syndrome	7	2	1.4%	12	8.4%	20	14.0%	18	12.6%
Allergies	4	39	26.7%	53	36.3%	62	42.5%	56	38.4%
Ulcers	4	6	4.1%	7	4.8%	13	8.9%	13	8.9%
Cancer	4	0	0.0%	0	0.0%	5	3.4%	6	4.1%
Frequent flu/colds	4	15	10.3%	20	13.7%	17	11.6%	12	8.2%
Pneumonia	3	6	4.1%	5	3.4%	9	6.1%	6	4.1%
Bad back	1	5	3.4%	26	17.4%	65	43.6%	52	34.9%
Surgery	2	17	11.5%	17	11.5%	33	22.3%	38	25.7%
Difficulty sleeping	2	40	27.0%	55	37.2%	76	51.4%	86	58.1%
Other	2	8	5.4%	8	5.4%	11	7.4%	12	8.1%

As illustrated, there are increases in physical illnesses, mostly between the adolescent/20s period and the period between 30 and 50, the strongest being for hearing problems, back problems, and difficulty sleeping. There is also a strong increase in rate of reported surgery. On the other hand, the incidence of flu and colds decreases. Most of these level off or even get less after 50, except for difficulty sleeping and difficulty hearing, two problems that seem to get worse after 50. A lot of these patterns may be attributed to aging. However, it could be that aging autistics have more physical problems that could be attributed to the mental stress of life on the spectrum.

Hearing/Speaking
30-50	15.2%
50+	25.5%

Lauren [51, NE*] told us: "When I was a kid, I had a lot of trouble hearing. I could not distinguish between different sounds. *b* and *v* sounded the same to me. Also, *th* and *f* and *s* all sounded the same to me, but *s* was very painful to my ears when I said it, so I used *th* instead when I talked, which gave me a lisp. I have continued to have trouble distinguishing sounds, and unless I am listening carefully, words sound garbled to me against the background noise around me." Tim [76, NE*] has problems with "inner ear, etc., caused by gunfire onboard ships. Bad back – wrecked a motorcycle while going to college. Appendix and eye surgery (injured by flying piece of wood at work in a lumber yard)." Kenneth [51, UK] has difficulty staying focused in places that have a lot of background noise. Louise [52, UK] had similar problems: "Difficulty hearing in childhood - this wasn't an inability to hear speech, but an occasional complete failure to understand it, as if I was hearing a foreign language."

Allergies

30-50	42.5%
50+	38.4%

Doris [55, AUS*]: "I am dangerously allergic to tick bites and need to keep epi-pens handy. I deal with ongoing skin cancer due to fair skin, but nothing life-threatening. A bout of pneumonia in my thirties brought on asthma, which occurs only when I have a respiratory disease. Bad back from housekeeping in hotels. Some gynie surgery. Difficulty sleeping when I'm dealing with stresses and problems. Also sleepless in childhood but had no real stress then to cause it."

Difficulty Sleeping

30-50	51.4%
50+	58.1%

Carlos [66, NE*] "is very prone to fatigue. Bad sleep pattern contributes to that but does not explain it totally." Helen [50, UK]: "I've always had difficulty sleeping. Cindy [52, NE]: "Difficulty with sleeping came with later years and, possibly, increased job stress."

Chronic Fatigue Syndrome

30-50	14.0%
50+	12.6%

Katrine-Estella [53, UK]: "I started to get chronic fatigue when I moved in...2000; it came and went and was not permanent. The condition was not diagnosed, but this year I have been diagnosed with fibromyalgia, which I probably had since 2013." Marilyn [65, W*]: "I have a dislocated clavicle and have broken my wrist and ankle, all due to accidents. Fatigue is a big issue."

MEDIA AND INTERESTS

SURVEY QUESTION #35: *What TV shows and movies do you like?*

This question was intended as a way to learn more about people's interests. A strikingly high number [26 adults, or 17% of the group] responded that they watch little or no TV/movies. Of those who are regular viewers, a number of genres and programs were particularly popular: science fiction [*Star Trek, Dr. Who*], fantasy [*Harry Potter, Lord of the Rings*], documentaries, history, military, comedies [especially *The Big Bang Theory*, which features an autistic-like character], and detective/crime programs [including *Sherlock*, whose lead character also has autistic qualities].

SURVEY QUESTION #36: *What books, magazines, newspapers do you read? [Are any of them especially helpful for people on the spectrum]?*

About 10% said they read little or not at all; a few respondents said they read mostly via the Internet or had visual difficulty that impairs their reading. A few others proclaimed, "I read everything; I used to read everything; or I can read anywhere, anytime." One noted, "Books are my escape, my happy place." Some of the more commonly mentioned topics include Asperger/autism [Temple Grandin books, Asperger's United, Asperger's magazine], science fiction, how-to, history, math, science, and news.

SURVEY QUESTION #37: *What Internet sites do you find helpful or interesting? [Are there any Asperger's/autism sites that you find helpful?]*

About 27 [18%] specifically mentioned that they don't look at Asperger/autism sites. The reasons they gave included: they don't use the internet much or they had specific reasons for not going to autism sites. Some of the reasons include: "I tend to say my mind and that can get me in trouble", "I get most of the support I need from the group meetings," and "I don't focus on my autism." Regular Internet users mentioned a wide range of popular/general interest sites, including news [CNN, +BBC], science/medicine, Google Earth, YouTube, and Amazon. [Only two mentioned sports.] Quite a few autism sites were reported, especially WrongPlanet, Facebook groups, and National Autistic Society.

SURVEY QUESTION #38: *What social media do you use? [Twitter, Facebook, Pinterest, SnapChat, etc.]*

At least 41 [27%] of our group reported not using social media at all, often declaring as much vociferously "[DO NOT USE SOCIAL MEDIA AND NEVER HAVE…don't see the point in it…seems like a complete time waster…I am scared of the very idea…I would rather volunteer and help real people]." Among the social media users, Facebook and Twitter were by far the preferred platforms. A few use social media for hobbies and interests [cars, watches, model aircraft], several use it for maintaining social contact, and a few find it helpful for autistic-related matters. I find many kindred spirits there – especially with Autchat…Twitter for contact with autistic community.

SURVEY QUESTION #39: *Do you regularly visit any blogs or forums that pertain to the spectrum? [Which ones?]*

Most of the group responded "no" to this question. Some responded in a general fashion ["long list"]. Specific blogs/forums mentioned included *Ask an Autistic*, *Everyday Aspie*, and *Wrong Planet*.

Other special interests or passions

Only two or three responded "none" or "not really" to this item, suggesting that nearly all of the participants have hobbies or deep interests. Some wrote at length about their interests. Contrary to the stereotype of autistics as sedentary geeks, quite a few cited exercises, including kayaking, ballet, bicycling, scuba diving, hiking, weightlifting, and walking. The range of other interests cited was vast: autism rights, gardening, reading, science, music, ham radio, Neanderthals, herbs, Egyptology, winemaking, cricket, motorcycles, *Scrabble*, homeschooling, railways, collecting sugar packets, and many more.

RESPONSE TO BEING ON THE SPECTRUM

SURVEY QUESTION #48: *How have you responded to being on the spectrum at various stages of your life [when you knew your diagnosis] or to just being different from others around you? [Indicate which statement is true.]*

	1. I don't know	2. Childhood	3. Teens & 20s	4. 30-50	5. 50+
I was ashamed of my differences	13	51	60	55	36
		37.2%	43.8%	40.1%	26.3%
I celebrated my differences	11	9	16	34	64
		6.5%	11.5%	24.5%	46.0%
I hated myself	4	33	53	48	33
		22.6%	36.3%	32.9%	22.6%
I wanted to kill myself	9	16	38	37	28
		11.3%	27.0%	26.2%	19.9%
I was OK with being different, but was upset by the discrimination	7	24	34	49	53
		16.8%	23.8%	34.3%	37.1%
Because of discrimination, I hated who I was	13	14	16	16	17
		10.2%	11.7%	11.7%	12.4%
I tried hard to look like others and hide my true self	8	54	87	76	44
		38.0%	61.3%	53.5%	31.0%
I accepted who I am	5	15	21	43	89
		10.3%	14.5%	29.7%	61.4%
I hated who I am	10	26	41	37	20
		18.6%	29.3%	26.4%	14.3%
I desperately wanted to be like everybody else	6	47	60	38	20
		32.6%	41.7%	26.4%	13.9%
I tried to hide who I am because of bullying and teasing	9	50	54	29	19
		35.5%	38.3%	20.6%	13.5%
I connected with others on the spectrum, and felt like I belonged	11	3	4	26	64

		2.2%	2.9%	18.7%	46.0%
I am ashamed of my autism	13	6	7	8	10
		4.4%	5.1%	5.8%	7.3%
I am proud of my autism	8	3	6	26	63
		2.1%	4.2%	18.3%	44.4%
I get depressed about social discrimination of autism	8	7	13	28	53
		4.9%	9.2%	19.7%	37.3%
Other	2	1	2	4	11
		0.7%	1.4%	2.7%	7.4%

How we feel about our autism is an important aspect of how we navigate degrees five, six, and seven. We are redefining ourselves, reviewing life from a different perspective, and becoming more fully integrated. The figures in the above chart show how this process has been for our participants at different points. The most positive changes seem to come after age 50: In general, respondents feel less ashamed of differences, more accepting of self, pride in identity of autism, active in the autistic community, as well as being more helpful to others.

Participant Comments

Proud of being autistic

Karen [62, W*] tells us: "It's my superpower." Yvonne [65, SW*] said: "I was always and am proud of my autism. I find autistic people are individuals, so I don't necessarily feel drawn to them if they have a social or background like NT, who I don't care for, especially dishonest ones. I find parenting has a lot to do with how a child turns out both autistic and neurotypical...nature vs. nurture." Marilyn [65, W*] says: "My diagnosis was a turning point for me. I now accept who I am and, for the most part, am proud of it." Karen [62, W*] is quite enthusiastic: "I can't explain my experience to you, but as I mentioned earlier, 'epiphany' is too small a word. I was elated, energized, and enlightened simultaneously. I knew – KNEW – who I was for the first time in my life. I suddenly had a sense of myself as a whole person."

Acceptance of self

Tim [76, NE*] is quite accepting in saying: "It is what it is." Rhys [52, UK*] expressed acceptance: "I'm not ashamed or proud of my autism any more than I'm ashamed or proud of having blue eyes or curly hair." Samantha [52, MW] explained that before diagnosis, she thought of herself as an "alien."...But now says she is not ashamed of autism nor proud of it: "it's just who I am." Doris [AUS, 55] explains her experience: "I wouldn't now say I'm proud of being autistic – I just live with it and I'm glad I now understand myself better. I don't want to be in the 'Aspie club' as such. We all have different issues in our lives and we all try to make the best of it. Before, I wanted to be like everybody else. Now, I just want to be me."

Ashamed of autism

Martha [57, SW*] resents that life seems so much more difficult for her than for others who are not autistic. Carlos [66, NE*] is alert to negative thinking: "autism is a great source of self-hate, but also a feeling that I have struggled and succeeded in coping with a condition that few will ever have to deal with. But I always have to remain vigilant about its effects on my current interactions with others."

Depressed about social discrimination

Julianne [69, AUS]: "I'm saddened and frustrated by the lack of understanding and empathy by the NT population to those who are different. Sometimes I'm angry."

Trying to be normal

Emma [60, CAN*] was trying to look normal: "was probably unaware of trying to be like everyone else (I actually thumb-nosed that idea from an early age), but at the same time, I was working hard to be accepted as 'normal.'"

Some tried to hide their autism. Janet [61, UK] tried to act normal and hide her autistic characteristics so she wouldn't be bullied at work. This has left her exhausted for social interactions. Louise's [52, UK] attitude is similar: "I have told practically no one around me that I am autistic. This is because I did tell people around me when I was diagnosed with depression and found that it completely changed the way some people behaved towards me, always in a negative way. Nowadays I'm interested in focusing on what I can do well rather than being defined by the autistic label." Mark Dean [54, UK]: "I feel that it is important for me to be open about being autistic, as it is only through people being open about it that progress can be made. I want to project a positive view of autism, and I think that I am achieving that slowly, in however small a way." Jack [57, UK] lives the universal story of our generation of autistics in saying, "I've lived for 50+ years without thinking/knowing I had autism." He tells us he's not proud of his autism, but very relieved to receive a diagnosis. He is now in less pain and sees possibilities for future growth in his life.

Don't/didn't like being autistic

Some have negative feelings about their autism. One gentleman wrote: "I hate being autistic and I get angry about it as I believe others sense I am vulnerable and weak and take advantage of me. I am easily led and influenced by others. I do not like who I am. I have always wanted to be normal like everyone else. I do not socialize with other autistics of the same age."

Mixed feelings

Mixed feelings to this question are common. Kenneth [51, UK] hates himself because of his differences, yet also is proud of being unique. Rhys [52, UK*] puts autism in a neutral context: "I'm not ashamed or proud of my autism any more than I'm ashamed or proud of having blue eyes or curly hair." Adam [56, OTH*] has similar views: "I am neither proud nor ashamed of my autism. It's simply a different 'culture.'"

Carlos [66, NE*] is cautious: "Autism is a great source of self-hate, but also a feeling that I have struggled and succeeded in coping with a condition that few will ever have to deal with." Lauren [51, NE*] had a deeply honest comment. "This is really a complex issue for me. I feel all of the ways I've felt, at different times and under different circumstances. I can feel one way in one moment and different in the next, depending on the condition."

What Karen [62, W*] shared about her experiences through stages five, six, and seven [after diagnosis] is especially poignant for ending this section:

> "I can't explain my experience to you, but as I mentioned earlier, 'epiphany' is too small a word. I was elated, energized, and enlightened simultaneously. I knew – KNEW – who I was for the first time in my life. I suddenly had a sense of myself as a whole person."

DEGREES EIGHT AND NINE: TURNING OUTWARD TO SOCIETY

DEGREE EIGHT: *Unconditional Service*. As mentioned, the final stages of autism are only reached by a minority of adults. For those who do, after letting go of past hurts, the focus becomes "active service to help others...passionately applying your gifts with an open heart. The key to success is being aware of our gifts and finding a way to apply them for the benefit of humanity" [Wylie et al., 2016, p. 161].

Dr. Sara Heath, author of the chapter on the eighth degree in Wylie et al. [2016, p. 152], states:

> "*When* an autistic individual embarks upon the eighth degree of autism this furthers acceptance and healing. However, there are also many challenges to come to terms with during this stage. Many people, especially those late to be diagnosed with autism, may be backward looking, and still often haunted by problems from the past."

Even fewer reach the final degree.

DEGREE NINE: *Recognition, mastery, unity*. It is powerful to have "achieved self-mastery, made a positive contribution to our environment, and gained a sense of unity with the larger world" [Wylie et al., 2016, p. 163]. While some of those who have reached the ninth degree have worldwide renown [e.g., Temple Grandin], others apply their mastery in a much smaller sphere such as their local community. It is difficult to determine from people's self-reports if they have reached the ninth degree. Heath writes:

> "But those who have reached the ninth degree of autism may never procure public recognition or renown. Their positive contributions may be local or even within their circle of friends and family. Their personal integrity and the healthy integration of autism into their overall life may be simply reflected in their ordinary daily actions" [Wylie et al., 2016, p. 167-68].

This chart shows that our participants have both positive and negative feelings about being on the spectrum.

SURVEY QUESTION #49: *HEALING AND WHOLENESS: Indicate at which points in your life each statement is true [or not].*

	1. I don't know	2. Childhood	3. Teens & 20s	4. 30-50	5. 50+
Autism is a positive part of my life	14	9	11	30	79
		6.6%	8.1%	22.1%	58.1%
I love that I am on the autism spectrum	16	3	3	15	43
		2.2%	2.2%	11.2%	32.1%
I hate being on the autism spectrum	16	7	7	12	22
		5.2%	5.2%	9.0%	16.4%
I have autistic friends	9	2	6	27	60
		1.4%	4.3%	19.1%	42.6%
I'm involved in an autism support group	6	0	0	17	53
		0.0%	0.0%	11.8%	36.8%
I am active in an autism community	9	0	0	11	29
		0.0%	0.0%	7.8%	20.6%
I'm involved in a community of disabled	7	0	2	11	18
		0.0%	1.4%	7.7%	12.6%
I try to hide my autism	10	13	16	23	31
		9.3%	11.4%	16.4%	22.1%
I feel proud of talking about my autism	13	0	0	12	53
		0.0%	0.0%	8.8%	38.7%
If I could get rid of my autism, I would	18	10	11	15	26
		7.6%	8.3%	11.4%	19.7%
I wouldn't give up my autism even if I could	21	5	5	19	56
		3.9%	3.9%	14.7%	43.4%
I'd like to see a cure for autism	16	6	5	8	17
		4.5%	3.7%	6.0%	12.7%
I'd like to see autistic people have greater acceptance	4	13	18	48	120
		8.9%	12.3%	32.9%	82.2%
I get angry when people try to change me.	9	27	38	47	76
		19.1%	27.0%	33.3%	53.9%
I try to help others on the spectrum	6	3	9	43	91
		2.1%	6.3%	29.9%	63.2%
I do volunteer work in my community	6	3	15	30	50
		2.1%	10.4%	20.8%	34.7%

I'm usually too depressed/tired to do volunteer work	8	2	6	20	38
		1.4%	4.2%	14.1%	26.8%
I have been content since knowing about my autism.	9	0	0	17	77
		0.0%	0.0%	12.1%	54.6%
I get depressed about discrimination against those on the spectrum	12	2	5	22	52
		1.4%	3.6%	15.9%	37.7%
I get angry about discrimination for those on the spectrum	6	3	7	38	88
		2.1%	4.9%	26.4%	61.1%
It empowers me to work towards changing discrimination	9	1	2	22	58
		0.7%	1.4%	15.6%	41.1%
I have some type of spirituality in my life	9	29	38	52	80
		20.6%	27.0%	36.9%	56.7%

While more participants feel pride in being autistic after age 50, a greater percentage also feels negatively about it. We believe that both arise as a result of having been diagnosed. Along with finding out who we are come both positive and negative feelings about ourselves, our capabilities, our gifts, and our limitations.

A third of the group or more seem to be taking some active role, either toward helping others, or toward promoting awareness, which would place them in one of the higher degrees. Well over a half are very accepting of their autism. We wanted to know more about whether our respondents were becoming comfortable with their life on the spectrum, and if they were reaching out into the world in Degrees Eight and Nine. Becoming active in the world is an important aspect of Degrees Eight and Nine, so we wanted to get a sense of what our participants are doing in that arena, as well as how comfortable they have become with being on the spectrum.

Participant Comments

Autism is a positive part of my life.
Childhood   6.6%
Teens & 20s   8.1%
30-50   22.1%
50+   58.1%

Some of our respondents have found a deep contentment with their autism. Looking at the chart, we see that positive feelings about autism increased after age 50 [when most of our folks were diagnosed.]. Rhys [52, UK*] writes: "Being diagnosed has made a very positive difference to my life. I can now look back on my younger days and finally stop beating myself up about why I didn't do better in school and other things that I have allowed myself to hate myself for. I am a lot more content in myself since diagnosis than I have ever been before. Since being diagnosed I have found out that I have a long-term friend who also has Asperger's. I have been registered with my local autism support group since the beginning of the year and am starting to make more use of their services and facilities. Although I would not class myself as an active part of that group, I would very much like to be so in the future."

Others are comfortable, yet struggle with some of the negatives with life on the spectrum. Samantha [52, MW] is happy on the spectrum, but doesn't exactly "love" it; however, she is involved in advocacy work. Lauren [51, NE*] muses: "Autism is absolutely a positive part of my life, but it's not easy. I wouldn't change it for the world, but I think the world could use some changing. The one thing that could be changed is that people stop thinking they've got it all figured out – or that they need to. We are all on a spectrum of some kind. Why not be generous and make an effort to help others? It does make me angry that people are discriminated against, but it's also a complex issue – and people who discriminate need help as well. I feel empowered to work towards changing things, but there's only so much I can do so long as autistic people are considered 'less capable' and 'impaired/disordered.'"

I love that I am on the autism spectrum.
Childhood	*2.2%*
Teens & 20s	*2.2%*
30-50	*11.2%*
50+	*32.1%*

A greater percentage of our respondents said that, at 50 and older, autism was a positive part of their life, as compared with those who responded that they loved being on the spectrum - 58.2% vs. 32.1%.

Pat [64, NE*] is open about her ambivalent feelings. "I do acknowledge that I have a love/hate relationship with the fact that I'm on the spectrum. Some days are better than others." Rhys [52, UK*] has positive feelings now about the part of the journey that brought self-hate. "Being diagnosed has made a very positive difference to my life. I can now look back on my younger days and finally stop beating myself up about why I didn't do better in school and other things that I have allowed myself to hate myself for. I am a lot more content in myself since diagnosis than I have ever been before. Since being diagnosed I have found out that I have a long-term friend who also has Asperger's. I have been registered with my local autism support group since the beginning of the year and am starting to make more use of their services and facilities. Although I would not class myself as an active part of that group, I would very much like to be so in the future."

I hate being on the autism spectrum.
Teens & 20s	*5.2%*
30-50	*9.0%*
50+	*16.4%*

The negative feelings of those at over 50 [16.4%] are much lower than the positive ones [58.2% and 32.1% for "Autism is a positive part of my life" and "I love that I am on the autism spectrum," respectively].

Many came to the point of: "I accept my autistic traits, but I would prefer not to have them." Doris [55, AUS*] reflects on one worry about "spectrumites": "I don't really think about my autism all that much, but I get concerned when many people in the news that have committed violence have been referred to as autistic or with Asperger's. Mainly males. Makes me think that people will be scared of us."

I am involved in an autism support group.
Childhood   *0%*
Teens & 20s   *0%*
30–50   *11.8%*
50+   *36.8%*

Mark [54, UK] is setting up a support group: "I am in the process of setting up a mutual support group at my place of work. I hope to develop this in both size and scope to become more of an outreach group and working with other organisations. In general, there is a lot of reaching out to help others on the spectrum. A common attitude is: 'When I see someone could benefit from support for their child or themselves...I make a point of bringing it to their attention.'"

I am active in the autism community.
Childhood   *0%*
Teens & 20s   *0%*
30–50   *7.8%*
50+   *20.6%*

Many respondents speak of the strength in support groups. Emma [60, CAN*]: "My community – online and in person – are sustenance, fun and so enriching. I have always been involved in activism – decades before I understood my own autism. It has been critical in my adult life."

I try to hide my autism.
Childhood   *9.3%*
Teens & 20s   *11.4%*
30–50   *16.4%*
50+   *22.1%*

Some of our participants are cautious about disclosure. They keep their autism to themselves when it could hurt them – such as in a job – but if they can be helpful to another autistic, they step up to disclose and offer help.

Lauren [51, NE*] is one such autistic. She says: "Autism is absolutely a positive part of my life, but it's not easy. I wouldn't change it for the world, but I think the world could use some changing. The one thing that could be changed is that people stop thinking they've got it all figured out – or that they need to. We are all on a spectrum of some kind. Why not be generous and make an effort to help others? It does make me angry that people are discriminated against, but it's also a complex issue – and people who discriminate need help as well. I feel empowered to work towards changing things, but there's only so much I can do so long as autistic people are considered 'less capable' and 'impaired/disordered.'"

Lauren is reflecting the values of community and service in the eighth and ninth degrees.

I'd like to see a cure for autism.
Childhood   *4.5%*
Teens & 20s   *3.7%*

30-50	*6.0%*
50+	*12.7%*

Issues around autism cause and cure have been vocal and controversial through the years. Kenneth [51, UK] would like to have a cure for autism available for any autistic who wants to take it. He himself wouldn't take such a remedy because he likes who he is now.

I'd like to see autistic people have greater acceptance.
Childhood	*8.9%*
Teens & 20s	*12.3%*
30-50	*32.9%*
50+	*82.2%*

Jamie [52, UK] is another participant reflecting eight- and nine-degree values: "I always say it's a mixed blessing, there are good things and bad things. I work with my wife doing Asperger awareness training to people like teachers, mental health workers, and other caring professions, including human resources professionals."

Many participants expressed regrets that they didn't know sooner. Some of the comments included: "I don't really care too much now that I know what I am. I do still try to blend in, but I don't really care as much as I used to. And I'm okay with being autistic, I just wish I knew sooner."

I try to help others on the spectrum.
Childhood	*2.1%*
Teens & 20s	*6.3%*
30-50	*29.9%*
50+	*63.2%*

I have been content since knowing about my autism.
Childhood	*0%*
Teens & 20s	*0%*
30-50	*12.1%*
50+	*54.6%*

I get depressed about discrimination against those on the spectrum.
Childhood	*1.4%*
Teens & 20s	*3.6%*
30-50	*15.9%*
50+	*37.7%*

I get angry about discrimination against those on the spectrum.
Childhood	*2.1%*
Teens & 20s	*4.9%*
30-50	*26.4%*
50+	*61.1%*

It empowers me to work towards changing discrimination.
Childhood	*0.7%*
Teens & 20s	*1.4%*

30-50   *15.6%*
50+   *41.1%*

Emma [60, CAN*] says: "My community – online and in person – are sustenance, fun and so enriching. I have always been involved in activism – decades before I understood my own autism. It has been critical in my adult life."

I have some type of spirituality in my life.
Childhood   *20.6%*
Teens & 20s   *27.0%*
30-50   *36.9%*
50+   *56.7%*

Karen [62, W*]: "Ah...the 'too logical for God' question. I used to go to an Evangelical Lutheran church, conservative, and always had doubts about the miracles and things, and then I read three of Bart Ehrman's books, and I believe doing so affirmed my basic faith. Not much for the Sistine Chapel Ceiling Guy, but more...the Universe." Edward [77, W] has another approach to autistic spirituality: "I believe the Dali Lama is an Aspie."

Some autistics with a spiritual bent are angry at God for putting them on the spectrum. Martha [57, SW*] says: "Maintaining a spiritual life has gotten harder with age and increased resentment toward God for making me who I am. Also, my sensory issues have increased with age, making it harder for me to tolerate being around groups of people and in worship service."

SURVEY QUESTION #50: *Do you feel you have reached a point in your life where you are comfortable with being on the spectrum and consider it a positive part of your life?*

Response:	Percent	Count
Yes	68.5%	98
No	31.5%	45
Total Responses		143

In terms of the degrees of autism, almost 69% see autism as a positive part of their lives [answered "Yes"], which implies aspects of Degree Six ["resolution to live with autism"] and Degree Seven ["acceptance"].

Participant Comments

68.5% said they were comfortable after the diagnosis.

Some people wonder about the benefit of diagnosing older persons. "They lived without a diagnosis most of their lives – just let them be," so goes their thinking. But participants who are living within the higher degrees of autism provide a different answer. Many celebrate the support that has been so important in their journey:

Wenn [64, AUS*] commented: "Setting and reaching personal goals with support from others who believe in me. I had to believe in myself first though." David [70, NE*] expresses gratitude for the Asperger/Autism Network: "Understanding is everything. The Over 50 group at AANE is terrific! It is a relief to finally begin to understand, but it is also empowering to know that I have survived almost 70 years and have a pretty good life."

Some compared their life now to earlier years.

Anya [69, NE*]: "I lived behind a glass wall with no way to get through to the rest of the human world. I always felt I was a unique individual and had a purpose in life but did not know how I would ever discover it since most doors seemed to be closed to me. I can see that all the things that I like about myself and all my abilities and the loves that are part of me now have been there inside me my whole life…All I could do was just plunge into the middle of life and hope that somewhere deep inside of me I knew how to swim. I took it upon myself to learn, to teach myself, and begin to do what I had wanted to do. In the process I gained many abilities and skills. I got pretty lost at times and I had a lot of scary and painful experiences…I'm now living a life where all the pieces do fit. But if I hadn't gone through all those experiences I'd still be behind the wall wondering."

Earl [57, NZ*] described his journey very poetically: "Stumbled along in the darkness of no knowledge, then the light came on, and I and my past selves were suddenly OK." Yvonne [65, SW*] observes that she "found out late in life and I did well in life not knowing, so I want others to know autistic people do quite well in life when they can be accepted as well as, unfortunately, act like an NT…we should not have to do so." Emma [60, CAN*]: "Meet and talk with other adults, both online and in person. The neurodiversity movement is so important, and I so wish more parents of autistic kids would take the time to make those connections and not automatically default to the idea that articulate, functional adults like me are "not like my child." Those parents didn't see us as children, and are opting into an Armageddon view of autism, which is very sad. As a newly recognized autistic, this community is a huge support."

Pat [64, NE*]: "I keep remembering the Serenity Prayer from my 12-step program." Bob [54, NE]: "My diagnosis was sufficient. I always knew I was different, but, then, so is everyone else. The dx clarified lots of things and formed a simple explanation out of what had been perceived as a bunch of character flaws and odd behaviors and emotions. My apparent flaws were either the opposite of what they seemed or inseparable from what were considered especially good traits." Eric [55, NE]: "I had to let go of my pride and see myself for who I really was. I see that those on the spectrum have much to contribute."

How they coped

Some survey takers shared the techniques that have helped them the most. Carlos [66, NE*] recalls: "I learned how to cope by taking some normal people as a model and imitating what they did in social situations. But I feel that my autism enables me to identify more than others can with people who are marginalized. I do good work with marginalized and outcast people, residents of nursing homes, many of whom have criminal and/or substance abuse histories. I feel that being on the spectrum has made me more compassionate than others generally." Graham [65, UK]: "As a practicing educational psychologist I gained huge insights into the strengths and difficulties of being on the spectrum. I was able to use my own diagnosis and life experience positively to help youngsters going through the school system and to support their parents from an unusually informed perspective." Helen [50, UK]: "I cope by having an autistic friend in my life. We talk about autism a lot. We work through issues we have while trying to live and work in a NT world. Reading books by autistic people, joining a support group, and meeting other autistic people has helped." Derek [53, NE*]: "I have learned how to have romantic relationships, which has helped a lot with depression and frustration."

Anita [57, NE*]: "I don't see autism as a disease or disorder. I see it simply as a different way to 'be.' I also see myself as better than those neurotypicals who discriminate against me or anyone else on the spectrum. I would NEVER do anything to hurt another person's feelings nor discriminate against them. For that, I see myself as a higher human being."

Some expressed contentment in old age, such as one man who said that, despite living in poverty, he was content with his life as a senior citizen. Kenneth [51, UK] had no 'journey' to accepting his autism. From the moment of diagnosis, he has been at peace with it. Marilyn [65, W*]: "Having to work at a low-paying job for which I was overqualified was very stressful and frustrating. Now that I'm no longer working, I no longer have to try and meet others' expectations. It also gives me time to be creative and do those things that give me the most pleasure."

Still coming to terms with it

Rhys [52, UK*]: "I am still very much coming to terms with my diagnosis as it's less than a year since my private diagnosis and only four months since my National Health Service diagnosis. There are days when I think they must have made a mistake, then I have days where I am so overwhelmed by the outside world that I cannot leave the house. Whereas in the past I would have been really hard on myself for being like that and considered myself a failure, I now know what the reason is for being the way I am, and that helps me be far more forgiving of myself. Large parts of my life were spent in total bewilderment, not knowing why things affected me certain ways or why I found things that other people did without a second thought so impossible. I hated myself for being weak, stupid, useless, and afraid. Now I know why I was like that I am finally able to start laying all these negative feelings to rest. Since my diagnosis rather than beat myself up, I feel that I must have been pretty strong to manage to get through life and still be here to talk about it. For the first time in my life I feel like I'm OK."

Jack [57, UK] has been learning more about autism since diagnosis, and he is feeling better about himself and his future. Doris [55, AUS*]: "It's another perspective on life. Now I know why I don't want to follow the herd. I embrace my differences and I accept my shortcomings. I just wish I could go back and tell my younger self that it's ok, you're not strange or lacking, just different." May [70, SW]: "I finally let go of the social judgment from others that different is bad. It is their need to belong...to not be ostracized...that causes them to believe that way. It is not what I believe though. I am free to act on my beliefs; I don't need acceptance from everyone, only those I choose to be a part of my life. I only choose those who accept and enjoy my differences. It works for me."

Stuart [53, UK]: "I've stopped approval seeking, living up to others' expectations; have to put my own needs first irrespective of what others might think, without being selfish." Janet [61, UK]: "Following diagnosis, I am beginning to accept who I am. I have stopped trying to change things that I cannot change." Lillian [55, UK]: "Diagnosis was an affirmation of me as a whole person; I could include all the bits of myself that I had hidden away or tried to escape from and didn't understand. It was life-changing on an internal level."

Nancy [57, NE*]: "It helped that I had a son on the spectrum and I spent almost a decade learning about his disability, advocating for him and learning to be compassionate for him. When I first realized that I was on the spectrum several years after my son's diagnosis, I was embarrassed and relived many past events where I had acted in a non-expected fashion. But as I got to meet and know other adults on the spectrum, I have come to accept myself more and celebrate all the challenges that I have overcome to get to this point in my life."

31.5% said they were not comfortable after the diagnosis.

Katrine-Estella [53, UK]: "I would like to have support for my autism by having a mentor, CBT Therapy, and social skills training. This would make life easier for me." A British man told us: "That's up to each individual to find their own contentment, some times are better than others. I am angry about my autism, not with anyone or even myself. I am just sad I have it and the grief it has caused my family and friends and those around me. I don't want pity or understanding. I just want acceptance for who I am, not me the autistic. I dislike people who are proud to be autistic; I don't like people who revel in it or wear it like a badge. I less like experts in autism who have not lived the life and just read books, have studied sufferers, or studied it. It's not a pleasant life to have to endure." Jamie [52, UK]: "Neither yes nor no. Very, very difficult question. Acceptance is probably as close to positive as I can be."

SURVEY QUESTION #51: *How do you think things are different for our generation – growing up before Asperger's was a term and when there was little understanding of autism?*

We had little support.

[Rob]: "I believe it was probably much more painful. There was probably much less acceptance of it growing up, and much less understanding of it." Wenn [64, AUS*]: "We were in the dark more and had little support." Adam [56, OTH*]: "We didn't understand ourselves." James Hunt [74, NE]: "Feeling alone and 'weird,' no explanation for our 'weirdness,' a lot of pressure to conform." Anya [69, NE*]: "It's totally different. If I was just starting out today, I'd probably be getting the help in school to where I could go on to college and become a veterinarian. But then look at what I would have missed. I wouldn't have lived through all those experiences or learned all the other abilities and gained the insights that make me who I am today. I would have chosen just one of the pieces – one of the roads – and not tried to link up the whole spectrum of misaligned parts that made me. So I think that it was right for me to be born at that time and it is right for the new kids to be born now. I think there was a plan."

Karen [62, W*]: "I think that we suffered more from bullying and feeling that every failed friendship or blurting out something inappropriate was our fault." Natalie [57, UK]: "It was difficult just being regarded as strange or weird, though with support from a family it would probably have been easier." Carlos [66, NE*]: "Things have been MUCH worse for our generation. Since there was no awareness of the spectrum, we were expected to conform to everyone else and were judged by standards we could not possibly meet. It has done a lot of damage." David B. [62, NE]: "I see all the support young people are getting, and it makes me sad. I wish I could have found out about my AS before my parents passed. We were never very close and now I know why. I wonder how often my parents tried figuring out what was up with me?" Derek [53, NE*]: "I really would have benefited from counseling like my son had at a young age. Perhaps I would not have been depressed and gotten lousy grades in college."

Anita [57, NE*]: "I'm happy I didn't know until I was 50. When I look at this younger generation, everyone is looking for services to get them better. The only way to get better is by getting out in the world and experiencing life, the good, the bad, and the ugly. No services can substitute for life-earned wisdom. I became a success without knowing I'm on the spectrum. Parents need to take notice of adults like myself and look at why this is. It's because I started working jobs since age twelve. Yes, I made plenty of blunders. And I'd get up and dust myself off and forge ahead."

One woman complained: "For most of my life I was just 'wrong' or 'broken,' or it was all my fault." Katrine-Estella [53, UK]: "I think it is much harder as many people still think autism affects only children and that adults cope better and don't need any help even if they want it. I also think that they expect adults not to have meltdowns due to sensory issues because they think it only happens to children. I could not do imaginary play as a child and found it very hard to copy my peers as I could not copy them. There is no support for older siblings who have younger siblings as it is only for children. I have no parents and the Asperger's support group is only for parents and adults, but if you do not have your parents, you cannot take another relative. If you were epileptic and/or had cerebral palsy (even if you had classic autism), you never got diagnosed with autism as your main disability; nor would you get special preference as they would not recognise it because they will say it is because of your epilepsy/cerebral palsy." Laurence [68, UK*]: "A great deal of wasted opportunities. There are so many points in my life I can point back at and say: If only I knew then what I know now about myself, I could have handled all that much better." One respondent noted sadly: "As a kid during the 50s and 60s, I often felt as if I had arrived from a different planet. There were no words to describe this experience."

Wayne [58, UK*]: "More understanding now – so many people I know have a family member with Asperger's/Autism. I still believe we are the victims of the vaccination scandal." Jackie [61, UK*]: "For us, it is like being born again...as much as it's too late, there is still hope and time for many of us, and I hope we are all infected by that hope." Doris [55, AUS*]: "I applaud everyone who has survived their experiences to arrive this far with their sanity intact. Well done! Our generation has mental strength." Louise [52, UK]: "A lot of us have received a diagnosis very late in life, sometimes when the opportunities to form close relationships are less than they were at, say 20. An early diagnosis would have made such a difference to my life, but Asperger's simply wasn't known about in those days – it's no one's fault. Mental health issues were also much more of a dirty little secret when I was young, and I'm glad to see that is changing."

Nicole [51, W]: "We were and are ignored. First because autism is still seen by many as a childhood condition, and now 'adult autism' is considered an issue for ages 18-25 and their neurotypical parents. I greatly resent that there is no help for our 'lost generation.' I am 51, extremely intelligent, and still trying to get and keep a 'real job.'"

SURVEY QUESTION #51 [continued]: *How do you think things are different for younger generations on the spectrum?*

More understanding and support now.

Wenn [64, AUS*]: "There is greater understanding of autism now. There is more support." Adam [56, OTH*]: "They have access to more info and support." Anya [69, NE*]: "They will be able to be themselves right at the beginning of their lives. They will be supported and hopefully be able to be safely and successfully independent. Hopefully, the world outside will welcome them and appreciate them." Lucy [61, NE*]: "They are more often identified and then connected with resources." Eric [55, NE*]: "There are a lot more services, support, and resources!" Carlos [66, NE*]: "If they are lucky, their condition will be recognized, and they will get help and support and maybe even a little understanding." William [67, NE*]: "I know some younger people diagnosed with

Asperger's. They have diagnoses and get some help. In the principal case known to me, he gets plenty of help from his stalwart mom."

Early labels can be harmful.

Yvonne [65, SW*]: "There is more understanding and education for younger people, but they are labeled early on and labels hurt." Natalie [57, UK]: "I hope it is better, but I think too much support might have a negative effect in that they will not learn to cope without it." Mathew [69, NE]: "They are being conditioned into a dubious identity at a younger age...handled badly, this could cause them problems, but handled well it might help them." Anita [57, NE*]: "I think the younger generation focuses too much on the fact that they have autism. They need to forget about it and start living. Life begins at the end of your comfort zone! Get out there and just do it!" An angry participant said: "Having an ASD means you are mentally ill in the UK; that means no life insurance, no mortgage, lots of jobs you cannot do. Has anyone explained that to the parents pushing schools/professionals for a diagnosis? A lifelong illness with no cure, so once you've got it you're stuck with it. A life sentence then."

More hope

Willie [67, UK]: "There is more diagnosis and support, but often rather rigidly applied – seeing the label rather than the individual." Deanna [73, UK*]: "Quite different. Autism is acknowledged." May [70, SW]: "More support but also more discrimination and focus on correcting what are perceived as deficits." Julianne [69, AUS]: "They have both context and accommodations, but possibly don't know themselves as well as those diagnosed very late. Those diagnosed late have had to live most of life without a 'reason/ excuse' (depending upon how the individual is placed...that is, do they or do they not accept a place of responsibility within their limitations on aspects that they may have control over?). Having a reason, an understanding, can be valuable if one is wanting to develop one's potential, but if one is not, it can be a reason to not develop, whichever way the autistic individual will either benefit or lose depending upon their personal decision regarding actions that recognise both limitations and possibilities. All is complex and individual."

And here is our final question.
SURVEY QUESTION #52: *What else would you like to add? What do you want readers of this future book to know about you and your life with autism?*

Wenn [64, AUS*]: "I'd like it known that autism isn't the monster some make it out to be...we are valuable, and we need to believe in ourselves. Being autistic is a disadvantage in a multitasking overly sensory stimulating world, but we have an advantage when it comes to being focused on stuff we are interested in and when sensory load is reduced." Karen [62, W*]: "Now that I know I have Asperger's, I feel whole. It's only been about eight months since I discovered I have Asperger's, but I feel blessed to have been given the gift of finally finding out who I am." Yvonne [65, SW*]: "Accept autism as merely a different brain operating system, it's not a disorder. We are brilliant in our own right." Emma [60, CAN*]: "• Find autistic activists • learn about neurodiversity • become involved in activism to counter negative stereotypes • understand and hear the stories of those of us who love ourselves and our lives and don't want to be cured • don't get sucked into the 'cure' and 'eradication' eugenics arguments so popular in the media • listen to the experts – autistic people. This is a redundant list – on purpose. :-)"

Pat [64, NE*]: "Being a senior citizen on the spectrum, I have good days and I have bad days. I just wish there were more support services for people like me. It would help make things a lot easier!" James Hunt [74, NE]: "Understand that everyone has issues and problems, including NTs; accept who you are and be proud of what you have accomplished." Lucy [61, NE*]: "I think I am going to write my own book someday and answer this question there." Eric [55, NE]: "I hope this book contributes to better understanding and acceptance of those on the spectrum. Realizing I was on the spectrum was initially very disconcerting, but ultimately may turn out to be one of the best things that have ever happened to me." Carlos [66, NE*]: "That people need to recognize we have our own special gifts and can make valuable contributions like everyone else. That it is WRONG to bully people because you are a coward and you prey on the weak to make yourself feel secure. That we have a lot to teach the world about being understanding, compassionate, and loving, and the world needs what we can bring to it in that regard. And finally, as Temple Grandin said so well: "DIFFERENT, NOT LESS THAN!""

Mathew [69, NE]: "I am not convinced at this point that ASD is a valid construct; the whole *DSM* is not anywhere near as scientific as it makes out to be, and its implementation is more folkish than rigorous. I am also not convinced my counselor is right that I 'have autism,' I don't know what it is if I do (though I would like to, but no one really does), and am skeptical about a lot of the science around it. I am skeptical of the identity as over-limiting though if it comforts some, fine. About the value of the community I do not know yet." Tim [76, NE*]: "It has been very difficult to get to the age of 75. I have been married 42 years and it has been very difficult for my wife. At my diagnosis my wife found out there was a reason for my being an 'asshole.' She is in her own counseling group of spouses of Aspies. If I had known of the terrible effects of an Aspie on a spouse, I don't think I would have gotten married."

Lauren [51, NE*]: "My life is absolutely amazing. My experiences are so vivid, so alive! I would never want to inhabit the 'shadows' of neurotypical existence, where the only thing that matters is when next you'll eat, sleep, or have sex. My special interests are the lights of my life, and they keep me young and vigorous. People paint such a dire and dour view of autism, when it has so many wonderful aspects. Volumes could be written about how wonderful it is to inhabit our world, but I think the neurotypical folks just wouldn't get it." Linda [56, W]: "I was told my whole life that I was a terrible bird. The wrong color, the wrong size, I needed to try harder to fly, I was a failure. And it wasn't until my 50s that I learned an astonishing fact – that I'm actually an elephant. And there is a whole herd – a huge herd – just like me out there. No wonder I was gray and not yellow and too heavy to ever fly. :) That's how I feel about learning about AS. I am really a good person, funny, creative, the hardest worker you'll ever meet. But I make so many mistakes. If people could hang in there and deal with me honestly ('did you mean to say that?') and patiently, they would learn that I don't hurt feelings intentionally. I don't like talking on the phone. I don't get when to say something and when not to, etc. But if you can work with me on those things, I am worth getting to know. I guess most people don't. Even my family. They like to sit back and latch on to any one word you use or one thing you say then go away and gossip about you to others – judging you for saying that one thing and talking about how awful you are. They have always done that. Always on the attack. Always ready to pounce. I have always hated that about people."

Anita [57, SE*]: "Read my book *ASPERGER'S SYNDROME: When Life Hands You Lemons, Make Lemonade.* Read what I'm doing now. I would never have achieved ANY of it if I sat around feeling sorry for myself that I'm autistic. I want to be an inspiration to others on the autism spectrum. Yes, you must work hard. But hard work is what makes dreams come true! Set goals and work towards them, one day at a time. Never give up. It's not about falling. It's about getting up." Mark [54, UK]: "I would like them to know that it is possible to carve out a niche for yourself. I somehow refused to be overcome by the challenges that I have faced. I have gained a lot of respect from those I have come into contact with. I have combined working for a living with compiling a cryptic crossword for a national newspaper every week (more or less) for the last 16 years, as well as having a book of them published, and have now branched out into theatre reviewing, journalism, and campaigning. My final message would be: We are here, and we are staying." Marilyn [65, W*]: "I can't think of anything else to tell readers. But to the author: I think this is a terrific idea for a book! I haven't found much written about older adults on the spectrum [i.e., past age 60]."

Rhys [52, UK*]: "My life until I was diagnosed was largely one of bewilderment, not understanding why I found things that other people found so easy I found so impossible. I could not, for instance, understand why my time at school started so well but became a nightmare for me. I could not understand why, despite being thought of as a typical 'life & soul of the party' person I found it increasingly difficult to socialise, and forcing myself to do so caused me to descend deeper and deeper into depression and misery. I could not understand why I found it so difficult to understand and follow what I knew were simple instructions at work, or why being taken off a job and put on something else without warning would cause me to go into meltdown. What my diagnosis has done for me, at the age of 50, is to give me the piece of the puzzle that has been missing all my life, and now that I have that piece I am finally able to start to make sense of my life and to start to forgive myself for the things that, for so long, I hated myself for. I finally know who I am." Jackie [61, UK*]: "I want to thank you from the bottom of my heart for doing this project. High-functioning adults on the autism spectrum over 50 have so much of the past thinking embedded...and the negative messages and feedback etched into our brains...and when we do try to stand up and matter, dealing with police and government bodies who know they have the power not to help or understand, it can sometimes be hard to find the energy to stand again. And yet, the wisdom that has come with age, if we are blessed enough to still have hope and clarity, makes the awareness of our diagnosis a gift so late in life because we know what happened before we knew, that there was nothing wrong with us, just something different and that maybe, just maybe, we can still make some major strides in our life with whatever time God allows us to remain...and I pray a lot I am here for a long while and conquer some of those barriers in my life. Thanks so very much for caring and I hope the rest of your life is a blessing of smiles and accomplishments and dreams come true."

Doris [55, AUS*]: "I think ASD is at a real crossroad these days. Neurotypical experts have no idea what makes us tick, really. Do they think the strange and withdrawn kids avoiding eye contact aren't actually acutely aware of the other person's presence? They are so aware, in fact, that eye-to-eye contact is mentally painful. And yet these kids are told to look people in the eye like a neurotypical! Give me a break. Actions like this by well-meaning experts can cause much of the angst and anxiety in Aspie people who need to be true to themselves. Let the kid spend hours cataloguing Star Wars cards or whatever. Special interests soothe the mind and provide the refuge needed to recalibrate. A year in the universe of Lord of the Rings helped me through a bad spot in life. I don't need Legolas and his friends these days, but I thank them for their help when I really needed it."

Deanna [73, UK*]: "I would like everybody to recognise that childhood problems may be due to autism and not original sin." Stuart [53, UK]: "My brother and I are both on the spectrum. My autism helps me be logical about things and understand and deal with problems (e.g., taking medication). Autism can be a positive – you can deal with the factual part of a problem." Jamie

[52, UK]: "The mask,'" and the mental exhaustion at the end of the day from keeping the mask up, and the need to chill and recharge. Or withdraw from situations for a short period to recharge – Meltdown – we are not Rain Man – as it's a spectrum disorder."

Janet [61, UK*]: "I have contributed a chapter in the book *Aspies on Mental Health* [Beardon, L., & Worton, D. (Eds.) (2011)] and found it a very cathartic experience. It was good to explain what worked and what didn't in psychiatric wards."

Martha [57, SW*]: "There is more I could come up with but not that I can think of now." Louise [52, UK]: "Coming to terms with being 'different' and the resulting difficulty in conforming to society's expectations about how life should be has been a long struggle. But I've found a new career that I love and that suits my autistic traits very well. Find what you're good at and do that."

Just before we went to press, Anya shared with us one of her artworks that speaks to her early struggle.

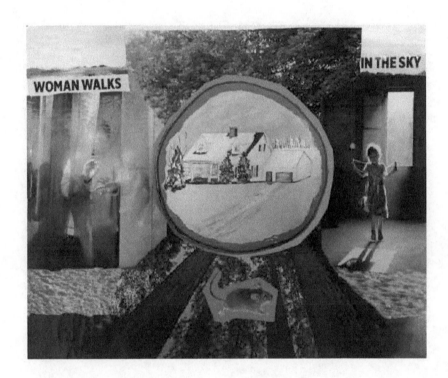

PART IV
THE FUTURE

Where do we go from here?

Summary of Findings

This study grew out of the life experiences of three older autistic adults. We struggled to put our lives in context after the powerful realization that we were on the autism spectrum. Rob was fortunate to get an initial diagnosis as a young adult that was confirmed later in life. Eric is the father of an autistic son, and just realized three years ago that he himself was on the spectrum. Wilma was diagnosed four years ago with autism/Asperger's syndrome.

The three of us are active in support groups in our area. In fact, we met each other through our support group connections. We share a passion for understanding the life events of our generation. We grew up with autism before high-functioning autism was recognized, and, like most of our generation, we discovered our diagnoses later in life. We knew there were thousands of others with similar stories. Where were they? How were they doing? Where was the research? These are *our lives,* and it seemed that someone ought to be studying us.

These were our questions as we began:

1. What was it like being children, teens, and adults with minimal diagnostic information existing for autistics, especially those without an intellectual disability?

2. How were they doing now – with relationships, jobs, health, and resources for autism?

3. What kind of help did they need? What wisdom did they have to share?

4. When and how did they get a diagnosis and how did they feel about it? How did it change their lives?

We wanted to explore three sources of answers:

1. The beliefs about autism that existed when we were born, and as we grew up. This would involve some historical research.

2. The experiences of our generational peers through their lives. This would require us to do a worldwide survey with some follow-up interviews.

3. An integrative framework to allow us to take all that we have learned into our lives. This would involve an understanding of the "nine degrees" as well as listening to the voices of 150 of us from the "lost generation."

Historical Perspective

The historical research showed us the context in which we were born and grew up, including considerable prejudice towards people who are different. Many of our lives came out of the context of eugenics and Nazism. We saw the birth – and death – of theories involving refrigerator mothers and vaccines. At the present time, we have witnessed a growing attitude of "nothing about us without us." We hope for a future of greater community and deepening understanding.

Survey and Interview Results

Our survey and interview results constitute the bulk of this book, with 150 respondents from nine countries. The questionnaire was primarily distributed digitally through Survey Gizmo. The link was sent to autism organizations around the world. Therefore, it was self-limiting in terms of who accessed the link. We attracted primarily people on the mailing lists of autism organizations who were literate and computer-savvy. We hope that future studies will have a broader outreach. The survey had other limitations: It relied on self-report; respondents were self-selected, typically educated, articulate, and high-functioning; and the sources of diagnosis varied.

We tried to balance the reporting in our book between statistical data and real-life stories. We feel this is an especially useful research model for this study in that the researchers are in the population being studied. In fact, the three of us completed the survey and our responses were included in the data. As a result, the lines between researcher and subject overlap. We authors are sometimes scientists reporting data, other times sociologists doing fieldwork, and throughout we are also the population being studied, with all the insight and blind spots that entails.

We limited the study to people at least 50 years old at the time they filled out the form. Therefore, we were primarily reaching Baby Boomers and older. Our respondents were 56% men and 44% women – a ratio closer to equal than is typical in autism studies. The survey allowed participants to describe what it was like for them growing up on the spectrum via multiple-choice questions with unlimited space for comments. Some participants were interviewed by phone or in person to get more extensive personal stories. The respondents' comments and stories reflect a range of life experience, but several common themes emerged.

• Most participants found the experience of diagnosis (either by a professional or by their own conclusion) to be liberating. Most also wanted support and understanding of their childhoods (which were often traumatic) and their present circumstances. Many of their comments convey wisdom and insights about autism and the effects of limited knowledge, prejudices, and stereotypes.

• Most respondents felt relieved and better about themselves following diagnosis but upset that they had lived such a great part of their lives without knowing about it.

• There was an overall improvement in the quality of life after age 50, both in terms of coping strategies and mental health.

• Women tended to get professionally diagnosed significantly less than men, were more varied in sexual orientation, and reported a higher incidence of PTSD. While women are also more likely than men to report PTSD in the general population, in our study both men and women had a significantly higher incidence of reported PTSD than the general population. We also found more diversity in sexual orientation for both genders than in the general population.

• Bullying was a significant issue, with 80% reporting having been bullied, compared to about 30% in the general population.

• Respondents had to cope with limited supports growing up. Because neither a high-functioning autism nor Asperger's Syndrome existed as diagnoses in our childhoods, few of us got appropriate help. Only a handful of us received special services, and most of us were over 50 before getting diagnosed. Most, however, suspected their autism before "official" diagnosis.

Integrative Framework

We explored how the participants' development compared to the nine degrees of autism model [Wylie et al., 2016].

Before Diagnosis
First Degree: Being born autistic
Second Degree: Knowing you are different
Third Degree: Developing secondary health issues

Diagnosis
Fourth Degree: Self-identification

After Diagnosis
Fifth Degree: Considering all the options
Sixth Degree: Crisis of identity/resolution to live with autism. Which parts of self to keep?
Seventh Degree: Self-acceptance
Eighth Degree: Unconditional service
Ninth Degree: Recognition, mastery, unity

Although a range of degrees characterize our participants, all had reached at least Degree Four, since they had to believe they were on the spectrum to participate. As reflected in their responses, some were still trying to sort it all out in the fifth, sixth, or seven degrees or had settled into the eighth or ninth, where they were at peace with their diagnosis and able to turn outward to help others along the way.

AUTISM AND THE NINE DEGREES: A NEW PARADIGM?

Can the nine degrees be a new paradigm for autistics? Based on what we have read, what we have heard from our respondents, and our own experiences, here are a few preliminary thoughts for discussion and research.

> ➢ The concept has been invaluable in this research and in our lives. It helps to solidify the healing journey of autistics. The book is written with a wide variety of authors – mostly autistics – who share from their own lives and others they know. It is affirming and encouraging.

> ➢ We need more conversations and research about the use of the nine degrees as a paradigm for autistics. Some of the questions we'd like to see addressed are:

> How common is it for autistics to move through the degrees sequentially, completing one degree before entering the next? We did not specifically ask that in our questionnaire, but our sense is that most adult journeys are complex and lengthy, going back and forth in the degrees, especially after "realization" in Degree Four.

> • There is more diversity in our own journeys than is reflected in the book. We suggest that it is because this research is new, and we need many more stories from around the world and from a range of ages.

> • We also wonder how useful the model is when diagnosis occurs in childhood. Dr. Shore was diagnosed at age 2.5, yet he found that he could use the degrees more as he grew older.

> With the benefit of early diagnoses at age two and a half, coupled with my parents openly using the word "autism," since age five and a half I knew I had autism. However, it was not until I reexamined how autism affected me during my struggles toward the end of a doctoral degree in music did I begin to develop an understanding of what it meant to me to be on the autism spectrum. [Wiley et al., 2016, p. 111]

> What is different for other children being diagnosed at age 2 or 3? Do degrees one and two have any meaning? Does the child need the same journey in degrees five, six, and seven as people diagnosed as adults do?

> • How useful is the model for those who have "classic" autism? Dr. Lawson writes:

> I suggest that individuals with a diagnosis of classic autism can be supported to work to the best of their ability and achieve outcomes far and beyond the expectations of many professionals [Wylie et al., 2016, p. 140]. We need research in this area.

> • Some topics need expansion in their discussion and examples. We would emphasize the need for interaction with friends and community in degrees six and seven in preparation for community service. Degree Five is primarily a processing of the diagnosis/realization of Degree Four, seeking for one's true self. The suggested work in Degree Six is on identity alignment. Degree Seven includes believing in ourselves, environmental support, and exercise. These topics are all vital to

the healing journey. However, in Degree Eight the focus is going into the community to be of service. Are we adequately prepared for Degree Eight after degrees six and seven? Wilma says:

> In my personal life, I must receive a significant amount of support prior to being of service. Many of us need some guidance around our interactional skills. We need to learn how to be part of a supportive relationship, and how to become immersed in community. In addition to giving service, many of us also need to learn how to become part of a community – how to receive support as well as serve others.

We older autistics tend to live in isolation without seeing that as a problem. Yet, we cannot be whole by ourselves; we can only find wholeness in relationships. Interaction is not a strong part of our neurology. Yet we still need community at least as much as neurotypicals, for whom it may be easier.

Just as we need community, the world needs our full participation. We have so many gifts to share; so many ideas to be heard. In addition to providing service, we need to raise our autistic voices in all areas of social justice. In today's conflicted world, we need all our voices.

We started this project to answer some questions. Instead, we have generated more questions. They are not questions that any one of us or any handful of us can answer. We all grew up with the attitudes and knowledge of a specific time, and we all suffered from the lack of information of the generations before us. How can we find or establish a worldwide community? Let's start sharing ideas with each other and letting our voices be actively included in the conversation.

Physicist Fritz Capra suggests ways to understand "community":

The web of life is, of course, an ancient idea which has been used by poets, philosophers, and mystics throughout the age to convey their sense of the interwovenness and interdependence of all phenomena. One of the most beautiful expressions is found in the celebrated speech attributed to Chief Seattle …

> Humankind has not woven the web of life. We are but one thread within it. Whatever we do to the web, we do to ourselves. All things are bound together. All things connect. [Capra, 1996, after "contents," quoting Ted Perry who was inspired by Chief Seattle][2]

We have lived in isolation too long. Let's now seek relationships and connections that will allow us to participate fully in the web of life.

Reflections from the Authors

Wilma Working with the stories of 150 elder autistics has brought me into the community. I have found my "tribe."

In addition to finding community in this project, I have come to have deep respect for the nine degrees. As I look back on the years since my diagnosis, I can see where I have walked through the degrees of coming to terms with it and reaching out into the world for community and healing.

Shore had *wise words to share about Degree Five, after diagnosis:*

---

2 This quotation has long been attributed to Chief Seattle in 1854. However, it is now considered to have been written by Ted Perry, a screenwriter in 1971. See Snopes, Chief Seattle Speech. https://www.snopes.com/fact-check/chief-seattle/

> It's a process of death in order for there to be life. As an example, I am reminded of Winter. At times when I'm cold in the Winter and feel the "greyness" of a particularly drab day, I remind myself that without Winter there would be no Spring [Wiley et al., 2016, p. 111].

There was a long winter in my life that year after diagnosis in Degree Five with many days of depression as I got stuck on the basic question: *Just who am I, anyway?* I would think: "I can't live as my true self! I don't know if I have a true self."

It is now four years post-diagnosis. Life is not as orderly and quiet as it was B.D. (before diagnosis). I don't have as much control over my day as I did before, as I now get many more emails, phone calls, and text messages. Yet, my life is enriched.

I am now spending a lot of time in Degree Seven, with some occasional visits to the eighth. I've found Dr. Lawson's words on self-acceptance to be healing:

> I began to appreciate that self-acceptance was about stopping trying and starting to receive. It was about ceasing to rush around and simply let things be. It meant giving up the fighting, the sorting, the battle, and giving in to "surrender." This was not an act of defeat so much as an act of bravery. It was in letting go that I actually could realize what I had. Accepting myself, warts and all, meant saying that just as I am, I'm OK! [Wylie et al., 2016, p 143]

For the first time, I'm surrendering to who I am instead of trying to create appropriate personas for different occasions.

Eric: I am starting to see myself more clearly, which is both grounding and liberating. After reaching the fourth degree (self-identification) three years ago, the fifth and sixth degrees – especially the crisis of identity - arrived quickly and tumultuously. My self-acceptance (seventh degree) is starting to feel much more stable these days.

Like Wilma, I have experienced feelings of profound isolation. In contrast, connecting with a community of other Aspies and neurodiverse couples in recent years has been a wonderful experience. I now strive to apply what I have learned to help others, both young and old, in my personal and professional life. Whether I succeed in reaching the eighth or ninth degrees I leave for others to judge.

Rob: I started out with the goal of doing primarily the I.T. part of this project, but just seeing and reading the comments from respondents describing their experiences was an unexpectedly therapeutic experience for me, as so much of it paralleled what I went through. I and many other autistics were challenged by, and struggled with, the same degree of denial and oppression that so many who are different have been through historically. It is fascinating to me to see the way in which many of our respondents so eloquently put their life experiences into words, and in many cases, they were describing my own experiences! I have felt a commonality with these experiences quite unlike anything I ever encountered growing up.

This has positively complemented my 10 years of leading the Adults with Asperger's group in Maine, where I was able to relate to and understand experiences of those of others in the group. This, in itself, reflected a profound difference from my experiences up to that point in the outside world; I was also able to make and have friends from the group; and I was in contact with many people of all ages and levels on the autism spectrum. It is through helping people in our support group and other venues of support for those on the spectrum that I believe I was able to attain one of the higher degrees of autistic development as described in this book. This also included helping them find and affirm their identity, pushing others in the direction of attaining a higher degree and better quality of life.

REFERENCES

American Psychiatric Association (1994). *Diagnostic and Statistical Manual of Mental Disorders.* Washington, D

American Psychiatric Association, (2013). Diagnostic and Statistical Manual of Mental Disorders. Washington, D.C.: American Psychiatric Publishing.

Asperger/Autism Network, *AANE Language Guide*, Feb. 2019.

Ariel, C. N., & Naseef, R. A. (Eds.). (2006). *Voices from the spectrum.* London, UK: Jessica Kingsley.

Aston, M. (2003). *Asperger's in love.* Philadelphia, PA: Jessica Kingsley.

Attwood, T. (2007). *A complete guide to Asperger's syndrome.* London, UK: Jessica Kingsley.

Attwood, T., Evans, C. R., & Lesko, A. (2014). *Been there. Done that. Try this!: An Aspie's guide to life on earth.* Philadelphia, PA: Jessica Kingsley.

Attwood, T., Grandin, T., et al. (2006). *Asperger's and girls: World-renowned experts join those with Asperger's syndrome to resolve issues that girls and women face everyday.* London: Jessica Kingsley.

Baron, Saskia (Jan. 17, 2016) . *In a different key: The story of autism* by John Donvan and Caren Zucker review. The Guardian. Retrieved from https://www.theguardian.com/books/2016/jan/17/different-key-story-autism-review-donvan-zucker

Baron, Saskia (June 4, 2018). Asperger's Children: The Origins of Autism in Nazi Vienna – Review. The Guardian. Retrieved from https://www.theguardian.com/books/2018/jul/27/aspergers-children-origins-autism-nazi-vienna-edith-sheffer-review

Baron-Cohen, Simon (2015, September 12). Did Asperger save children from the Nazis -- or sell them out? *The Spectator.* Retrieved from https://www.spectator.co.uk/2015/09/did-hans-asperger-save-children-from-the-nazis-or-sell-them-out/

Baron-Cohen, S., Wheelwright, S., Skinner, R., Martin, J., & Clubley, E. (2001). The Autism-Spectrum Quotient (AQ): Evidence from Asperger syndrome/high-functioning autism, males and females, scientists, and mathematicians. *Journal of Autism and Developmental Disorders, 31*, 5-17.

Beardon, L., & Worton, D. (Eds.). (2011). *Aspies on mental health: Speaking for ourselves*. London, UK: Jessica Kingsley.

Beauty Lips, Crayola. Feb. 23, 2014. The History of Autism. Parents [magazine on-line]. Retrieved from https://www.parents.com/health/autism/the-history-of-autism/

Brugha, T., Spiers, N. (2012). *Estimating the Prevalence of Autism Spectrum Conditions in Adults: Extending the 2007 Adult Psychiatric Morbidity Survey.* [data collection]. UK Data Service. SN: 7082, http://doi.org/10.5255/UKDA-SN-7082-1

Caldwell-Harris, C., Fox Murphy, C., Velazquez, T., & McNamara, P. (2012). Religious belief systems of persons with high functioning autism. *Cognitive Science Journal Archive*. Retrieved from http://www.academia.edu/628798/Religious_Belief_Systems_of_Persons_with_High_Functioning Autism

Cameron, Julia. (1992). The Artist's Way: A Spiritual Path to Higher Creativity. New York: Tarcher/Putnam.

Capra, Fritz. (1996). The Web of Life: A New Scientific Understanding of Living Systems. New York: Anchor Books.

Centers for Disease Control and Prevention. (2015). Suicide: Facts at a glance. Retrieved from https://www.cdc.gov/violenceprevention/pdf/suicide-datasheet-a.pdf.

Child Trends. (2014). *Child maltreatment*. Retrieved from https://www.childtrends.org/indicators/child-maltreatment/

Christmas, J. (2011). Mental health services and me: What worked, and what didn't. In l. Beardon & D. Worton (Eds.), *Aspies on mental health: Speaking for ourselves* (pp. 17-36). London: Jessica Kingsley.

Christensen, D.L., Baio, J., Braun, K.V., et al. (2012). Prevalence and characteristics of autism spectrum disorder among children aged 8 years. Autism and Developmental Disabilities Monitoring Network.

Cohen, A. (2016). *Imbeciles: The Supreme Court, American eugenics, and the sterilization of Carrie Buck.* New York, NY: Penguin Press.

Crisis: The Journal of Crisis Intervention and Suicide Prevention, 35(4), 273-277.

Cutler, E. (2004). *A thorn in my pocket: Temple Grandin's mother tells the family story.* Arlington, TX: Future Horizons.

Dean, M., Harwood, R., & Casari, C. (2017). The art of camouflage: Gender differences in the social behavior of boys and girls with autism spectrum disorder. *Autism, 21*, 678-689.

Donvan, J., & Zucker, C. (2010, October). Autism's first child. *The Atlantic.* Accessed online at https://www.theatlantic.com/magazine/archive/2010/10/autisms-first-child/308227/

Donvan, J., & Zucker, C. (2016a, Jan. 19). The doctor and the Nazis. *Tablet.* https://www.tabletmag.com/jewish-life-and-religion/196348/the-doctor-and-the-nazis

Donvan, J., & Zucker, C. (2016b). *In a different key: The story of autism.* New York, NY: Crown.

Ecker, C., Bookheimer, S. Y., & Murphy, D.G.M. (2015). Neuroimaging in autism spectrum disorder: Brain structure and function across the lifespan. *The Lancet, 14*, 1121-1134.

Eliot, S. (2002). *Not the thing I was: Thirteen years at Bruno Bettelheim's Orthogenic School.* New York, NY: St. Martin's Press.

Fitzgerald, M. (2016). *The first degree of autism: Being born on the spectrum.* In P. Wylie, W. B. Lawson, & L. Beardon (Eds.), *The nine degrees of autism: A developmental model for the alignment and reconciliation of hidden neurological conditions* (pp. 39-56). London, UK: Routledge.

Gilmour, L., Schalomon, P. M., & Smith, V. (2012, January-March). Sexuality in a community based sample of adults with autism spectrum disorder. *Research in Autism Spectrum Disorders, 6,* 313-318.

Grandin, T. (2012). *Different not less: Inspiring stories of achievement and successful employment from adults with autism, Asperger's, and ADHD.* Arlington, TX: Future Horizons.

Grandin, T., & Moore, D. (2016). *The ninth degree of autism: Recognition, mastery, and unity.* In P. Wylie, W. B. Lawson, & L. Beardon (Eds.), *The nine degrees of autism: A developmental model for the alignment and reconciliation of hidden neurological conditions* (pp. 163-174). London, UK: Routledge.

Grove, R., Baillie, A., Allison, C., Baron-Cohen, S., & Hoekstra, R. A. (2014). The latent structure of cognitive and 'emotional empathy in individuals with autism, first-degree relatives, and typical individuals'. *Molecular Autism, 5,* 42.

Happe, F., & Charleton, R. A. (2012). Aging in autism spectrum disorders: A mini-review. *Gerontology, 58,* 70-78.

Happe, F., & Baron-Cohen, S. (2014, July 15). *Remembering Lorna Wing: 1928-2014. Spectrum: Autism Research News, "Opinion."* Retrieved from https://www.spectrumnews.org/opinion/remembering-lorna-wing-1928-2014

Heath, S. (2016). The eighth degree of autism: Unconditional service. In P. Wylie, W. B. Lawson, & L. Beardon (Eds.), *The nine degrees of autism: A developmental model for the alignment and reconciliation of hidden neurological conditions.* London, UK: Routledge. Pp. 151-162.

Hendrickx, S. (2015). *Women and girls with autism spectrum disorder.* London, UK: Jessica Kingsley.

Hendrickx, S., & Newton, K. (2007). *Asperger syndrome – A love story.* London, UK: Jessica Kingsley.

History of autism. (n.d.) Retrieved from https://www.timetoast.com/timelines/history-of-autism-dd96b3ad-5d13-4a81-ba87-27503867c5fb

History of autism. Online. (n.d.). Retrieved from https://www.preceden.com/timelines/64064-a-history-of-autism

Hofvander, B., Delorme, R., Chaste, P., et al. (2009). Psychiatric and psychosocial problems in adults with normal-intelligence autism spectrum disorders. *BMC Psychiatry, 9,* 35.

Howlin, P. (1997). *Autism: Preparing for adulthood.* London, UK: Routledge.

Howlin, P. (2000). Outcome in adult life for more able individuals with autism or Asperger syndrome. *Autism, 4* (1), 63-83.

James, I. A., Mukaetova-Ladinska, E., Reichelt, F. K., Briel, R., & Scully, A. (2006). Diagnosing Asperger's syndrome in the elderly: A series of case presentations. *International Journal of Geriatric Psychiatry, 21*(10), 951-960.

Kaelber, L. (2015). *Kinderfachabteilungen (special children's wards): Sites of Nazi children's 'euthanasia' crimes and their commemoration in Europe*. Retrieved from http://www.uvm.edu/~lkaelber/children/

Kanner, Leo. (1943) Autistic Disturbances of Affective Contact. Nervous Child: Journal of Psychopathology, *Psychotherapy, Mental Hygiene, and Guidance of the Child* 2, 217-50.

Kats, D., Payne, L., Parlier, M., & Piven, J. (2013). Prevalence of selected clinical problems in older adults with autism and intellectual disability. *Journal of Neurodevelopmental Disorders, 5,* 27.

Lawson, W. (2015). *Older adults and autism spectrum conditions: An introduction and guide*. London, UK: Jessica Kingsley.

Lesko, A. (2011). *Asperger's Syndrome: When life hands you lemons, make lemonade*. Bloomington, IN: Iuniverse. Kindle version.

Los Angeles Times Staff. (2011, Dec. 8). Autism: Rise of a disorder. *Los Angeles Times*, Retrieved from http://timelines.latimes.com/autism-history/

Lovegrove, E. (2013). *Help! I'm being bullied*. Cardiff Bay, UK: Accent Press.

Lyons, T. W. (1984). *The pelican and after: A novel about emotional disturbances*. Richmond, VA: Prescott Durrell & Co.

Moore, D., & Grandin, T. (2016). *The loving push: How parents and professionals can help spectrum kids become successful adults*. Arlington, TX: Future Horizons Publishers.

Mukaetova-Ladinska, E. B., Perry, E., Baron, M., & Povey, C. (2011*). Ageing in people with autistic spectrum disorder. International Journal of Geriatric Psychiatry, 27,* 109-118.

Mullin, J. (2014). In J. Mullin (Ed.), *Drawing autism*. New York, NY: Akashic Books, pp. 13-18.

Nansel, T. R., Overpeck, M., Pilla, R. S., Ruan, W. J., Simons-Morton, B., & Scheidt, P. (2001). Bullying behaviors among US youth: prevalence and association with psychosocial adjustment. *JAMA, 285,* 2094-2100.

National Institute on Drug Abuse. (2015). *Nationwide trends*. Retrieved from https://www.drug-abuse.gov/publications/drugfacts/nationwide-trends

Nicolaidis, C., Raymaker, D., McDonald, K., Dern, S., Boisclair, W. C., Ashkenazy, E., & Baggs, A. (2012). Comparison of healthcare experiences in autistic and non-autistic adults: A cross-sectional online survey facilitated by an academic-community partnership. *J Gen Intern Med, 28*(6) 761-9.

Paquette-Smith, M., Weiss, J., & Lunsky, Y. (2014). History of suicide attempts in adults with Asperger syndrome. *Crisis: The Journal of Crisis Intervention and Suicide Prevention, 35*(4), 273-277.

Pew Research Center. (2014). *Religious landscape study*. Retrieved from http://www.pewforum.org/religious-landscape-study/

Project Autism. (n.d.). *History of autism*. Retrieved from http://projectautism.org/history-of-autism

Piven, J., & Rabins, P. (2011). Autism spectrum disorders in adults: Toward defining a research agenda. *Journal of the American Geriatrics Society, 29,* 2151-2155.

Pollak, R. (1997). *The creation of Dr. B.: The biography of Bruno Bettelheim.* New York, NY: Simon and Schuster.

Prizant, B. M. (2015). *Uniquely human: A different way of seeing autism.* New York, NY: Simon and Schuster.

Raines, T. (2002). *Rising to the light: A portrait of Bruno Bettelheim.* New York, NY: Knopf.

Redford, R. C. (2010). *Crazy: My seven years at Bruno Bettelheim's orthogenic school.* Bloomington, IN: Trafford Publishing.

Rimland, Bernard. (1964) *Infantile Autism: The Syndrome and Its Implications for a Neural Theory of Behavior.* Englewood Cliffs, NJ: Prentice-Hall.

Robison, J. E. (2011). *Be different.* New York, NY: Broadway Books.

Sheffer, E. (2018). *Asperger's children: The origins of Autism in Nazi Vienna.* New York, NY: W.W. Norton Publishing Co.

Silberman, S. (2015). *NeuroTribes: The legacy of autism and the future of neurodiversity.* New York, NY: Penguin Publishing Group. Kindle Edition. Silberman, S. (2016). Was Dr. Asperger a Nazi? The Question Still Haunts Autism. Retrieved from https://www.npr.org/sections/health-shots/2016/01/20/463603652/was-dr-asperger-a-nazi-the-question-still-haunts-autism

Simone, R. (2010). *Aspergirls: Empowering females with Asperger Syndrome.* London, UK: Jessica Kingsley.

Stillman, W. (2006). *Autism and the God connection: Redefining the autistic experience through extraordinary accounts of spiritual giftedness.* Naperville, IL: Sourcebooks, Inc.

Snopes (website) Sept. 26, 2007. Retrieved from https://www.snopes.com/fact-check/chief-seattle

Stuart-Hamilton, I., Griffith, G., Totsika, V., Nash, S., Hastings, R. P., Felce, D., & Kerr, M. (2009). The circumstances and support needs of older people with autism. Report for the Welsh Assembly Government. Cardiff, UK: Welsh Assembly.

Sutton, N. (1996). *Bettelheim: A life and a legacy.* New York, NY: Basic Books.

Time Magazine (April 26, 1948). Frosted Children. Retrieved from http://content.time.com/time/magazine/article/0,9171,798484,00.html

Travers, J. C., Tincani, M., & Krezmien, M. P. (2011). A multiyear national profile of racial disparity in autism identification. *Journal of Special Education, 20,* 1-9.

van Niekerk, M.E.H., Groen, W., Vissers, C., van Driel-de Jong, D., Kan, C. C., & Voshaar, R.C.O. (2011). Diagnosing autism spectrum disorders in elderly people. *International Psychogeriatrics, 23*(5), 700-710.

van Heijst, B.F.C., & Geurts, H. M. (2014). Quality of life in autism across the lifespan: A meta-analysis. *Autism, 19,* 158-167.

Vermeulen, P. (2012). *Autism as context blindness.* Future Horizons

Ward, B. W., Dahlhamer, J. M., Galinsky, A. M., & Joestl, S. S. (2014). Sexual orientation and health among U.S. adults: National Health Interview Survey, 2013. *National Statistics Reports, 77,* 7/15/14.

Wing, L. (1992). Manifestations of social problems in high-functioning autistic people. In E. Schopler & G. Mesibov (Eds.), *High-functioning individuals with autism.* New York, NY: Plenum Press. 129-142.

Wylie, P., & Beardon, L. (2014). *Very late diagnosis of Asperger Syndrome (Autism Spectrum Disorder): How seeking a diagnosis in adulthood can change your life.* London, UK: Jessica Kingsley Publishers.

Wylie, P., & Heath, S. (2013). *Very late diagnosis of Asperger's syndrome: 2013 UK survey report.* Shropshire, UK: Autonomy.

Wylie, P., Lawson, W. B., & Beardon, L. (Eds.). (2016). *The nine degrees of autism: A developmental model for the alignment and reconciliation of hidden neurological conditions.* London, UK: Routledge.

APPENDIX #1

WHO ARE OUR RESPONDENTS? – *THE STORIES*

OUR RESPONDENTS: THE STORIES

Some people elected to have their first name used, and a few wanted their full names used. The others were given pseudonyms, and some details of their lives were obscured. We could not give extensive detail on the lives of 150 people, but we chose a selection of our participants randomly to include here. All of those participants gave their permission for their story to be told – whether or not they had a pseudonym.

For everyone we quote, regardless of whether they have a life story written about them, we give the person's age as of 2016 (when the survey was done) and indicate where they lived then by the following schema:

United Kingdom	UK
Australia	Aus
New Zealand	NZ
Wales	Wales
Canada	CAN
United States:	
Northeast	NE
Southeast	SE
Midwest	MW
Southwest	SW
West	W
Other	OTH

Alan [62, NE]

Alan was born in Scotland, and still speaks with a bit of a brogue. He is a member of the support group in Portland, ME. He has been involved with the group for many years, and at one time was one of the facilitators. In retirement now, he is decreasing his commitments, but still attends the group and other activities. He was randomly selected for an interview and chose to use his real name.

His mother saw differences in him when he was young. She told him that as a young child, he didn't like sitting in laps or cuddling, but his family was largely supportive and nurturing. Alan was a good student in school but was bored a lot and sometimes got in trouble for breaking rules. He had some depression in late childhood, but by his teens he discovered music, which became a lifelong passion.

Alan found success as a computer programmer, where he could avoid most contact with people and could also use his Aspie gift for attention to detail. He was in his fifties when he dated a woman with whom he spent many pleasant hours strolling on the Maine seashore and driving in his car. She chatted a lot; he was mostly silent. She introduced Alan to a friend who had taught autistic children, and who sensed quickly that he was on the spectrum. His girlfriend printed out material about autism for him to read. After seeing the similarity with his life, Alan spent a couple of days in denial. Then he recognized himself clearly and was relieved. He called the local Asperger's support group. It was December and they weren't having a meeting that month, but he started in January.

He began reading on the topic and diagnosed himself. He said: "Autism support groups and the Internet helped me find out more about myself. I spent a fair bit of time on WrongPlanet.net when I was first made aware of my Aspie nature." After a couple of years, he became a facilitator of the group, a position he continued until his recent retirement from work.

He feels he has reached a point in his life where he is comfortable with being on the spectrum and considers it a positive part of his life. "Knowing I'm Aspie helped me to decide when to interact and when to be alone. I had learned to cope well, but always needed a lot of alone time. The realization made many mystery parts of my past make sense. That helped me to accept it."

Alan's interests include: sci-fi/fantasy shows [e.g., *Babylon 5*, *Firefly*] and sci-fi/fantasy/superhero movies [e.g., *Serenity*, *Star Wars*, *Guardians of the Galaxy*, *X-Men*, etc.] as well as music technology/ synthesizers and guitar/bass/mandolin. He especially loves playing music and has performed in a couple of bands for many years. Friends from the Aspie support group often went to hear him play.

Anya [69, NE]

Anya's early years were spent in a rural area, where she attended a small school. "I felt at home where we lived out in the country in a farming area. No close neighbors, but I had many animals for company. I relied on knowing and being safe in a small town and country environment." But at age 15, her family had to move to a city, and she was devastated: "Suddenly, the fact that I was smart did not help because the education system was different. I was totally lost because school was suddenly [not] about learning but about social life and sex, and I was very immature."

Although she had earned good grades in the rural school, she had trouble keeping up in the city high school: "I went to the school counselor many times but was always told I just wasn't trying hard enough."

"Towards the end I was told that because I had not gotten good grades I would not be able to graduate from high school, much less go to college. In fact, thanks to the interventions of a teacher I did graduate, but the diploma was not of much use. I didn't know where I would fit in. I was very depressed." She tried to get a job and live on her own, but she ended up spending 19 years in a group home while she worked. Later she got married and moved out.

Being diagnosed made a big difference for her. "I felt like I lived behind a glass wall with no way to get through to the rest of the human world. I always felt I was a unique individual and had a purpose in life but did not know how I would ever discover it since most doors seemed to be closed to me. I can see that all the things that I like about myself and all my abilities and the loves that are part of me now have been there inside me my whole life."

When asked how she thought things would be different for the current generation, she said: "They will be able to be themselves right at the beginning of their lives. They will be supported and hopefully be able to be safely and successfully independent. Hopefully the world outside will welcome them and appreciate them."

Anita Lesko [57, SW]

Anita is a 57-year-old woman who lives in Florida. She gave us permission to use her real name. Her story has been told in Temple Grandin's book *Different...Not Less,* and she has written books herself, including *If Life Hands You Lemons, Make Lemonade.* She also co-wrote with Tony Attwood: *Been There. Done That. Try This!: An Aspie Guide to Life on Earth.* She is featured in the final chapter of the book on the nine degrees [Wylie et al., 2014] as an example of an autistic who has reached the final ninth degree.

Anita, a nurse, realized she had Asperger's Syndrome one day at work. She wrote on our questionnaire:

"A coworker's son had just been diagnosed with Asperger's. She was very upset and started telling me of his diagnosis. I'd never heard of Asperger's. She handed me papers with info about it. That was the moment, as I read it, that my life suddenly changed, that moment I learned why I'm so different and never fit in."

She left work that day and went directly to a bookstore. She recalled: "I stopped at the bookstore and purchased every book they had about Asperger's. I stayed up all night reading Tony Attwood's book." A week later, she saw a neuropsychologist, who confirmed she had AS. After her diagnosis, she realized that her mother and adult nephew were on the spectrum too.

Anita was 50 when she received that diagnosis, and it fit her concept of herself. "I always knew I was different and never fit in, but didn't know why." Some adults become depressed after the diagnosis, but not Anita: "I had thought I was the only person in the world like me! I was TOTALLY relieved!!!!!!!" She goes on to say, "My whole life changed," She began to blog, write books, speak, and consult. She started a support group. She met her husband, who is also autistic, and they married publicly at an autism conference in 2015.

But it wasn't always easy for Anita. She wrote that as a child: "I'd daydream a lot...gazing out the window imagining I was on a big white horse galloping across lush green pastures. I sensed that I was different as young as age 4...I was simply the weird kid that didn't fit in. My mom was constantly called to the principal's office to complain about me! All school physical education activities I nearly flunked. I was uncoordinated."

As an adult: "My sensory issues have always been BIG issues at my job." Prior to being diagnosed, bosses and coworkers were extremely harsh to her. She experienced discrimination, harassment, and bullying at various times in her life. Outside of work, she pursues a variety of interests, including horses, soap making, and military aviation photojournalism. One of Anita's more recent passions is writing books about autism. She has fully accepted being autistic:

155

"I don't see autism as a disease or disorder. I see it simply as a different way to be."

Anita is glad she didn't learn about her autism until later in life:

"I'm happy I didn't know until I was 50. When I look at this younger generation, everyone is looking for services to get them better. The only way to get better is by getting out in the world and experiencing life, the good, the bad, and the ugly. No services can substitute for life-earned wisdom. I became a success without knowing I'm on the spectrum. Parents need to take notice of adults like myself and look at why this is. It's because I started working jobs since age twelve. Yes, I made plenty of blunders. And I'd get up and dust myself off and forge ahead."

Anita shares her website with us: www.anitalesko.com

Carlos [66, NE]

Carlos is a 66-year-old, happily married man of Middle Eastern descent living in the Northeast. Being diagnosed at age 64 "was a great relief. It confirmed what I suspected. The doctor called me 'almost a textbook case' of Asperger."/ASD He further noted, "I am positive that my father had the condition as well."

Carlos's sentiments about late diagnosis echo those of many of our respondents. "I just regret that the condition was unknown when I was a child. Had the professionals in my life been aware of it, it would have spared me a lot of suffering." He believes that things have been MUCH worse for our generation. "Since there was no awareness of the spectrum, we were expected to conform to everyone else and judged by standards we could not possibly meet. It has 'done a lot of damage.'"

Fortunately, Carlos was able to access useful resources. "I found help in support groups and confirmation I was not alone, that it wasn't just me who was defective and hateful, but a condition people have that they didn't ask for and had no control over. It made sense out of so many things in my life, most especially the repeated rejection I have experienced throughout and that has devastated my self-image. This rejection included, as a child, being excluded from social activities and as an adult, not considered for jobs for which I was qualified. As is common for Aspies, I was very withdrawn, was bullied, and always felt disliked. I hated competitive sports and avoided playing with boys my own age. I related better to older adults than to kids my age. In school, I could have done much better overall if I didn't believe I was stupid."

Carlos experienced challenges at home as well as at school: "My father was also on the spectrum, so he didn't know how to relate to me, and he was extremely overprotective...My family was always supportive but didn't understand me very well."

Despite four graduate degrees, "Because of my autism, my work history is dismal. I was never paid what I was worth and never made a living wage." Retired, Carlos now does "excellent" volunteer work for nursing home residents. As a result of the flexibility inherent in the volunteer work, "I am definitely outshining my peers in this work."

Carlos has developed many interests as an adult, including politics, music therapy, Spanish novels, web design, eldercare, and theology. "Spirituality helps me more than psychology."

Being autistic is a mixed bag to Carlos. "Autism is a great source of self-hate, but also a feeling that I have struggled and succeeded in coping with a condition that few will ever have to deal with. But I always have to remain vigilant about its effects on my current interactions with others...But I also feel that my autism enables me to *identify more than others can with people who are marginalized.*"

Carlos's message to readers is: "People need to recognize we have our own special gifts and can make valuable contributions like everyone else. It is WRONG to bully people because you are a coward and you prey on the weak to make yourself feel secure. We have a lot to teach the world about being understanding, compassionate, and loving, and the world needs what we can bring to it in that regard." Not surprisingly, Carlos is enthusiastic about the title of Temple Grandin's book: *Different, Not Less!*

David Stamps [70, NE]

School went well for David through grade 3, but after that he describes a "slow slide downhill. I think I might have had ADD, but home life was so chaotic between a father on the spectrum and a mother who resorted to alcohol more and more as a coping mechanism. By fourth grade my handwriting deficit due to mixed dominance began to manifest...by middle school, I was just lost. Between large crowds, aggressive middle school students, and a fragmented home life, I think I was just shut down most of the time. I was interested in math and science and studied quite advanced electronics, building radios and things but was just flunking and didn't know why."

He was sent to a private school but did *very poorly* in the ninth grade and almost wasn't invited back.

"But beginning in the 10th grade," David told us, "I woke – only way to describe it. I made honor roll the first term and never left it. Graduated fifth overall, despite almost flunking out the first year. Despite much awkwardness, I began developing coping mechanisms to an extent, excelling in soccer...I took National Forensics Debating and excelled in that, which gave me life-long verbal skills."

After graduation he was always underemployed, "seldom working more than 18 months in a job. I just couldn't get along with anyone and find anything that didn't bore me in three months." This all changed in 1975 when he discovered computer programming. He now has his own business, is happily married, and is close to his grown children.

"I am a dedicated Kindle reader and read voraciously. Reading is also a coping mechanism. Since it is also on my phone, I can read anywhere, anytime. I read very widely from Kate Wilhelm mysteries, Fredrick Forsyth, Jodi Picoult, John LeCarre, David Baldacci, John Grisham, and hundreds more a year!"

When asked if he was comfortable being on the spectrum, he told us "yes" and added:

"Understanding is everything. The Over 50 group at AANE is terrific! It is a relief to finally begin to understand but it is also empowering to know that I have survived almost 70 years and have a pretty good life."

David Stamps, dbstamps@dbstamps.com; David is an occasional speaker for AANE and would welcome dialogue with anyone.

Derek [53, NE]

Derek self-diagnosed at age 44. He is now 53. Prior psychotherapy failed to uncover the autism: "I feel that therapists were not trained to recognize Asperger's in adults in the 1980s."

His son was evaluated in the third grade when Derek was a freshman in college. As he and his wife filled out the forms for their son, his wife said, "all these characteristics describe you, too." Derek had to agree with her. He worked on computers with Rob Lagos and talked to him about it. Rob said, "I have Asperger's, too, and facilitate a support group!" It was a year or so before Derek could attend. He started thinking about his dad, who had the same characteristics. He read John Elder Robison's book *Look Me in the Eye*. He connected to the title since his Dad was always telling him to "look me in the eye." He thought about his children, his brother, his father, and himself, and then "a light bulb went off." He began to identify himself as an Aspie. A few years later, his daughter was diagnosed in high school.

Derek told us that as a child, he was shy in school. At recess, he'd walk around the playground keeping his head down. "I was scared of other kids; I had social anxiety." He was bullied. In the fourth grade a bunch of kids held him down on the ice and other kids rammed into him. His mom let him switch schools, and the situation improved. "But I still had few friends. I was always anxious; afraid to talk to others."

As he grew older, he didn't understand the dynamics of social, and especially romantic relationships. Matters got worse before they got better: "I had no friends in high school, no girlfriends in college, became depressed about my social situation and let my grades slide, drank too much alcohol, and was angry." Finally, "things got better; I got married at 28." He pursued a master's degree in statistics in his forties and is now employed full-time and is still married.

In some ways, self-identification didn't change much for Derek. "I was still the same person. I don't need to label myself." Yet, the awareness helped him access important resources: "I realized that the final pieces of the puzzle as to why I am the way I am fell into place, and that others feel the same way. OTHERS FEEL THE SAME WAY. That is why I attend a support group. Because others can relate to what I feel."

He enjoys live music, theater, and politics. He's actively involved in a support group and has autistic friends. His message to readers? "Things can and do get better."

Doris [55, AUS]

Doris is a 55-year-old woman in Australia who grew up in the sixties. She says: "Life was less complicated in those days. Asperger's hadn't been invented then. Socialization at school mainly consisted of playground games. I had lots of friends. It was the best time of my life and it all went sadly downhill after that..."

She hated sports. "Scared to stand out as socially lacking. Tried to hide in the library at lunchtimes. I thought I was an idiot. Hard times."

She had major problems as a teen at school but didn't tell anyone about it – not even her parents. "I internalized everything and kept it all a secret because I thought that every problem I experienced was my fault. I've since told mum a few things, and she says she had no idea of my difficulties. I believe her, because I successfully pretended to be ok. But God, it was hard work at the time!"

Her sister suggested she was on the spectrum, and she found "plenty of tests online and scored highly for Asperger's on every one." A clinical psychiatrist eventually diagnosed her. Their father is also on the spectrum. "My neurotypical Mom let us be ourselves, tolerated our strange habits and praised our strengths and achievements, God bless her. I feel this upbringing preserved our unique personalities."

At that point she was at "a crossroads, with a failing marriage and burnout at work. I needed answers. Thank God I got them."

After the diagnosis, she continued to visit her psychiatrist. She got a disability support pension and found a less stressful job. She filed for divorce and started a new relationship. "I was still depressed but continued to push ahead with life. My inner self was still in turmoil regarding the diagnosis, but I educated myself online and became more reconciled to my alternative." She got an associate diploma in animal husbandry from an agricultural college. "I liked working with animals."

Reflecting on her autism, she muses: "I knew I was different and thought I was a deficient person. I wouldn't now say I'm proud of being autistic. I just live with it, and I'm glad I now understand myself better."

She has more thoughts about being on the spectrum: "I don't want to be in the 'Aspie' club as such. We all have different issues in our lives and we all try to make the best of it. Before, I wanted to be like everybody else. Now, I just want to be me."

She has insight into an important social issue: "I get concerned when many people in the news that have committed violence have been referred to as autistic or with Asperger's. Mainly males. Makes me think that people will be scared of us." She also reflects on the greater resources for children diagnosed early: "I wonder if active intervention does more harm than good. Being told 'you have a problem' and to follow programs, etc., may stigmatise young adults. They simply need to be told they are OK as is, maybe get some support for various aspects of life that they find a challenge. I think it's fair to say that most of us would revert back to our true selves once these interventions stop. Our mental wiring and, therefore, our outlook on life can't be fundamentally changed. Where would Einstein and his theory of relativity be if his parents had tried to change him in his developing years?"

Earl [57, NZ]

Earl was born in the U.S. but currently resides in New Zealand. He feels so strongly about the innate origin of autism that he stated, "If your book focuses on non-genetic causes or cures, I withdraw my consent to participate."

Earl was a good student through school and achieved a master's degree. However, he experienced "serial job loss," due to conflicts with bosses. He now struggles financially.

Prior to diagnosis, he "stumbled along in the darkness of no knowledge, then the light came on and I and my past selves were suddenly OK." At 50, a psychiatrist diagnosed Earl because he had been having problems at work. In terms of the year after diagnosis, he wrote: "Was relieved, but work issues led to depression, and this led to marital separation. But I also began to explore who I was and what made me happy." In addition to feeling excited and relieved, he was: "curious to learn everything about Asperger's." He has had some experiences with mild depression, OCD and ADHD, but felt helped by an "Artist's Way" support group.

Earl's interests include Grateful Dead music, Neanderthals, cooking, ecology, and comics. He reads "Aspie books" and visits Facebook Aspie groups and "Ask an Autistic" on YouTube.

He's not convinced that Asperger's is the same as high-functioning autism. "I don't agree that Asperger's can be clustered in with the other terms. I still believe it may not be the same as HFA. Perhaps there are shared genetics between some types of autism, but likely some remain discrete and less related."

When asked how he thought things are different for our generation of Aspies, he said: "Likely childhood was more fun and free for us. I would have hated knowing then and being sent for a bloody cure of which there are none nor are there any needed."

Earl believes that being on the spectrum confers certain advantages: "I can see beauty all around me, which I'm fairly sure many, if not most, neurotypicals are unaware of. I see how everything, thought or material, is connected...We are not sick, dysfunctional, mentally ill, disabled, or deficit-ridden. We are just as beautiful as anyone."

Note: In a recent email [3/2017], Earl let us know that he has a job now and is comfortable financially.

Emma Van der Klift [60, CAN]

Emma is a speaker and advocate in the disability rights community. She thinks of herself as a "modern-day storyteller," continuing the long-held tradition of using humor and narrative to initiate self-reflection and social change [from her website -see link at bottom]. She and her partner travel throughout North America providing training on inclusive education, employment equity, conflict resolution, and other disability rights issues. She has several publications.

"I have vacillated about whether I should pursue a diagnosis. It's difficult where I live, and expensive, but I could do this. However, the more time that has passed, the less need I have for 'official' diagnosis. I also know that so few professionals understand the way women show up, and the developmental nature of autism." [Before going to press, Emma let us know that she ended up getting a diagnosis.]

She added: "I have always been connected with other autistic people because I have been on the speaker's circuit in disability/inclusive education/human services for decades. I would not characterize my contact with Asperger's/autism support groups; it's more like disability rights groups. I've always gravitated to other autistic people, and they often to me. However, largely because [I believe] women are so misunderstood, and older individuals like me pre-date diagnosis, I didn't see it specifically in myself. I am proud of being autistic. And, like so many, reconfiguration my life experiences in the context of this understanding transformed many of the issues I've faced from 'moral failings' to differences. Liberating."

Emma seems to be an outstanding example of an autistic person living happily in Degree Nine and giving much of herself to make a better world. Her website is http://www.broadreachtraining.com/.

Emily Lovegrove [70, UK]

Emily got along well with teachers when in school, but classmates bullied her. She eventually got a Ph.D. and became a psychologist. Prior to that she taught piano. She is now self-employed, with her partner being the primary source of income. Her work focuses on acting as a mentor to those who are bullied and those who are anxious about musical performance.

She was researching "Asperger's" for her daughter, whom she suspected was on the spectrum, when she began to realize she also had the characteristics, and then diagnosed herself. In terms of how her life changed after self-diagnosis, she said: "Wish I'd known sooner. Or didn't have it so I understood others better. Also, as a psychologist, feel stupid at not guessing earlier."

When asked: "When you were diagnosed [or realized] you were on the spectrum, which of the following did you feel?" She wrote: "Huge sadness that no one had understood and had laughed at me for years."

She adds: "I wish it was OK to explain lack of sociability openly and others to understand without judgment...and schools and hospitals to receive a LOT of training to make education/ health care easier."

Emily has published a book, *Help! I'm Being Bullied*, based on her own experiences as a child. She also has a website [http://thebullyingdoctor.com/] about her work with bullying. The following is from her website:

"The Lovegrove Approach is based on a range of successful anti-bullying strategies that increase your self-confidence to tackle bullying that happens to you and to help others. Because this system was developed with young people, it's very popular with school pupils [As well as adults!].

I work in schools, hospitals and organisations in the UK, USA and Europe delivering staff training as well as one-to-one help on bullying issues. I am part of an ongoing EU group that meets in Brussels to discuss children, safety, and justice. I also work with organisations such as Welsh Government and Children in Wales."

When asked, "Do you feel you have reached a point in your life where you are comfortable with being on the spectrum and consider it a positive part of your life?" she replied "No," adding, "I dislike division into ASD and NT. It still feels like we're not 'normal'..."

Jackie Shanley [61, UK]

Jackie was interviewed by phone; she talked about her childhood trying to look normal: "I was 'the girl with the laugh.' I used all my strength to appear normal and to be liked. I was always on the outside looking in...I was never a child...I tried to find a fit in my teens, but also made my first suicide attempt at 14, so no, things weren't going well. I was used a lot and I had a laughter everyone talked about in school...they thought I was funny and so I had some people like me but at the same time, I was suicidal, and no one knew it."

"I always say it was my personality that saved me...even though it was an act and after I acted happy and cared about everyone except myself for those hours, I went home and recharged for the next show."

She did get through school and managed to hold jobs for many years, supporting herself and having several short-term relationships. She married at age 48 and is still happily married. However, she had to move a considerable distance when she got married, and life became too hectic for her to continue working. She and her husband have a house and modest lifestyle based on his income.

When she was 51, she happened to watch a documentary on Asperger's. She describes her experience:

"The psychiatrist described infant and baby behaviours that literally left me with my mouth hanging open and on that day, approx. 9 or 10 years ago, I began my own research on the autism spectrum and took a Cambridge-sponsored test online that placed both myself and my husband high in the category of high-functioning autism...it changed my life. It is like being born again. As much as it is too late, there is still hope and time for many of us and I hope we are all infected by that hope. I am confident that in the generations to come, we will just be a different type of human...with those different needs nurtured and respected and honored."

In response to the question "How is life different now?" she responded: "I am allowed to realize I'm a human being. My God, everything fell into place! Now I don't have to do all the things I want to do in life...I'm catching up with so much. I feel like I've been born."

To another interview question, "Did you come to accept this diagnosis? What did that mean for you?" Jackie responded: "Happier; more accepting of self...Big Bang Theory is us. I'm like Sheldon. So complex at my age... Sheldon can be who he is and still function in the world. Wrote the producer a letter when it first came out...I can say 'I'm like that'...it makes such a difference in my life."

She was grateful for our survey: "I want to thank you sincerely for doing this project. High-functioning adults on the autism spectrum over 50 have so much of the past thinking embedded...and the negative messages and feedback etched into our brains. The wisdom that has come with age, if we are blessed enough to still have hope and clarity, makes the awareness of our diagnosis a gift so late in life...I wouldn't want anyone else to go through what I went through up to 55. Over here there is so little support...diagnosis not good...easier just to do it online."

Perhaps she best sums up her post-diagnosis life with these words: "I wouldn't be anyone else for anything...just wish I'd known it younger."

Janet Christmas [61, UK]

Now 61, Janet grew up in a mainstream British school where she was badly bullied.

"My problems with coordination meant that I could never catch a ball, or even throw a ball so that another child could catch it. I could never work out what was going on in tag games and tried at all times to stand with my back against a warm, safe wall or to hide under my desk so that I would not be forced to join in the play. But this was the late 1960s, and because I was intellectually bright and had a haughty, precocious language, the school psychiatrist who saw me did not assign me for education in a specialist school."

Bullying continued in middle school. It was at its worst at this age. "I was ostracized and called names. I couldn't work out what was going on in team games and was terrified of play time. I wanted to die and thought about committing suicide every day. At home, I was bullied and put down by adults in the family. I did not get on well with my mother, who was disappointed that I was not a girly girl. My intellectual abilities managed to get me through most things, and although school was torture, I finally found my niche at university where I read for two degrees in geology."

Things did not improve for her in the work world.

"People called me haughty and aloof. I didn't recognize myself in my staff reports, which were invariably awful. I was never promoted and my pay lagged far behind other staff on my level. [As a result], I hated myself before my diagnosis, and didn't understand what was going wrong. The revelation for me finally came in 1999 when I read a newspaper article about Temple Grandin [a lady in America who has AS]. It so accurately reflected my problems that, as I read the article, the hairs on the back of my head stood on end."

"I never had children as I didn't know what was wrong with me and did not want to pass it [whatever "it" was] on to any offspring. I did not want them to suffer as I did at school and work."

Diagnosis by a psychologist finally came at age 56, and proved to be a great relief. "This was after a decade of suspecting I was on the spectrum, but psychiatrists, doctors, insisting that I was not autistic. I was told by a psychiatrist in 2002, 'Children with autism grow up to be adults with autism. You were not diagnosed as a child; therefore, you do not have autism.' Problem was, no one knew about autism and Asperger syndrome when I was a child in the late 1950s and early 1960s. That was why I wasn't diagnosed."

Janet found it helpful to join an online British group. [The diagnosis] "opened doors to work adjustments...I finally realized why I was different to everybody else...I finally realized it wasn't 'all in my head.' Following diagnosis, I am beginning to accept who I am. I have stopped trying to change things that I cannot change." Sadly, Janet still feels compelled to "act normal" and hide her autism around coworkers to avoid bullying.

Janet's main interests revolve around railways and travel, as well as the history of India, Buddhism, and Hinduism. She enjoys collecting postcards and sorting them.

She views autism not as a deficit, but as an adaptation: "I think autism is an evolutionary mechanism. In primitive societies thousands of years ago, society needed autistic individuals with their heightened senses to look out for danger and come to the rescue of the community. The geekier individuals went off and invented things to help society develop, such as tools and metal forging. As Temple Grandin has said, 'if it weren't for those with Asperger's, we would all still be living in caves, socializing with each other but not progressing in any way.' "

Jonathan [54, UK]

Jonathan, a 54-year-old man in the UK, grew up feeling "different detrimentally." Regarding school, he says: "Because I felt so unsafe, I would hide during break times to study and then reappear for classes." He was miserable during most of his school years. Despite such challenges at an early age, he developed a career as a scientist.

Jonathan was diagnosed at 53. He found it difficult to get a proper diagnosis by anyone who understood autism, even though his girlfriend suggested he might be on the spectrum. "I am afraid this exposes a much deeper problem, and that is low levels of academic/clinical/interactional understanding of ASD amongst health professionals outside the autism field."

Jonathan's reaction to diagnosis changed dramatically over time. "For a couple of weeks after my diagnosis, I felt relief. But this was quickly followed by despair as the signposting for support that was promised quickly evaporated and I am left completely on my own in having to deal with my diagnosis of Asperger's."

Jonathan reported significant discrimination in employment, which he believes to be widespread. "In my career I have been in one toxic environment after another." Fortunately, he owns a home and is financially secure. He has had relationships but is currently living alone.

"As the *DSM*-5 has omitted the category Asperger's, this means individuals who have a mild form of autism such as Asperger's are now labelled with ASD. As discrimination is still rampant, a diagnosis of ASD rather than Asperger's will exacerbate discrimination against Asperger's individuals."

He perceives a lack of understanding and services for people like himself. "There is support out there for individuals severely afflicted with autism. But the much milder forms such as Asperger's and high-functioning autism, there is very little support out there, except to just get on with it." In his spare time, Jonathan enjoys watching thrillers and war movies, and listening to soundtracks and pop music. He copes in part by withdrawing. "At the moment, I am minimizing/eliminating any form of human contact to reduce my anxieties/stress/depression."

Karen [62, W]

Karen is working on a B.A. in Education, hoping to be an educator. She said that getting educated about autism spectrum disorder [ASD] has improved her mental health considerably. Karen was quite excited upon finding out her diagnosis, but she also felt some apprehension and uncertainty. "It took about six weeks to internalize/accept the label; I could see how well it explained my entire life." A big change for her is that she was able to let go of a lot of self-blame. "I consider Asperger's my 'superpower,' given that since I've embraced who I am and what it is, a lot of things seem better in part because of being able to let go of the self-blame." She also indicated feeling more creative due to a relaxing of social expectations.

Karen recalled: "The woman who made me aware I might have Asperger's was in an early childhood education class...All of a sudden the pieces fell into place; I'd read about autism before but didn't know about colors and textures...Like a typical Aspie, I blurted out 'That's me, too!' Now that I know I have Asperger's, I feel whole...I feel blessed to have been given the gift of finally finding out who I am."

Consistent with what many of us on the autism spectrum experienced, she said that she had few friends, and got bullied a lot; she said she didn't understand people, and why they did things she thought were "stupid." She read a lot in middle school, but she always thought there was something wrong with her. "I think that we suffered more from bullying and feeling that every failed friendship or blurting out something inappropriate was our fault."

She recounted an experience of being traumatized by a teacher, involving her finishing a reading assignment before the rest of the students: "When I got to first grade, I could already read although I don't recall learning how. I remember sitting in a semi-circle of students reading a Dick and Jane book, the teacher having told us to read a certain part. When I was done, I sat and waited for the rest of the children to finish. The teacher asked me why I wasn't reading. I said I was done, but she said I was lying and made me pull my chair beside her and read the material again. I felt humiliated, and I was angry that the teacher didn't believe me. That kind of set the tone for the rest of my educational career. To this day, my interactions with teachers are affected by that first experience."

Laurence [68, UK]

Laurence was excited when he realized he was on the spectrum. "Many things from my past became very easy to understand." He was diagnosed at age 57 by a mental health professional. In the year after diagnosis: "I felt better about myself and I was more outgoing."

He loved classes and was a good student. He was supported at home: "My parents encouraged me in everything I did, even to the extent of my father building me a laboratory."

"I was a contract computer programmer for most of my working life." After he was diagnosed, he used his skills to help others on the spectrum.

For a while after diagnosis, he was active on Internet sites for those with Asperger's.

His interests include *Have I Got News for You, Buffy the Vampire Slayer, Mythbusters, Lexx, Doctor Who,* and films (primarily sci-fi).

When asked if he had come to accept being on the spectrum as a positive part of his life, he said "yes." When asked what he would like to share with others, he said: "Accept it. Wallow in it. Tell others just how easy it is to stop 'feeling' different and accept 'being' different."

What has been different for our generation? "A great deal of wasted opportunities. There are so many points in my life I can point back at and say: 'if only I knew then what I know now, about myself, I could have handled all that much better.'"

How are things different for kids today? "They have a chance to accept themselves and grasp opportunities without feeling unsure. That's not to say that they can all do that."

Lucy [61, NE]

Lucy, 61, lives on the east coast of the U.S., but previously lived in other countries. Her grand-parents emigrated from Europe, and she hopes to obtain dual citizenship.

As a child, she focused on doing well in school "as my ticket to escape my abusive family." Like most of our respondents, she found socializing difficult. "I couldn't just chit chat, make conversation, hang out. 'Hanging out' never made a bit of sense to me." She was one of the few adults we surveyed who reported doing well in sports as well as in dance.

Her belief in God also stood out. "I have a strong belief in God, based on experiencing him personally; my childhood family life had a lot of addiction, mental illness, and abuse in it, but through that all I felt God's message to me that I was special and unique to Him even if not to others. It's interesting to me because it seems very few people on the spectrum believe in God."

Lucy was diagnosed with autism in her early fifties by a therapist during a research study. She pursued a diagnosis at that age "because I was experiencing harassment in my workplace and I could not understand what was going on enough to defend and protect myself." However, she had long suspected something was different about her. "I knew something was 'wrong' when I was in college, back in the 70s before there was the Internet, so I sought out anything I could find in psychology textbooks and journals at the library. I finally gave up, and just started thinking of myself as having a brain that short-circuited every now and then, as well as having what I called 'no filters' so everything got into my brain and stayed there."

Diagnosis brought her instant relief. "It was so nice to have a name for it! And it allowed me to join a support group and start learning more about myself, as well as being clearer about which aspects of being on the spectrum I could work on, and which I would just have to live with. Driving and parking, for instance, will always be stressful, while reading nuances in social conversation is something I am getting better at."

Lauren [51, NE]

Lauren, 51 years old, is self-diagnosed and lives on the east coast of the U.S. "I have repeatedly assessed myself via a number of tests [online and in print] since 2/1998, and I always score well in the range of the spectrum." She tried to obtain a professional diagnosis but was discouraged from doing so. "Except in the case of AS support groups, as well as AS-specific online resources [social media, forums, etc.], my diagnostic forays fared poorly. I was met with resistance and disbelief at every turn, and I was actively discouraged from pursuing an official diagnosis. I was denied diagnosis, in fact, by a neuropsychologist I really trusted, and that was crushing. He insisted that I was too empathetic, I was too social, I made eye contact, and I didn't fit the 'theory of mind' criteria. Of course not! I'm a grown woman with a lifetime of life experience and learning, not a 7-year-old white male from an upper-middle-class family."

She has mixed feelings about her recent awareness of her autism. She has felt better about the things she could now understand, but worse because of implications of being "broken" and beyond help. She believes that people pathologize differences characteristic of autism and Asperger's.

She feels that her autistic traits led to being bullied throughout middle school. In relationships, she has been taken advantage of and sometimes ridiculed, but in high school she learned how to socialize. She feels that friends, family, and therapy were generally useless, although family has helped from time to time. She has had some bad experiences with therapists, who were ignorant about Asperger's, and seems disdainful of their ignorance. However, neuropsychiatric rehabilitation (working on executive function and communication skills) has been helpful to her, as have exercise and diet.

She is quite successful in her work as a technical program manager, yet stressed because her success depends on her ability to socialize. She is hoping to get involved with book information design, which will involve less socializing. She feels that her autism has made employment difficult; she would get "maxed out" and unable to deal with a job any longer, then move to another job.

She hides her autism, particularly at work, because she does not want to call attention to her difficulties in social interactions. She feels that because of her autism, she has been isolated from "cool folks" at jobs.

"I alternate between feeling better than others and feeling like there is something terribly wrong with me. I am usually at such odds with the world around me that I spend a lot of time blending and trying to accommodate the world around me, just so I can get by. When I was young, autism was not spoken about openly. It was something discussed in hushed tones in private, and it was a cause for shame among parents and family members. If I'd known about the full spectrum, as well as Asperger Syndrome, at a younger age, it would have really 'clicked' for me."

Marilyn Cosho [65, W]

Marilyn is an artist. Her work has been published in *Drawing Autism* [Mullen, 2014] and *Been There, Done That Try This!: An Aspie's Guide to Life on Earth* [Attwood et al., 2014].

Her parents, she says, were extremely nurturing and supportive, and she never wanted to leave home. But growing up was a challenge nonetheless. "When I was in grade school, the learning environment was usually very structured which suited me well. I generally kept to myself and was an observer more than a participator." Yet, she remembers feeling that, at age 11, her 5-year-old sister had more common sense than she.

In middle school, her teachers would comment about what a hard worker she was, yet she was "only" a "B" and "C" student. She would sweat and become flushed during tests, and sometimes her mind would go blank. Her level of fear and anxiety got worse around sixth grade. In high school, she was a "B" student, but "My parents hired a tutor to come to our house to keep me from failing Spanish. My uncle, an engineer, helped me with math. I probably had about three dates during high school, which were stressful. I didn't feel psychologically or emotionally old enough to date. I preferred doing things alone, like skiing, playing the violin, collecting stamps and dollhouse miniatures, and being with my cat." She graduated with a degree in elementary education.

Marilyn was diagnosed at 54 by a psychologist and felt joyful. "I finally understood that there was something different about me." Unfortunately, her attempts to share it with others didn't turn out as planned. She worked in a school and was happy to share her diagnosis with other staff. She was hoping they would be more understanding and appreciate her strengths more, such as her creativity, attention to detail, and reliability. Instead, most became very critical and more demanding. At the end of the year, she was laid off, after 16 years. She indicated to us that the job was very stressful.

After she was laid off from work, she was eventually granted disability status, which was a huge relief to her. Receiving recognition for her art and getting continued support from her family and close friends was also very helpful. In addition, art and dance have been quite therapeutic. "Now that I'm no longer working, I no longer have to try and meet others' expectations. It also gives me time to be creative and do those things that give me the most pleasure." Being diagnosed has clearly helped. "My diagnosis was a turning point for me. I now accept who I am and, for the most part, am proud of it."

Now at age 65, Marilyn seems content in retirement. One of her current interests is studying ballet: "I enjoy working on small technical details such as a graceful arm motion. There is no pressure to interact with others. The beautiful music and repetitive movement helps me get in touch with my body. Sometimes I feel like I become the music. I think it might help others on the spectrum."

She has many other hobbies as well. "I make miniature dioramas based on actual historical places, I write books about history and my family, I create art...all of these things reflect my love of sorting and organizing." She also makes miniature fairy chairs out of twigs and has created a seven-minute DVD called *Welcome to the Asperger Syndrome Mind*.

A good summary of Marilyn's journal is this: "My diagnosis was a turning point for me. I now accept who I am and, for the most part, am proud of it." Marilyn invites readers to explore some of her art at this site: https://treasurevalleyartistsalliance.org/Gallery/marilyn-cosho/"

Martha [57, SW]

Martha is one of our randomly selected interview participants; her story comes both from her questionnaire and the interview. She got diagnosed earlier than many of us, some time in the mid to late 90s. This was probably shortly after "Asperger's" appeared in the *DSM-IV.* "I had an initial diagnosis of Asperger's in my late 30s by a therapist I was seeing. He was part of a group practice, and he and his colleagues did research to figure out what my diagnosis was, and that is what they came up with. At the time they told me, I asked what could be done about it and they said 'nothing' (as I presume that was the extent of their knowledge). Since nothing could be done about it, it seemed like useless information to me and I just discarded the notion. I did not have Internet access at the time and put it out of my mind.

Later on, I heard Temple Grandin interviewed on NPR, and when I looked up 'Asperger's' and 'autism' on the Internet, I realized that this is what fit me the best of anything else I had ever read or heard about. So, one could say I was self-diagnosed in the end. And subsequent psychiatrists and therapists have agreed that this is my diagnosis."

When asked how she felt about the diagnosis she said that at first, she was relieved and happy about it – she finally knew who she was. But after the initial euphoria, she realized it wasn't unhealthy habits that got her to this point; there was nothing she could do. "Since nothing could be done about it, it seemed like useless information. At one point: I felt better about myself because I no longer felt I was as much to blame for the fact that my life did not turn out as well as expected. At another point: Later on, I have been rageful about the sense of being robbed of so many aspects of life that other people enjoy, especially the ability to live comfortably in my own body without sensory torments and to have normal sexual relations and family life. I struggle with my relationship with God because I cannot understand why he did this to me."

Life hasn't been easy: "I always hated myself for being different even though at times I did feel 'special and unique' and 'better than others.' As I have gotten older, the positive feelings have diminished and life is just a grind."

She was a good student in school, but, like so many of our respondents, "I was bullied at home, at school (all the way through college), and at a few workplaces. Bullied constantly for being sensitive, for being 'different,' for reasons I could not identify throughout my young life."

She grieves over what she has lost in life. "I'd never find life as easy as others...grieving...Still grieving ..."

When asked if she was comfortable being on the spectrum and saw autism as a positive part of her life, she said "no."

Martha completed a bachelor's degree and now works full-time, but her comments reinforce the common issue of underemployment among people on the autism spectrum: "Work has been difficult due primarily to my sensory issues and to social issues. I am underemployed. With an IQ of 150, I have done clerical work all my life."

She never had romantic relationships and has no children. "I've never really been close to anyone."

She enjoys listening to public radio and reading historical fiction, mysteries, memoirs, and self-help books. She is also interested in Russian language, architecture, cats, psychology, history, and religion.

With respect to services and resources, Martha responded, "There has been WAY too much emphasis on autism in children with little to no attention paid to helping and supporting older people on the spectrum." She considers herself part of the lower middle class and is managing financially, but she worries about retirement down the road. She is still grieving the person she thought she was before this late-in-life diagnosis.

Nancy [57, NE]

"During my childhood, my identity was defined primarily by my academic success in school. I was a straight 'A' student up until middle school, and always exceptional at math. Things changed in high school, which was very difficult for me because I didn't understand the social norms and knew I was different than my peers but couldn't figure out how to change myself to fit in." Things went better for her in college, "because the focus shifted back to academics and I was successful in that area."

"I was mostly always one of the teacher's pets because I was so well behaved and such a smart student. I have always been a 'goody two-shoes.' I thought it had to do with my Catholic upbringing but maybe it has more to do with my AS brain!"

She suspected she was on the spectrum when her 7-year-old (adopted) son was diagnosed on the spectrum and she learned more about the condition. She saw parallels to some male members of her family and began to identify them as having autistic traits. Then she read Rudi Simone's book *AsperGirls* and found confirmation that she was indeed on the spectrum.

Nancy shared more thoughts during the interview:

> I am articulate and present very high-functioning; however, social interactions cause me anxiety, the more people in the room, the higher my anxiety. I am much more relaxed with one other person or small groups (fewer than five people). Otherwise, it becomes too tiring to engage in conversation and I end up tuning everyone out, due to overload.

She has a unique perspective on the recent history of autism diagnosis, having raised an autistic child in addition to her own long struggle. "As a parent of a boy on the spectrum, I have seen many sides of the autism diagnosis. When my son was 3 years old, he was clearly experiencing extreme stress with dozens of meltdowns a day, but later he had help at articulating his need. THAT made everything so much EASIER for him and for us! We were more than willing to accommodate his needs and advocate for him. Now, neither we, nor our son, look at his autism as a disability – it is just another way of thinking."

When asked how things were for our generation, she said: "First, our generation did not get service and we had to develop coping strategies on our own. Those of us who were higher-functioning have been able to be successful in specific fields, but others who are not higher-functioning have had a great disadvantage of not being understood. Second, our generation did not benefit from neurodiversity and, as such, have experienced much discrimination for the way our brains work and have been marginalized, under-employed and/or not valued for our talents."

She added: "I am a successful person with AS...I have a well-paying respectable job, am in a long-standing marriage with my 'best friend,' have raised two confident, capable sons who both have learning disabilities, and have volunteered in the autism community for the past decade helping families affected by autism."

It was not, however, an easy journey. "It helped that I had a son on the spectrum and I spent almost a decade learning about his disability, advocating for him, and learning to be compassionate for him. When I first realized that I was on the spectrum several years after my son's diagnosis, I was embarrassed and relived many past events where I had acted in a non-expected fashion. But as I got to meet and know other adults on the spectrum, I have come to accept myself more and celebrate all the challenges that I have overcome to get to this point in my life."

Nancy is quite active in the Maine support community. After her son's diagnosis, she started a parents' support group and after her own diagnosis she began an adult women's group. Both have been greatly appreciated through the years.

Pat McCoy [64, NE]

Pat is a 64-year-old racially mixed woman living on the east coast of the U.S. "Not knowing why I'm different" left her feeling worse and alone. She suspects her father was autistic, too, but he died when she was 4 years old. She has felt "isolated in a crowd of NTs who don't understand," but has found some comfort in an online Aspie support group.

Pat was called *"retarded"* throughout childhood; autism was never mentioned in school. "Any learning difficulties were met with physical punishment, ridicule, and bullying. I was often frustrated and remember breaking down and crying a lot. The meltdowns were often met with more punishments." Unfortunately, things did not improve in later grades: "Junior high school was a nightmare...and I was mostly isolated in high school...I was never able to make friends."

She grew up with one older sibling and their mother, who she felt was NEVER a mother, "making it crystal-clear that she never wanted to give birth to me after my sibling."

Pat graduated summa cum laude from college and obtained a master's degree despite an undiagnosed learning disability. Nevertheless, work has proven a challenge. "Voc. Rehab. does NOT understand the autism/Asperger spectrum in adults and don't understand how that impacts employability...I have encountered age-ism and able-ism repeatedly."

Relationships have proven equally difficult: "I've tried living with roommates, but that situation became too stressful. I've had only two or three intimate relationships that fell apart. The last one knew about the autism spectrum but just didn't 'get it.' Eventually, he left, too."

She "nearly died" from substance abuse [alcohol, marijuana, and benzodiazepines], but has been in recovery for over 30 years. She felt misunderstood by mental health professionals and "finally gave up on them." She notes that the younger generations "have resources that were never available to us Golden Oldies. As for attitudes about autism, I acknowledge that I have a love/hate relationship with the fact that I'm on the spectrum. Some days are better than others...I just wish there were more support services for people like me."

Pat enjoys *Star Trek*, crocheting, weaving, genealogy, and drumming. When we checked in with her before going to press, she asked us to also include that she is learning how to spin yarn with an electric spinning wheel and drop spindle.

Ritamarie Cavicchio [50, NE]

Ritamarie, who is 50 years old, is a well-educated woman. She has taken many classes at a master's level in various areas of study: business management, history, language, and technology. She could not find the time to finish her degree program, but she hopes some day to go back and achieve a degree.

She had an online business for many years but stopped when her son was born. He was diagnosed around age 9, and she puts a lot of time into being with him. She also finds time to go online to build community around her special interests.

She is hopeful for her son's generation: "I hope things will be easier for my son's generation. I worry about people who may use their disability as an excuse to not work hard for something. I worked hard to overcome my problems and I might not have if I had known I was disabled."

Her special interests are extensive: "I have many! I'm an animal lover and I've had corgis for 20 years. I love being part of the online corgi community. I love to knit, sew, garden, decorate for the holidays, and send out cards and letters to my friends around the world. I send out over 800 Christmas cards every year. I am a self-taught herbalist and soap maker. I love languages and spend time learning them online. I like to write, and I post many opinions online. In the past couple of years, I've become more interested in local news and politics. I enjoy music. I love photography and art. I like to preserve food and hope to someday have a small farm to tend chickens, goats, and sheep. I love LEGO sets, too. I enjoy crossword puzzles, and regularly do puzzles and play card and word games online."

Ritamarie has learned a lot from realizing she is on the spectrum. "If I only had known sooner, I could have saved myself and others a LOT of hassle and maybe even accepted myself more...It was so difficult growing up like this [she was bullied at home and at school]. I still have [some] shame about my diagnosis and struggle with figuring things out. I was taken advantage of often in life and I blamed myself, but I now realize people were doing it to me not the other way around. I didn't know and so I couldn't protect myself. I know now, but I learned my lessons the hard way.

I know who I am now and I'm very glad for that. But I don't always let people know that because I still have plenty of fears and anxiety about it. I'm afraid people will judge me more if I say I'm autistic. Like I am trying to capitalize on a trend, which I am not.

Five years ago, I lost my best friend and champion, my dad. I'm still not over it, and I miss him so much. He accepted me for me and loved me always. Other than him, my son, and my dogs, I've never felt true love. I don't believe I ever will."

Rhys [52, UK]

Rhys lives in the U.K. with his partner of 18 years. He is now retired. He recounted his work history as follows:

"I have been employed for most of the time since I was 18. I was lucky in that the job I had for 23 years was, purely by coincidence, very well suited to somebody with Asperger's (I was a bookbinder). I was very good at my job and very highly regarded." Later his position was eliminated, and he had to work in more traditional office-type environments. "I quickly came to find that the amount of noise and the constant interaction with people in these circumstances was completely overwhelming and began to suffer badly with stress and depression."

He had meltdowns on the job that led to sick leave, during which he received a professional diagnosis of Asperger's Syndrome. Soon after that, he retired due to his health.

Rhys's interests include music, astronomy, historical literature, photography, cats, and bridges. He loves *Star Wars* and superhero movies but dislikes graphic violence. He signed up for Facebook reluctantly but uses it because he does not like using the phone. He stopped using autism-related social media because he felt appalled at the level of animosity and in-fighting on them.

He used alcohol and marijuana from his late teens to early thirties to deal with his anxiety in social situations. "It was only when I stopped self-medicating because I knew it was not a healthy way to live that I really began to have trouble coping in social and job situations."

Rhys is neutral about his autism: "I'm not ashamed or proud of my autism any more than I'm ashamed or proud of having blue eyes or curly hair." However, being diagnosed was very helpful to him: "In fact, finding out I am on the spectrum has made a very positive difference to how I feel about myself...Being diagnosed has made a very positive difference to my life. I can now look back on my younger days and finally stop beating myself up about why I didn't do better in school and other things that I have allowed myself to hate myself for. What my diagnosis has done for me, at the age of 50, is to give me the piece of the puzzle that has been missing all my life, and now I have that piece I am finally able to start to make sense of my life, and to start to forgive myself for the things that, for so long, I hated myself for. I finally know who I am."

Despite a relatively recent diagnosis, Rhys seems to have rapidly incorporated autism into his identity in a positive and healthy way.

Samantha [52, MW]

Samantha grew weary filling out our extensive questionnaire, so we did a follow-up by phone and had a chance to chat a bit about her life. Samantha grew up in New York and now lives in the Midwest. At 8, she was diagnosed as mentally retarded. She said she has "nonverbal autism" and is unable to speak under stress. Her mother taught her to read and write, but it took her many years of hard work to become verbal. She explained to us by email:

> Nonverbal autism means the wiring in my brain that allows my mouth/throat to make speech sounds didn't work and my processing delays made traditional speech training a process of lots of meltdown because my brain couldn't keep up. Eventually I got it working, but even now there are times when I cannot speak verbally.

As a child, "school was hell." She performed below average in most academic areas. "I could not read, write, or even really speak by age eight," she told us. Nevertheless, she received no special services at school. "I was the invisible alien child," she comments. She coped in part by isolating herself and when asked if she felt different from other children and teens, she responded, "The humanoid alien stuck on an alien planet."

Growing up different had the negative impact we have seen in most of our survey takers. Samantha told us, "I have long had concomitant comorbid [other diagnoses] because of decades of abuse because I'm different. I have been on disability since 2002 for PTSD, major depression, anxiety, and more."

She graduated from a seminary college with training in theology.

At age 50, she came along for an appointment with her girlfriend's adult daughter who was seeking a diagnosis, and this led to obtaining a diagnosis herself. The diagnosis was very illuminating: "Now that I know, I have answers to so much of my life starting with my first remembered meltdown at age two. It only makes more sense from then on. In retrospect it is clear both my mom and her father were clearly on the spectrum, too." However, coming to terms with the diagnosis was painful. "I had to go through the grieving process, or most of it. I am incapable of certain emotions, so I did not experience rage...I kept seeing my autism doctor so I could chart a new path in life."

As an adult, she has experienced discrimination in most major areas of her life. "I had a long and fascinating work life until I hit burnout because NO ONE heard or understood me. Crashed hard and burned." Although she has struggled with homelessness and institutionalization in the past, she now gets by on disability, lives independently, drives, and uses public transportation. She has "thousands of books" and writes her own blog. Her hobbies include cycling, maps, photography, and meditation. As for her attitudes about autism: "It's not a disease, it shouldn't be cured. Autism is a gift. I'm not ashamed of autism, not exactly proud; it's who I am. I'm like an ambassador at large for the autism community."

Stephen Shore, Ed.D [guest interviewee]

Dr. Shore was not in our original group of participants in the study, but we wanted to hear his experiences on the topics we looked at.

By Eric Endlich

I had the privilege of interviewing Dr. Stephen Shore in person at Panera Bread in Newton Centre, MA. We had the usual communication glitches that seem to be common between Aspies, including his thinking we were meeting a day earlier than scheduled. On the appointed morning, I entered the coffee shop and walked among the tables looking for someone who resembled the photo on his website. When I didn't see him, my anxiety gradually mounted. *What if he's shaved his beard and I don't recognize him? What if he's right here in front of me and my face blindness is preventing me from seeing him?* Then I saw someone walking up and down the sidewalk outside who looked an awful lot like him; I went out and confirmed it was him. Apparently, he had gone to the wrong door (as I had also done when I arrived) and concluded Panera was closed.

Stephen is a soft-spoken, modest, middle-aged man whose glasses and beard lend him a professorial appearance. That cold January morning he was wearing a short-sleeved T-shirt and sandals [with socks].

Stephen is an assistant professor of Special Education at Adelphi University in New York. One of his current projects is to study [with Anita Lesko] healthcare access for autistic people, in hopes that this may improve their shorter life expectancies. Autistic adults may not know when they need medical care, may not know how/where to get it, and may lack the necessary financial resources [e.g., because they are more likely to be unemployed]. Stephen also plans to explore how much the medical community knows about providing care to autistic people. He has received a grant for this research, as well as the support of Augusta State University, and plans to recruit subjects via AANE and other organizations.

Stephen is also interested in greater inclusion for autistic people in research – not just as subjects, but also as research designers; this is often called "participatory research." Human subjects training is available online [for those planning to conduct research], but the tests associated with this training may not be sufficiently accessible to the autistic population [e.g., for those who have impaired working memory]. Stephen is also currently writing a book on the social experiences of people with disabilities.

He has been in touch with adult Aspies in Russia, who consider him the "honorary president" of their support network. While individuals in Russia and other countries may be quite knowledgeable about current trends in autism and self-advocacy, on an institutional level many countries are far behind the United States.

Stephen noted the "3 As" of autism: awareness, acceptance, and appreciation. Not only individuals, but also organizations, may move through these stages; for example, Autism Speaks initially focused on "curing" autism and didn't include autistic people on their board. They have now eliminated the word *cure* from their mission statement and added two autistic people [including Dr. Shore] to their board.

"I was hit with the autism bomb" at 18 months, Stephen explained, when he regressed and stopped speaking. His parents desperately sought answers, and a year later, his pediatrician told his parents Stephen might be autistic. They were sent to a specialist who confirmed the diagnosis and recommended institutionalization, a common suggestion in 1964. [Sadly, when our son was diagnosed with autism 35 years later in 1999 – also at age two and a half – the pediatrician made the same suggestion.]

It took a year for his parents to convince a school to accept him. In the meantime, his parents created their own home-based program to help him. They imitated his behaviors, which helped him become aware of them. At age four, he realized he could speak, and he resumed talking.

Being aware of his differences as a child "explained things," but differences also led to negative consequences such as bullying. In elementary school, he was typically about a year behind his peers. He read extensively in areas of interest, including astronomy, aviation, electricity, mechanical devices, natural history, weather, earthquakes, and cats. He abandoned his plans to become an astronomer when a teacher told him that was impossible because he would never be able to learn math. He now teaches statistics at a university!

Fortunately, his parents supported his interests. When they discovered him at age four taking apart a watch with a sharp knife, they supplied him with plenty of other objects he could also disassemble. At this point in the interview, he illustrated his ongoing love of devices by removing his watch. I looked through the clear crystal at the gears and mechanisms inside. "That's really cool looking," I said, "but I can't quite see how you are supposed to tell the time." He flipped it over. I had been looking at the back of the watch!

Stephen's ability to play team sports was affected by his motor control, sensory issues, and difficulty reading nonverbal communication. When he was supposed to catch a fly ball at a summer camp baseball game, he experienced sensory overload watching the ball, so he turned to look at the trees instead. He had a better experience when he pursued individual sports such as rock climbing and bicycling.

Stephen identified as autistic at two different points in his life. After his diagnosis in early childhood, he and his doctors readily accepted the diagnosis. In high school, he started receiving less counseling, and by the time he was in college, he believed he had outgrown the diagnosis. But when he started preparing for his qualifying exams for a doctorate in music, he ran into difficulty with their unstructured nature and realized "the autism was still there and it was causing problems for me." He underwent neuropsychological testing, but the graduate school didn't quite know what to do with the recommendations. In fact, when he visited their disabilities office, they offered the "analogy" of a quadriplegic who was rejected in his application to become a firefighter. At that point, Stephen started becoming more interested in autism and "defected" to the field of special education. When he applied for a doctoral program at Boston University, someone asked him, "Are you sure you want to put on the application that you're autistic? They might not accept you." He replied, "If they can't accept my autism, then I don't want to go there anyway."

Stephen offered this view: "Autism is not an excuse to get out of doing things; it's a key to how to get things done." One doesn't outgrow autism, but one can grow into strategies and accommodations to accomplish goals.

I asked him what older autistic adults needed, he answered, "resiliency." There was so little understanding of autism when we were growing up that we had to be resourceful. It pays to use our strengths and natural interests for employment, like Anita Lesko or Temple Grandin. Stephen could have just as easily become a bicycle mechanic or run a bike shop – in fact, he did, for a time. [Interestingly, so did Orville and Wilbur Wright, whom some writers believe had AS.]

We also need better knowledge of autism and aging, he said, as well as more companies such as SAP that actively seek out and hire autistic adults for their unique strengths. We need greater understanding in schools and workplaces.

Later that day, Stephen was scheduled to give a talk on sensory issues at Lesley University, then on to teach a weeklong course at NYU, then speaking a conference in Taiwan, and finally, back to teaching graduate courses at Adelphi.

There's no doubt, I reflected after meeting with him, that Stephen Shore has reached the ninth degree of autism.

Tim [76, NE]

Tim was randomly selected for an interview, which we did by phone. For Tim, now 76 and living in Northern New England, "Grade school learning was very difficult...I had no idea that I was different really. I coped by acting out and being disruptive. Many hours of writing on the blackboard after school...I was glad to get out of there and teachers were glad too." He lived in an affluent neighborhood where many of the kids went to private school. However, he couldn't do the work there, so he ended up back in public school – where he was in the principal's office frequently.

He had a tough time in school. He was bright but couldn't seem to do the work. He was bullied a great deal. Yet, after an eight-year stint in the military, he went on to college and graduated with distinction.

Diagnosis at age 73 was beneficial for Tim's marriage. "I felt better, and my wife felt better because we had found the name of the cause of much of our marital problems." He and his wife were in couples therapy because their long marriage was falling apart, especially after his retirement. After receiving the diagnosis, they now have couples therapy with a LCSW who knows Asperger's, and his wife is attending a support group for spouses of those on the spectrum. Medication has also helped Tim.

Nowadays, Tim keeps busy with reading, boating, and working on his house. While he accepts and even celebrates his differences, he voices some regrets about life choices: "It has been very difficult to get to the age of 75. I have been married for 42 years and it has been very difficult for my wife...if I had known of the terrible effects of an Aspie on a spouse, I don't think I would have gotten married."

Wayne [58, UK]

In early childhood, Wayne would line up plastic dinosaurs and cars. "I wasn't part of the crowd; I spent a lot of time on my own. I had a few choice friends. Didn't follow trends. I was different but didn't know why – thought it was because I was an only child. I did very well in school, was the top student in my year. A bigger school was more difficult as I wasn't good at mixing. I didn't know I was on the spectrum until my 40s – I had to make the jigsaw pieces fit. At first, I took people for face value, then I realized they didn't say what they mean. Now I'm distrusting of people, don't give them the benefit of the doubt." In adulthood, he has learned: "I shouldn't say the first thing that comes in my head – now I'm more considerate."

At 44, after his son was diagnosed, Wayne received a professional diagnosis, which answered a lot of questions for him. He'd had a difficult marriage, but despite marital therapy, he felt that his wife took the diagnosis as a "stick to beat him with," and they divorced. Wayne has been in another relationship for the past eight years and feels she is a lot more understanding.

Wayne was in sales and now owns an art gallery.

"Diagnosis helped make the pieces fit...I was able to understand my son better. I can relate to others who have kids/spouse with Asperger's. Being diagnosed made me even more determined to succeed in life."

Wayne is keenly aware of the widespread nature of autism. "Everyone knows someone on the spectrum. I have two children with Asperger's. I wish I could help more people through their problems – I help when I can on a one-to-one basis when asked. I believe people like me could mentor some of the more able Aspies to fulfill their potential."

Dr. Wenn B. Lawson [64, Aus]

The information about Dr. Lawson comes from his questionnaire, the interview, his books, and his website. www.wennlawson.com

Wenn felt different from other children and teens growing up: "I didn't have words or connections to explain the sense of 'difference.' I think that I always knew that I was not like others...but I didn't know why or how."

Here is a response to a question he gave on his website:

As a child, did you find it hard to make friends with other children, or were you not really interested in that?

"This was very difficult. I didn't want lots of friends, in fact I was much more drawn to animals than to people, but one friend would have been great. But, I had very little success. I was viewed as 'a know all,' and the only way that I could relate to other children was if we had an interest in common. I was interested, at a distance, in having a friend, but I lacked the social know-how of reciprocity and quite often would go overboard to 'buy' friends; influence others with knowledge; or, become their 'helper' to earn a friend."

As a child, he was diagnosed as intellectually disabled and later with schizophrenia. He was in and out of mental Institutions; eventually at age 42 getting diagnosed with an autism spectrum condition (ASC), ADHD, dyspraxia, and learning difficulties. Despite these struggles, today he is a Teaching Fellow with Birmingham University's online master's autism course. He serves on the Autism Open Access board and the board for SEAL [Community College in Warrnambool, Australia], and the ICAN board, South West [Australia]. He is a participant and advisor for Autism CRC, Australia, and he has written numerous books [and papers] on ASC.

When asked what he'd like to share with others about autism, he said: "I'd like it known that autism isn't the monster some make it out to be...we are valuable, and we need to believe in ourselves. Being autistic is a disadvantage in a multitasking overly sensory stimulating world, but we have an advantage when it comes to being focused on stuff we are interested in and when sensory load is reduced."

In terms of young autistics today, he observed: "It's now brilliant for the younger generation; it's far more known about these days."

His primary interests include birds, writing, and researching autism. His books include: *Older Adults and Autism Spectrum Conditions: An Introduction and Guide.*

William Moye [67, NE]

William is a 67-year-old Aspie in New York. He was randomly selected for an interview after completing our questionnaire. However, it wasn't convenient for him to talk by phone, so we interviewed him via a series of emails.

He didn't have good memories of school. "I despise school in all forms. Never again will I enter a classroom...Mostly, I remember grammar school as a medium for boredom punctuated by brutality and humiliation. However, a possibly enlightened fourth-grade teacher allowed me to paint murals on large sheets of paper, which were then displayed on the walls. This probably wouldn't happen in public school today either. Before that a second-grade teacher also recognized my artistic talent and insight into the natural world."

When asked, "Did you feel different from other kids and teens?" his response was: "How about HELL YES?"

He learned about Asperger's before many of us did. "I probably began to hear of Asperger's in the nineties and immediately recognized myself. I marvel that anyone thinks it requires treatment. In learning about Asperger's, overall, I felt comforted that someone defined the conditions of my life...I take it more seriously now, especially since I realize that I will never attain a state requiring no more adaptation. My current life requires considerable adaptation most of the time."

He has not had an official diagnosis, but has diagnosed himself and believes he is on the spectrum. "Certain clues loom large in this assessment. I jump and scream with sudden loud noises. I prefer solitude to the vast 'dreck' of humanity. I dread meeting new people but sometimes get a delightful surprise when I force myself to do it. I conceptualize everything visually in my mind as Temple Grandin does."

He lives modestly in an apartment with a partner. He is self-employed, but his primary joy lies in his art and photography. He'd like to share them with you here. [https://www.flickr.com/photos/wsmoye/albums]

Yvonne Mikulencak [65, SW]

Yvonne, 65, is using her real name. She grew up in Texas in a Czech community because of her family's ethnic heritage. As a child, she went to a private Catholic school with a great deal of structure and ritual, which she also had at home and found very helpful. She loved school and did well in math, art, drama, and athletics. She remembered: "Honors student in everything. I got along and had friends, but I did not understand many people and students. I kept it to myself and just acted." She earned a bachelor's in drama and a master's in studio art and art history. She worked full-time until retirement and has been married 41 years. She is interested in art, theater, scuba diving, and swimming, and she owns a ranch.

She was diagnosed by a psychiatrist at age 56, after comments from friends. Yvonne went through a variety of reactions following diagnosis: "Felt I lost my lifelong identity and went through a year of mourning the loss of knowing who I was before and there is a new identity...I had many questions answered about me. I felt good." However, she could not find much information on females, so she started what she says is "the first and largest Internet group worldwide for women on the autism spectrum for education and support: *the Autism Women's Association* Blog and Facebook page: https://www.facebook.com/autisticwomensassociation/ and https://autisticwomensassociationworldwide.wordpress.com/."

Her message to readers is, "Accept autism as merely a different brain operating system; It's not a disorder. We are brilliant in our own right." She adds: "I was always and am proud of my autism."

WHO ARE OUR RESPONDENTS? – *THE STATISTICS*

Response Statistics

GENDER

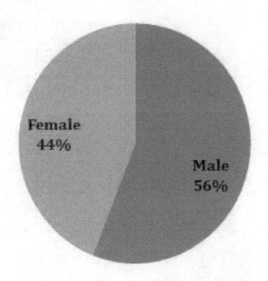

Gender	Percent	Count
Male	56.0%	84
Female	44.0%	66
	Total	150

Age Range

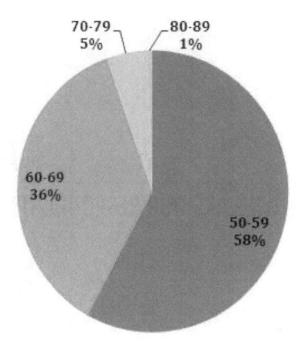

Age category	Percent	Count
50-59	58.0%	87
60-69	36.7%	55
70-79	4.7%	7
80-89	0.7%	1
	Total	150

Religious Preference

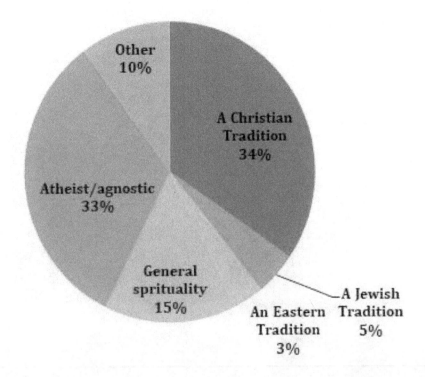

Religious preference	Percent	Count
A Christian Tradition	34.7%	52
A Jewish Tradition	4.7%	7
An Eastern Tradition	3.3%	5
General spirituality	14.7%	22
Atheist/agnostic	32.7%	49
Other	10.0%	15
	Total	150

Sexual Identity

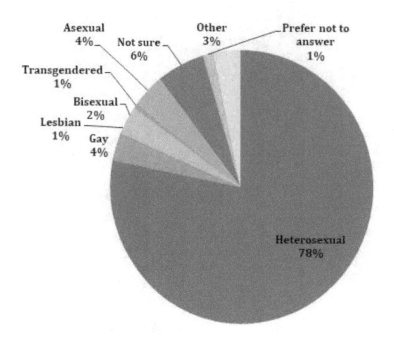

Sexual identity	Percent	Count
Heterosexual	78.0%	117
Gay	3.3%	5
Lesbian	1.3%	2
Bisexual	2.0%	3
Transgendered	0.7%	1
Asexual	4.0%	6
Not sure	6.0%	9
Prefer not to answer	1.3%	2
Other	3.3%	5
	Total	150

Ethnic Background - Responses

Ethnic Group	Count	%
African American	1	0.7%
Australian	1	0.7%
Caucasian	66	44.0%
Celtic	1	0.7%
Czech	1	0.7%
Dutch	1	0.7%
English	34	22.7%
French	1	0.7%
German	1	0.7%
Irish	4	2.7%
Japanese	1	0.7%
Jewish	5	3.3%
Latvian/Russian	1	0.7%
Middle Eastern	1	0.7%
Native American	2	1.3%
Other European mix	19	12.7%
Scandinavian	1	0.7%
Welsh	1	0.7%
White/Hispanic	2	1.3%
Unknown	6	4.0%

COUNTRY OF RESIDENCE

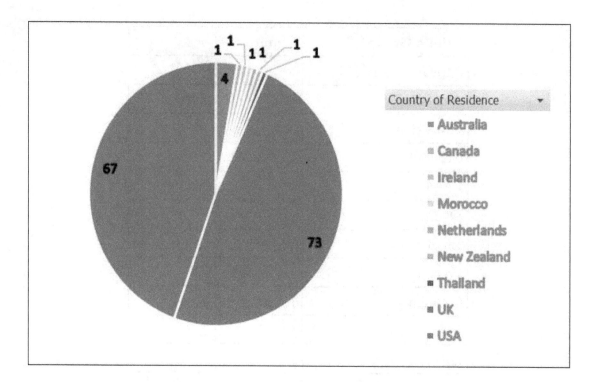

Row Labels	Count of Country of Residence
Australia	4
Canada	1
Ireland	1
Morocco	1
Netherlands	1
New Zealand	1
Thailand	1
UK	73
USA	67
Total	**150**

APPENDIX #3

ADDITIONAL DATA

<u>More Detail on Diagnosis:</u> **Have you been diagnosed with autism? If "yes," at what age?**

Responses to "Yes, at this age:"	Count
Left Blank	34
childhood, again age 59	1
25	1
28	1
33	1
37	1
38	2
40	2
41	1
42	4
44	1
45	3
46	4
47	6
48	8
49	5
50	11
51	7
53	10
54	6
55	9
56	6

57	2
58	4
59	4
60	1
61	1
62	3
64	2
65	1
66	2
67	2
69	1
70	1
72	1
73	1
Total	150

By what kind of professional were you diagnosed?

Responses to "Yes, diagnosed by a professional. What kind of professional?"	Count
No answer	36
M.D. Psychiatrist (specialization unspecified)	29
M.D. Psychiatrist specializing in autism	7
Psychologist (specialization unspecified)	42
Psychologist specializing in autism	6
LCSW	5
Neuropsychologist	4
Neurologist	2
Unspecified professional	14
Unspecified professional specializing in autism	5
Total	150

Because of friend or family member?

Responses to "Yes; because of comments by friend or family member:"	Count
No answer	139
Autistic friend	2
Friends and family	1
My children	1
Mother	1
My girlfriend	1
Sister's diagnosis	2
Ex-partner	1
Sister	1
Wife and son	1
Total	150

Other Statistics on Diagnosis

- Number professionally diagnosed with autism or Asperger's Syndrome: 122 [81.3%]
- Number with other diagnosis or condition besides autism (comorbidity): 121 [80.7%]
  - [These include anxiety, OCD, PTSD, Personality Disorder, Bi-Polar, Dissociative Disorder, ADHD; 73.3% reported anxiety.]

Male/Female Differences

Sexual orientation: Males identified themselves as heterosexual significantly more than females:
Males: 85.7%
Females: 68.2%
P value = .0101

Distribution of Reported Sexual Orientation

Row Labels	Female	%	Male	%	Total	%
Asexual	6	9.1%	0	0.0%	6	4.0%
Bisexual	2	3.0%	1	1.2%	3	2.0%
Gay	1	1.5%	4	4.8%	5	3.3%
Heterosexual	45	68.2%	72	85.7%	117	78.0%
Lesbian	2	3.0%	0	0.0%	2	1.3%
Not sure	5	7.6%	4	4.8%	9	6.0%
Other	3	4.5%	2	2.4%	5	3.3%
Prefer not to answer	1	1.5%	1	1.2%	2	1.3%
Transgendered	1	1.5%	0	0.0%	1	0.7%
Grand Total	**66**	**100.0%**	**84**	**100.0%**	**150**	**100.0%**

[Note: there is question about whether "Transgendered" belongs under sexual orientation. This will be reevaluated in future surveys.]

Diagnosis

Gender	Count	Percent
Female	48	72.7%
Male	74	88.1%

Sensory Issues

Gender	Count	Percent
Female	52	78.8%
Male	51	60.7%

PTSD

Gender	Count	Percent
Female	28	42.4%
Male	17	20.2%

Diagnosis

Although the difference in age of diagnosis between men and women was not significant, men tended to get professionally diagnosed significantly more than women: p = .0165.

Sensory Issues

Females had more sensory issues than men: For period of life 50s and beyond: p = .0165; for period of life 30-50, p = .0109.

PTSD:

There was a significant difference between males and females of rate of reported PTSD, for both periods of life, 50 and over, and 30s and 40s. This difference is consistent with the general population; however, for both males and females the rates are higher than the general population [which is around 10% for females and 5% for males]:

Females: 42%
Males: 20%
P value = .0032 for period of life 50 and beyond; p = .0056 for period of life of 30–50. [Values reported above are for 50 and beyond period.]

Differences in Period of Life: 30s and 40s vs. 50s and Beyond

From the survey, it appears that life, in general, got better after 50. This may be due in large part to having also been diagnosed after 50 for most respondents. So, we could probably say that life got better after diagnosis, and it may be a confounding factor with age. It also makes sense, however, that acquired life experience is often empowering, and that things do get favorably resolved due to this.

Significant improvements were seen in the following areas [using paired t-test and McNemar's test]:

Interactive

Less bullying and teasing: p < .0001
Less being taken advantage of: p < .0001
Improvement in communication difficulties: p < .0001
Less being misunderstood: p = .0069

187

Less hard to understand others: $p = .0003$
Less difficulty articulating: $p = .0121$
Less need for rigid routines: $p = .0121$
Less need for much alone time: $p = .0012$
Less anxiety/stress: $p = .0026$

Mental Illness

Less depression: $p < .0001$
Less suicide attempts: $p < .0001$
Less on psychiatric medication: $p = .0153$

Acceptance and Involvement

Less ashamed of differences: $p = .0003$
Celebrated differences: $p < .0001$
Acceptance of self: $p < .0001$
More autistic friends: $p < .0001$
More active in autism community: $p < .0001$
Would like greater acceptance of autism: $p < .0001$
Tried more to help others: $p < .0001$

The following did not register as "significant"; trends were observed:
Less anxiety: $p = .0881$ [a trend, close to significant]
Less in mental hospital: $p = .1091$ [a trend but difference not significant]
Less suicidal thoughts: $p = .2019$ [a directional trend but difference not significant]
Less bothered by sensory issues: $p = .2865$ [not significant]
Less PTSD: $p = .8093$ [not significant]

Numerical Findings

Anxiety

Period of Life	Count	Percent
30-50	118	78.7%
50+	110	73.3%

Depression

Period of Life	Count	Percent
30-50	106	70.7%
50+	85	56.7%

Suicide Attempts

Period of Life	Count	Percent
30-50	23	15.3%
50+	6	4.0%

On Psychiatric Medication

Period of Life	Count	Percent
30-50	54	36.0%
50+	41	27.3%

Suicidal Thoughts

Period of Life	Count	Percent
30-50	62	41.3%
50+	56	37.3%

In Mental Hospital

Period of Life	Count	Percent
30-50	12	8.0%
50+	6	4.0%

PTSD

Period of Life	Count	Percent
30-50	46	30.7%
50+	45	30.0%

Ashamed of Differences

Period of Life	Count	Percent
30-50	55	36.7%
50+	36	24.0%

Celebrated Differences

Period of Life	Count	Percent
30-50	34	22.7%
50+	64	42.7%

Acceptance of Self

Period of Life	Count	Percent
30-50	43	28.7%
50+	89	59.3%

More Autistic Friends

Period of Life	Count	Percent
30-50	27	18.0%
50+	60	40.0%

More Active in Autism Community

Period of Life	Count	Percent
30-50	11	7.3%
50+	29	19.3%

Would Like Greater Acceptance of Autism

Period of Life	Count	Percent
30-50	48	32.0%
50+	120	80.0%

Tried More to Help Others

Period of Life	Count	Percent
30-50	43	28.7%
50+	91	60.7%

Age Category Differences: Born Before 1/1/1960 and Born After 1/1/1960

Born before 1/1/1960 ["older"]: 95
Born after 1/1/1960 ["younger"]: 54
Unknown: 1

Exploratory Analysis – Explanation

We performed some exploratory analyses to find if there were differences between the older and younger members of our cohort, in an effort to find out the effect that growing up in a different decade may have had. We picked a cutoff date of 1/1/1960. For the attributes mentioned below, chi-square tests were done, and p values were computed, as though we had formulated the hypothesis about each beforehand. Since this is an exploratory analysis, results should be interpreted with caution. Still, the findings may be useful in forming other hypotheses, and guiding further study and analyses. Details are in this appendix.

Roughly 50 attributes were examined, but only those indicating a p value of about .05 are illustrated below. If the p value is .001 or less, it is denoted by two asterisks [**]; if it is between .001 and .002, it is denoted by one asterisk [*]. By chance alone and nothing else, the probability of any of 50 p values being .001 or less is close to .05; the probability of any of them being .002 or less is close to .10. But it appears that the collection of values as a whole has much greater significance than chance alone.

The exploratory analysis showed that the younger group had "significantly" greater awareness and "significantly" greater acceptance *and* rejection of their autism in their 30s and 40s than the older group – as well as more activism during the earlier age period. This finding makes sense if one considers that autism became increasingly known with each passing decade.

In addition to more pride of having autism during their 30s and 40s, the younger group wanted to be like everyone else and tried to hide their autism more so than the older group. The reason for this apparent disparity is that, in each case, less than half of the respondents were involved, and there were simply more responses in both areas, by different people responding in each area. This may be attributed to increase in awareness, whether for better or for worse. Regarding ailments, the younger group had a greater reported incidence of trouble hearing and trouble sleeping. Further, the older group seemed to excel significantly more in reading and language than the younger group.

There seems to be a significant difference in country of residence by age group: people in the younger group were disproportionately from the UK compared with people in the older group. Also, the younger group depended significantly more on disability income than the older group. (National policies, along with cultural climate, may also play a role.) This last finding may reinforce a concern expressed by a few respondents: While having help and resources is great, some may depend too much on them to the point that development of their own resources and the ability to survive and advance through struggle are diminished.

Age Category: Younger [Born post 1960] vs. Older [Born pre-1960]

Exploratory Analyses [findings having greater statistical significance]

Country of residence [totals]: creating three groups, US, UK, and Other:
US: 69
UK: 77
Other: 4

Demographics

Country of Residence[3]

Country Category	Age Older	Group younger	Total
Other	2	2	4
UK	41	35	76
USA	52	17	69
Total	**95**	**54**	**149**

There was a significant difference in country of residence and age group: people in the younger group were disproportionately from the UK as compared with people in the older group [p = .0233].

Depended on Disability

Age group	No	Yes	Total
older	73	22	95
younger	32	22	54
Total	**105**	**44**	**149**

The younger group depended more on disability income than the older group [p = .0237].

School Performance

Reading and Language: Elementary School

How they did	older	younger	Total
Above average	71	29	100
Average	14	14	28
Below average	8	11	19
Total	**93**	**54**	**147**

p = .0153 [older group more above average].

---

3   Note: for the purpose of this exploratory analysis, if a respondent's current residence was not the U.S. or the U.K. but the person reported growing up in one of those, that person was categorized in one of the two. This is why totals for UK and USA appear a bit higher here than as reported earlier.

Reading and Language: Middle School

How they did	Older	Younger	Total
Above average	61	28	89
Average	24	14	38
Below average	7	12	19
Total	92	54	146

p = .0342 [older group more above average].

Reading and Language: High School

How they did	Older	Younger	Total
Above average	63	23	86
Average	21	16	37
Below average	7	12	19
Total	91	51	142

p = .0063 [older group more above average].

Behavior and Emotional State [significance findings]

Awareness

Suspected or knew had autism at 30-50 age period

Age group	No	Yes	Total
older	58	37	95
younger	13	41	54
Total	71	78	149

The younger people reported that they suspected or knew they had autism in their 30s and 40s, more than the older group: $p < .0001$ [**].

Use of Resources

Used Friend Resources at Childhood

Age group	No	Yes	Total
older	92	3	95
younger	48	6	54
Total	**140**	**9**	**149**

The younger group had more friend resources than the older group during childhood as treatment for mental illness. $p = .0501$

Used Family Resources at Teens/20s

Age group	No	Yes	Total
older	85	10	95
younger	41	13	54
Total	**126**	**23**	**149**

The younger group used more family resources as teens as treatment for mental illness. $p = .0278$

Used Family Resources during 30s and 40s

Age group	No	Yes	Total
older	84	11	95
younger	34	20	54
Total	**118**	**31**	**149**

The younger group used more family resources in their 30s and 40s as treatment for mental illness. $p = .0002$ [**].

Used family resources 50s and beyond

Age group	No	Yes	Total
Older	78	17	95
Younger	35	19	54
Total	**113**	**36**	**149**

The younger group used more family resources at 50+ as treatment for mental illness. $p = .0178$.

Use of psychotherapy – 50s and beyond

Age group	No	Yes	Total
Older	47	48	95
Younger	37	17	54
Total	84	65	149

The older people used psychotherapy at age 50+ more than the younger group. *p* = .0242.

Ailments

Trouble hearing at teens/20s

Age group	No	Yes	Total
Older	90	5	95
Younger	44	10	54
Total	134	15	149

The younger group reported more trouble with hearing at teens/20s more than the older group. *p* = .0097.

Trouble sleeping at teens/20s

Age group	No	Yes	Total
Older	67	28	95
Younger	28	26	54
Total	95	54	149

The younger group reported more trouble sleeping at teens/20s than the older group. *p* = .0226.

Trouble sleeping at 30s and 40s

Age group	No	Yes	Total
Older	57	38	95
Younger	17	37	54
Total	74	75	149

The younger group reported more trouble sleeping in their 30's and 40's than the older group. *p* = .0008 [**].

Connection and Activism

Wanted to be like everyone – childhood

Age group	No	Yes	Total
older	71	24	95
younger	31	23	54
Total	**102**	**47**	**149**

The younger group wanted desperately to be like everyone else at childhood more than the older group. p = .0287.

Wanted to be like everyone – teens and 20s

Age group	No	Yes	Total
older	63	32	95
younger	27	27	54
Total	**90**	**59**	**149**

The younger group wanted desperately to be like everyone else at teens more than the older group. p = .0503.

Wanted to be like everyone – 30s and 40s

Age group	No	Yes	Total
older	76	19	95
younger	36	18	54
Total	**112**	**37**	**149**

There was a slight trend for the younger group to want to be like others more than the older group during their 30s and 40s, but it reversed at 50s. p = .0702 during 30s and 40s/ p = .2610 at 50s.

Wanted to be like everyone – 50s and beyond

Age group	No	Yes	Total
older	80	15	95
younger	49	5	54
Total	**129**	**20**	**149**

Tried to hide autism during 30s and 40s

Age group	No	Yes	Total
older	88	7	95
younger	38	16	54
Total	126	23	149

The younger group tried to hide autism in their 30s and 40s more than the older group. p = .0003 [**].

Connected to others on spectrum at teens/20s

Age group	No	Yes	Total
older	85	10	95
younger	38	16	54
Total	123	26	149

The younger group connected more to those on the spectrum than the older group during teens/20s. p = .0031.

Wanted to help others during 30s and 40s

Age group	No	Yes	Total
older	77	18	95
younger	29	25	54
Total	106	43	149

The younger group wanted to help others more in their 30s and 40s than the older group. p = .0004 [**].

Proud of autism at 30s and 40s

Age group	No	Yes	Total
older	86	9	95
younger	37	17	54
Total	123	26	149

The younger group was proud of their autism in their 30s and 40s more than the older group. p = .0007 [**].

Loved being autistic at 30s and 40s

Age group	No	Yes	Total
older	91	4	95
younger	43	11	54
Total	134	15	149

The younger group loved being autistic in their 30s and 40s more than the older group. p = .0016 [*].

Autistic friends during 30s and 40s

Age group	No	Yes	Total
older	83	12	95
younger	39	15	54
Total	122	27	149

The younger group had more autistic friends in their 30s and 40s than the older group. p = .0210.

Involvement with autism during 30s and 40s

Age group	No	Yes	Total
older	89	6	95
younger	43	11	54
Total	132	17	149

The younger group was more involved with autism in their 30s and 40s than the older group. p = .0095.

Proud of talking about autism during 30s and 40s

Age group	No	Yes	Total
older	91	4	95
younger	46	8	54
Total	137	12	149

The younger group were proud of talking about autism in their 30s and 40s, more so than the older group. p = .0222.

Wouldn't give up autism during 30s and 40s

Age group	No	Yes	Total
older	89	6	95
younger	41	13	54
Total	130	19	149

The younger group wouldn't give up autism in their 30s and 40s more than the older group. $p = .0018$ [*].

Wanted greater acceptance of autism during 30s and 40s

Age group	No	Yes	Total
older	73	22	95
younger	28	26	54
Total	101	48	149

The younger group wanted greater acceptance of their autism in their 30s and 40s more than the older group. $p = .0017$ [*].

Wanted a cure for autism during 50s and beyond

Age group	No	Yes	Total
older	80	15	95
younger	52	2	54
Total	132	17	149

More of the older group wanted a cure at 50+ than the younger group. $p = .0257$.

Too depressed to volunteer during 30s and 40s

Age group	No	Yes	Total
older	89	6	95
younger	40	14	54
Total	129	20	149

The younger group was too depressed to volunteer in their 30s and 40s more than the older group. $p = .0007$ [**].

This difference is not seen as much at 50+: $p = .0983$.

Content with autism during 30s and 40s

Age group	No	Yes	Total
Older	90	5	95
Younger	42	12	54
Total	132	17	149

The younger group was more content w/autism in their 30s and 40s than the older group. $p = .0017$ [*].

Feel positive about autism during 30s and 40s

Age group	No	Yes	Total
Older	82	13	95
Younger	37	17	54
Total	119	30	149

The younger group felt more positive about autism in their 30s and 40s than the older group. $p = .0092$.

Angry about discrimination of autism during 30s and 40s

Age group	No	Yes	Total
older	78	17	95
younger	33	21	54
Total	111	38	149

The younger group was more likely to be angry about discrimination in their 30s and 40s than the older group. $p = .0047$.

Empowered to work for change during 30s and 40s

Age group	No	Yes	Total
older	87	8	95
younger	40	14	54
Total	127	22	149

The younger group felt more empowered to work toward change in their 30s and 40s than the older group. $p = .0038$.

Feel spirituality in connection with autism during 50s and beyond

Age group	No	Yes	Total
Older	38	57	95
Younger	31	23	54
Total	**69**	**80**	**149**

The older group felt more spirituality in connection w/autism at 50+ more than the younger group. $p = .0405$.

Instructions for the Questions

Some questions are "yes" or "no", and some questions ask you to check all that applies to you in a list, or which period in your life certain things were true.

Don't spend too much time thinking through questions. Just give the answer that seems the most right for you.

Most questions give you an opportunity to write anything you'd like. Feel free to use the backs of pages.

If you have problems or questions on the questionnaire, feel free to contact us.

Below is the survey we used in our study. For this book, we have added which degree each question or section addresses. The degree labels were not in the original survey.

INTERNATIONAL QUESTIONNAIRE FOR OLDER ADULTS ON THE AUTISM SPECTRUM: 50 YEARS OR OLDER

This is an opportunity to participate in a study about what the generation <u>born before 1965</u> has experienced and how we express our experiences.

Acknowledgement: I am extremely grateful for the help provided by Philip Wylie who prepared an initial draft for this questionnaire based on his works: *Very Late Diagnosis of Asperger Syndrome [Autism Spectrum Disorder]: How Seeking a Diagnosis in Adulthood Can Change Your Life* [2014] and *The Nine Degrees of Autism: A Developmental Model* [2016]. I'm also grateful for the help of Rob Lagos, who used his extensive computer skills to refine this questionnaire and put it in digital format. The insights and support of both Phil and Rob were invaluable. But I'm responsible for whatever weaknesses or mistakes remain.

Thank you for your willingness to participate in this study!

IDENTIFYING INFORMATION IS OPTIONAL [But we need to have those marked with asterisk.]

<u>General Information</u>

Today's Date (key in date in month/day/year format or use calendar)
*
_____

Date of Birth (key in date in month/day/year format)
*
_____

*Gender**

[ ] Male
[ ] Female

*Age Range**

[ ] 50-59
[ ] 60-69
[ ] 70-79
[ ] 80-89
[ ] 90-99
[ ] 100 or higher

*Place of Residence**

Country of your residence	Region of country [state, province]
_____	_____

*Place of Birth**
List other countries where you have lived and when you lived there
(put "none" if none)*
Ethnic Background*

_____

Religious Preference*

[ ] A Christian Tradition
[ ] A Jewish Tradition
[ ] An Eastern Tradition
[ ] General spirituality
[ ] Atheist/agnostic
[ ] Other
Please specify other religious preference:

_____

Please clarify your answer as you wish:

_____

Sexual Identity*

[ ] Heterosexual
[ ] Gay
[ ] Lesbian
[ ] Bisexual
[ ] Transgendered
[ ] Asexual
[ ] Not sure
[ ] Prefer not to answer
[ ] Other
Please specify other sexual identity: **Please clarify your answer as you wish:**

Would you be willing to participate in an interview by phone or in person?
[ ] Yes
[ ] No
Would you like a summary of the results?
[ ] Yes
[ ] No
If "yes" to either, please include some contact information, and how you would like to be contacted.

GENERAL QUESTIONS

DEGREE #2

1) Awareness

	1. I don't know	2. Childhood	3. Teens & 20's	4. 30-50	5. 50+
I knew I was on the autism spectrum at these points in my life	[ ]	[ ]	[ ]	[ ]	[ ]
I suspected I was on the autism spectrum at these points	[ ]	[ ]	[ ]	[ ]	[ ]
I felt I was different from others, but didn't know why at these points	[ ]	[ ]	[ ]	[ ]	[ ]
a. I felt that there was something wrong with me	[ ]	[ ]	[ ]	[ ]	[ ]
b. I felt special and unique	[ ]	[ ]	[ ]	[ ]	[ ]
c. I felt better than others	[ ]	[ ]	[ ]	[ ]	[ ]

Please add additional comments:

_____

DEGREE #1

2) Do you believe that you were born on the autism spectrum?
[ ] Yes. I believe/know that I am on the autism spectrum and believe that one is born with autism.
[ ] Yes. I believe/know that I am on the autism spectrum and believe that autism is in part hereditary.
[ ] No. I believe/know that I am on the spectrum but I believe that circumstances in my childhood are the cause such as:
Please add additional comments:

_____

DEGREE #4

3) Have you been diagnosed with autism?
[ ] Yes, at this age: _____
[ ] Yes, diagnosed by a professional. What kind of professional?

_____
[ ] Yes; because of comments by friend or family member:

_____
[ ] No, but I have diagnosed myself and believe I am on the spectrum.
[ ] No.
Please add additional comments:

4) When you started thinking you might have autism; what resources did you use to explore it?

[ ] Friend
[ ] Family
[ ] Partner or spouse
[ ] Social media
[ ] Internet
[ ] Print media [newspaper, magazine, books, etc.]
[ ] Workshop or conference
[ ] Health Professional
[ ] Mental Health Professional
[ ] Asperger's, Autism support groups
[ ] Other: _____

Please add additional specifications or comments below:

5) When you were diagnosed [or realized] you were on the spectrum, which of the following did you feel?

[ ] Relief
[ ] Disbelief
[ ] Fear
[ ] Rage
[ ] Disappointment
[ ] Excitement
[ ] Other: _____

Please add specifications or additional comments below:

6) In the year after diagnosis/realization, how did your life change?

[ ] My life did not change
[ ] I felt better about myself
[ ] I felt worse about myself
[ ] I became depressed
[ ] I was more withdrawn
[ ] I was more outgoing
[ ] I developed mental health problems
[ ] I developed health issues

Please add additional comments:

7) In the year after diagnosis/realization, which support resources did you use?

[ ] Family
[ ] Friends
[ ] School
[ ] Therapy
[ ] Coaching
[ ] Mentoring
[ ] I was in psychiatric day treatment
[ ] I was in a psychiatric hospital
[ ] Support groups [incl. for autism]
[ ] Other: _____

Please add additional comments:

8) *This is one approach to diagnosis. Check any of these that you feel are true of you:*
[ ] Difficulty in ordinary social interactions
[ ] Difficulty in understanding and expressing emotions
[ ] Difficulty understanding non-verbal social interactions, such as body language, eye contact, gestures, and facial expressions
[ ] Difficulty in initiating and maintaining regular social relationships, such as making friends and adjusting to different social contexts
[ ] Repetitive use of the same gestures or words or objects, e.g. lining up objects
[ ] Insisting on routine and being upset by small changes
[ ] Getting fixated on particular interests or objects
[ ] Overly-reacting or under-reacting to stimuli such as noise, lights, smells, textures, touch, temperatures
[ ] These behaviors have always been part of your life in some way. However, they may not have been clear early-on, and may have improved over time.
[ ] These symptoms have caused significant problems in your social life, work life, or other aspects of living.
[ ] These symptoms aren't totally explained by something else, like intellectual impairment.
Add anything you would like to:

9) *Not everyone agrees with a symptom and deficit based approach to autism. Check any of these statements that you agree with.*
[ ] Autism isn't an illness. It's a different way of being human...to help them, we don't need to change them or fix them. We need to work to understand them, and then change what we do. (1)
[ ] Instead of classifying legitimate, functional behavior as a sign of pathology, we'll examine it as part of a range of strategies to cope, to adapt, to communicate, and deal with a world that feels overwhelming and frightening. (2)
[ ] Diagnosis with...the...DSM-5 is not precise like a diagnosis for bacterial infections where precise lab tests can be used. Psychiatric diagnostic labels were determined by both scientific studies and the opinion of committees sitting around conference room tables in hotels. Nobody debates the results of lab tests for a strep throat. Over the years, many psychiatric diagnoses have changed. (3)
[ ] When individuals on the milder end of the autism spectrum are labeled, you must remember that the following words all mean the same thing: Asperger, Aspie, geek, nerd, mild autism, social communication disorder or socially awkward. The science clearly shows that the social problems on the autism spectrum are a true continuum. (4)

Provide whatever detail you can to explain your answers above:

_____

(1) Barry M. Prizant, Ph.D. Uniquely Human: A Different Way of Seeing Autism; 2015 [New York: Simon and Schuster, 2015]. P. 4
(2) Ibid, p. 6
(3) Temple Grandin's website.
(4) Ibid.

10) *Do you feel you have experienced discrimination due to being on the autism spectrum?*
( ) Yes
( ) No
How have you been discriminated against? [Check all that apply]
[ ] School
[ ] Job
[ ] Relationships
[ ] Housing
[ ] Other: _____
Please add any further clarifications:

Other Developmental Disorders

DEGREE #1

11) *Were you born with any other developmental conditions or health issues?*
( ) Yes - please specify: _____
( ) No
Provide whatever detail you can to your answers above:

QUESTIONS BASED ON TIME PERIODS OF YOUR LIFE

Childhood: School

DEGREE #3
12) *Were you sent to a mainstream school or a special needs school?*

[ ] Mainstream school
[ ] Special needs school
[ ] Home school
[ ] Mainstream school but special education program
[ ] Other school (please specify): _____
Provide whatever detail you can to explain your answers above:

DEGREE #2
13) *Did you feel different from other children and teens?*

[ ] Yes
[ ] No
Provide whatever detail you can to explain your answers above:

DEGREE #3
14) *How did you do in elementary school? [ages 6 to 11]*

	Above average	Average	Below average
Reading & Language	[ ]	[ ]	[ ]
Math	[ ]	[ ]	[ ]
Science	[ ]	[ ]	[ ]
Art-drama	[ ]	[ ]	[ ]
Socially with peers	[ ]	[ ]	[ ]
Team activities	[ ]	[ ]	[ ]

Provide whatever detail you can to answers above:
15) *Which of these describes your experience of elementary school? [Check all that apply]*

[ ] I was bored a lot in classes
[ ] I had trouble understanding what teachers were talking about
[ ] It was hard for me to follow the instructions of teachers
[ ] It was easier for me to do homework on my own than to pay attention in class
[ ] I got in trouble a lot for not following rules
[ ] I got in trouble a lot for being verbally or physically aggressive
[ ] I loved classes and was a good student
[ ] Other; or add additional specification (box will pop up below)
Please specify:

16) *Were you ever given any special services in elementary school to work on social skills, behavior, academic help, or anything related to autism?*

( ) Yes
( ) No
If yes, describe the services and whether they helped:

210

17) *How did you do in middle school?* [ages 12 to 14]

	Above average	Average	Below average
Reading & Language	[ ]	[ ]	[ ]
Math	[ ]	[ ]	[ ]
Science	[ ]	[ ]	[ ]
Art-drama	[ ]	[ ]	[ ]
Socially with peers	[ ]	[ ]	[ ]
Team activities	[ ]	[ ]	[ ]

Provide whatever detail you can to answer:

18) *Which of these describes your experience of middle school? [Check all that apply]*

[ ] I was bored a lot in classes
[ ] I had trouble understanding what teachers were talking about
[ ] It was hard for me to follow the instructions of teachers
[ ] It was easier for me to do homework on my own than to pay attention in class
[ ] I got in trouble a lot for not following rules
[ ] I got in trouble a lot for being verbally or physically aggressive
[ ] I loved classes and was a good student
[ ] Other; or add additional specification (box will pop up below)
Please specify:

19) *Were you ever given any special services in middle school to work on social skills, behavior, academic help, or anything related to autism?*

( ) Yes
( ) No
If yes, describe the services and whether they helped.
Overall, how did you experience elementary and middle schools? Include how you got along with teachers and peers.

CHILDHOOD: FAMILY

20) *How was your relationship with your family up to age 12:*

[ ] My family was largely nurturing and supportive
[ ] My family largely ignored me
[ ] I was bullied and put down by other children in the family
[ ] I was bullied and put down by adults in the family
[ ] I was verbally abused
[ ] I was physically abused
[ ] I was sexually abused
[ ] Other [explain below]
Please explain other:

Provide whatever detail you can to explain your answers above:

21) *What was your living situation [up to age 12]? Mark all that are applicable.*

[ ] Lived with parents and sibs
[ ] Lived with one parent
[ ] Parents separated
[ ] One or both parents dead
[ ] Living with a relative
[ ] Living in foster care
[ ] Adopted
[ ] Orphanage
[ ] Lived with friends/neighbors
Provide whatever detail you can to explain your answers above:

TEENS: SCHOOL

22) How did you do in high school? [ages 15 to 18]

	Above average	Average	Below average
Reading & Language	( )	( )	( )
Math	( )	( )	( )
Science	( )	( )	( )
Art-drama	( )	( )	( )
Socially with peers	( )	( )	( )
Team activities	( )	( )	( )

Provide whatever detail you can to explain your answers above:

23) *Which of these describes your experience of high school? [Check all that apply]*
[ ] I was bored a lot in classes
[ ] I had trouble understanding what teachers were talking about
[ ] It was hard for me to follow the instructions of teachers
[ ] It was easier for me to do homework on my own than to pay attention in class
[ ] I got in trouble a lot for not following rules
[ ] I got in trouble a lot for being verbally or physically aggressive
[ ] I loved classes and was a good student
[ ] Other; or add additional specification (box will pop up below)
Please specify:

24) *Were you ever given any special services in high school to work on social skills, behavior, academic help, or anything related to autism?*
( ) Yes
( ) No
If "yes", please describe the services and whether they helped:

TEENS: FAMILY

25) *How was your relationship with your family during your teens:*
[ ] My family was largely nurturing and supportive
[ ] My family largely ignored me
[ ] I was bullied and put down by other children in the family
[ ] I was bullied and put down by adults in the family
[ ] I was verbally abused
[ ] I was physically abused
[ ] I was sexually abused
[ ] Other [explain below]
Please explain other:
Provide whatever detail you can to explain your answers above:

ADULTHOOD

DEGREES #5-7

26) *Educational experiences after high school [check all that apply]:*
[ ] I attended a community college
[ ] I graduated from a community college - degree:

_____

[ ] I attended a 4-year college
[ ] I graduated with a degree from year college - degree:

_____

[ ] I was in a program for masters and/or doctorate
[ ] I graduated with masters and/or doctorate - degree:
_____

[ ] Other post high-school degree:
_____

Other educational experiences you would like to specify:
_____

27) EMPLOYMENT: Check all that apply:
[ ] I am currently employed full time
[ ] I am currently employed part time
[ ] I am retired
[ ] I am looking for work
[ ] I am self-employed
[ ] My autism has made employment difficult for me
[ ] My autism has helped me in my work life
Provide whatever detail you can to explain your answers above:

28) INCOME: What have been your primary source/s of income in your adult life:
[ ] Job or jobs
[ ] Self-employment
[ ] I am retired
[ ] Disability benefits
[ ] Retirement benefits
[ ] Spouse or partner
[ ] Family support
[ ] Savings and/or investments
[ ] Illegal endeavors
[ ] Gambling
[ ] Other: _____
Provide whatever detail you can to explain your answers above:

29) INCOME: Check whichever statements are true for you now:
[ ] I am quite comfortable financially
[ ] I rarely worry about money
[ ] I have to "pinch pennies" to get by; I barely manage
[ ] I am homeless
[ ] I go hungry many days for lack of food
Provide whatever detail you can to explain your answers above:

30) *LIVING SITUATIONS in your PAST AND PRESENT adult life: Check all that apply:*
[ ] Apartment
[ ] Renting home
[ ] Own home
[ ] Landlord
[ ] Living on a boat
[ ] Boarding house
[ ] Homeless
[ ] Living with Friends
[ ] Living with children
[ ] Living with partner
[ ] Living alone
[ ] Other: _____
Provide whatever detail you can to explain your answers above:

31) *CURRENT LIVING SITUATION: Check all that apply:*
[ ] Apartment
[ ] Renting home
[ ] Own home
[ ] Landlord
[ ] Living on a boat
[ ] Boarding house
[ ] Homeless
[ ] In assisted living
[ ] In nursing home
[ ] Living with children
[ ] Living alone
[ ] Living with friend/s
[ ] Living with partner
[ ] Other: _____
Provide whatever detail you can to explain your answers above:

32) *RELATIONSHIPS in ADULT LIFE: Check all that apply:*
[ ] I'm in a close relationship
[ ] I have a committed partner
[ ] I am married
[ ] I know my partner/relationship is on spectrum
[ ] I think my partner/relationship is on spectrum
[ ] I have been married but now divorced or widowed
[ ] I have been married more than once
[ ] I'm happy with my relationship/partner
[ ] I have had a number of intimate relationships
[ ] I've never really been close to anyone
[ ] Other:: _____
Provide whatever detail you can to explain your answers above:

33) *FAMILY in ADULT LIFE: Check all that apply:*

[ ] Mother still living
[ ] If "yes", I'm close to her
[ ] Father still living
[ ] If "yes", I'm close to him
[ ] I think my partner/relationship is on spectrum
[ ] I have children up to age 18
[ ] I have children over age 18
[ ] I'm close to my children
[ ] I'm not close to one or more of my children
[ ] I think/know one or more of my children are on the spectrum

Provide whatever detail you can to explain your answers above:

QUESTIONS BASED ON TOPICS THROUGH YOUR LIFESPAN

34) *SENSORY EXPERIENCES: Which of these have you experienced, and when?*

	1. I don't know	2. Childhood	3. Teens & 20's	4. 30-50	5. 50+
Bullying and teasing	[ ]	[ ]	[ ]	[ ]	[ ]
Being taken advantage of	[ ]	[ ]	[ ]	[ ]	[ ]
Communication and social difficulties	[ ]	[ ]	[ ]	[ ]	[ ]
Being misunderstood	[ ]	[ ]	[ ]	[ ]	[ ]
Finding it hard to understand others	[ ]	[ ]	[ ]	[ ]	[ ]
Difficulty articulating clearly	[ ]	[ ]	[ ]	[ ]	[ ]
Need for rigid routines	[ ]	[ ]	[ ]	[ ]	[ ]
Sensory issues [e.g. bothered by noise, smells, etc.]	[ ]	[ ]	[ ]	[ ]	[ ]
Need for a lot of time alone	[ ]	[ ]	[ ]	[ ]	[ ]
Anxiety and stress	[ ]	[ ]	[ ]	[ ]	[ ]
Other (specify below)	[ ]	[ ]	[ ]	[ ]	[ ]

Specify other sensory experience(s):

YOUR INTERESTS

What are your interests?

216

35) *What TV shows and movies do you like?*

36) *What books, magazines, newspapers do you read? [Are any of them especially helpful for people on the spectrum?]*

37) *What internet sites do you find helpful or interesting? [Are there any Asperger's/Autism sites that you find helpful?]*

38) *What social media do you use? [Facebook, Twitter, Pinterest, SnapChat, etc.]*

39) *Do you regularly visit any blogs or forums that pertain to the spectrum? [Which ones?]*

40) *Other special interests or passions:*

DEGREE #3

41) COPING STRATEGIES

According to Dr. Tony Attwood, psychologist who specializes in autism, autistic individuals might use any of the following strategies to cope with feeling different. Indicate which ones you used and when.(5)

(5) Tony Attwood, "Introduction," in The Nine Degrees of Autism: Developmental Model [Routledge; London, 2016] l, p. 6-9

	1. I don't know	2. Childhood	3. Teens & 20's	4. 30-50	5. 50+
Escape into imagination [e.g. imaginary world]	[ ]	[ ]	[ ]	[ ]	[ ]
Denial and rigidity – blaming others	[ ]	[ ]	[ ]	[ ]	[ ]
Imitating neurotypical peers or acting "normal"	[ ]	[ ]	[ ]	[ ]	[ ]
Depression	[ ]	[ ]	[ ]	[ ]	[ ]

42) Are there other coping strategies you have used in your life to deal with being on the spectrum?
[Check all that apply]
[ ] Spending more time with younger children/adults than of your own age
[ ] Spending more time with older children/adults than your own age
[ ] Video games, TV
[ ] Immersed in hobby (explain below)
[ ] Immersed in academics rather than social life
[ ] Second-guessing things you had said/didn't say
[ ] Alcohol or drugs
[ ] Other (explain below)

Please explain hobby:
Please explain other:

43) DRUG USE:
Which of these did you use excessively during periods of your life?

	1. I don't know	2. Childhood	3. Teens & 20's	4. 30-50	5. 50+
Over the counter medication	[ ]	[ ]	[ ]	[ ]	[ ]
Prescription Medication	[ ]	[ ]	[ ]	[ ]	[ ]
Alcohol	[ ]	[ ]	[ ]	[ ]	[ ]
Cigarettes	[ ]	[ ]	[ ]	[ ]	[ ]
Illegal Marijuana	[ ]	[ ]	[ ]	[ ]	[ ]
Legal marijuana and/or medical marijuana	[ ]	[ ]	[ ]	[ ]	[ ]
Heroin or other opiates	[ ]	[ ]	[ ]	[ ]	[ ]
Amphetamines	[ ]	[ ]	[ ]	[ ]	[ ]
Barbiturates	[ ]	[ ]	[ ]	[ ]	[ ]
Ecstasy	[ ]	[ ]	[ ]	[ ]	[ ]
"Bath salt" drugs	[ ]	[ ]	[ ]	[ ]	[ ]
Other [please give details below]	[ ]	[ ]	[ ]	[ ]	[ ]

Other: please specify:

_____

Provide whatever detail you can to explain your answers above:

_____

44) ILLEGAL BEHAVIOR

	1. I don't know	2. Childhood	3. Teens & 20's	4. 30-50	5. 50+
Using illegal drugs	[ ]	[ ]	[ ]	[ ]	[ ]
Selling illegal drugs	[ ]	[ ]	[ ]	[ ]	[ ]
Robbery	[ ]	[ ]	[ ]	[ ]	[ ]
Assault	[ ]	[ ]	[ ]	[ ]	[ ]
Domestic Violence	[ ]	[ ]	[ ]	[ ]	[ ]
Smuggling	[ ]	[ ]	[ ]	[ ]	[ ]
Embezzling	[ ]	[ ]	[ ]	[ ]	[ ]
Arrests	[ ]	[ ]	[ ]	[ ]	[ ]
Conviction	[ ]	[ ]	[ ]	[ ]	[ ]
Served time	[ ]	[ ]	[ ]	[ ]	[ ]
Other	[ ]	[ ]	[ ]	[ ]	[ ]

Other: please specify:

Provide whatever detail you wish to explain any answers above:

45) _MENTAL ILLNESS/PSYCHIATRIC DISORDER:_

Which of these have been an issue for you at various life stages? Give details below of symptoms, any treatment, and progress.

	1. I don't know	2. Childhood	3. Teens & 20's	4. 30-50	5. 50+
Anxiety	[ ]	[ ]	[ ]	[ ]	[ ]
Depression	[ ]	[ ]	[ ]	[ ]	[ ]
Obsessive Compulsive disorder	[ ]	[ ]	[ ]	[ ]	[ ]
Post-traumatic stress disorder	[ ]	[ ]	[ ]	[ ]	[ ]
Personality disorder	[ ]	[ ]	[ ]	[ ]	[ ]
Bi-polar	[ ]	[ ]	[ ]	[ ]	[ ]
Dissociative Disorder	[ ]	[ ]	[ ]	[ ]	[ ]
ADHD or ADD	[ ]	[ ]	[ ]	[ ]	[ ]
Suicide Attempt	[ ]	[ ]	[ ]	[ ]	[ ]
Suicidal thoughts	[ ]	[ ]	[ ]	[ ]	[ ]
Hospitalization	[ ]	[ ]	[ ]	[ ]	[ ]
Insomnia or other sleep disorders	[ ]	[ ]	[ ]	[ ]	[ ]
Mental hospital	[ ]	[ ]	[ ]	[ ]	[ ]
On psychiatric medication	[ ]	[ ]	[ ]	[ ]	[ ]
Low self esteem	[ ]	[ ]	[ ]	[ ]	[ ]
Other	[ ]	[ ]	[ ]	[ ]	[ ]

Other: please specify:

Provide whatever detail you wish to explain any answers above:

46) *MENTAL ILLNESS/PSYCHIATRIC DISORDER:*

Treatment…Which of these treatments have you had? Indicate below whether they were helpful for you.

	1. I don't know	2. Childhood	3. Teens & 20's	4. 30-50	5. 50+
Psychotherapy/Counseling	[ ]	[ ]	[ ]	[ ]	[ ]
Coaching/mentoring	[ ]	[ ]	[ ]	[ ]	[ ]
Friends	[ ]	[ ]	[ ]	[ ]	[ ]
Family	[ ]	[ ]	[ ]	[ ]	[ ]
Intensive outpatient hospital	[ ]	[ ]	[ ]	[ ]	[ ]
In-patient psychiatric ward	[ ]	[ ]	[ ]	[ ]	[ ]
Psychiatric hospital	[ ]	[ ]	[ ]	[ ]	[ ]
Art therapy	[ ]	[ ]	[ ]	[ ]	[ ]
Dance therapy	[ ]	[ ]	[ ]	[ ]	[ ]
Medication	[ ]	[ ]	[ ]	[ ]	[ ]
Exercise	[ ]	[ ]	[ ]	[ ]	[ ]
Improving diet	[ ]	[ ]	[ ]	[ ]	[ ]
Social skills training	[ ]	[ ]	[ ]	[ ]	[ ]
Over the counter meds	[ ]	[ ]	[ ]	[ ]	[ ]
Other	[ ]	[ ]	[ ]	[ ]	[ ]

Other: please specify:

Provide whatever detail you can to explain your answers above:

47) PHYSICAL ILLNESS:

Indicate which of these you have had at various points in your life:

	1. I don't know	2. Childhood	3. Teens & 20's	4. 30-50	5. 50+
Epilepsy	[ ]	[ ]	[ ]	[ ]	[ ]
Inner Ear imbalance	[ ]	[ ]	[ ]	[ ]	[ ]
Difficulty hearing	[ ]	[ ]	[ ]	[ ]	[ ]
Chronic fatigue syndrome	[ ]	[ ]	[ ]	[ ]	[ ]
Allergies	[ ]	[ ]	[ ]	[ ]	[ ]
Ulcers	[ ]	[ ]	[ ]	[ ]	[ ]
Cancer	[ ]	[ ]	[ ]	[ ]	[ ]
Frequent flu/colds	[ ]	[ ]	[ ]	[ ]	[ ]
Pneumonia	[ ]	[ ]	[ ]	[ ]	[ ]
Bad back	[ ]	[ ]	[ ]	[ ]	[ ]
Surgery	[ ]	[ ]	[ ]	[ ]	[ ]
Difficulty sleeping	[ ]	[ ]	[ ]	[ ]	[ ]
Other	[ ]	[ ]	[ ]	[ ]	[ ]

Other: please specify:

Provide whatever detail you can to explain your answers above:

DEGREES #5-7

222

48) *How have you responded to being on the spectrum at various stages of your life [when you knew your diagnosis] or to just being different from others around you?*

	1. I don't know	2. Childhood	3. Teens & 20's	4. 30-50	5. 50+
I was ashamed of my differences	[ ]	[ ]	[ ]	[ ]	[ ]
I celebrated my differences	[ ]	[ ]	[ ]	[ ]	[ ]
I hated myself	[ ]	[ ]	[ ]	[ ]	[ ]
I wanted to kill myself	[ ]	[ ]	[ ]	[ ]	[ ]
I was OK with being different, but was upset by the discrimination	[ ]	[ ]	[ ]	[ ]	[ ]
Because of discrimination, I hated who I was	[ ]	[ ]	[ ]	[ ]	[ ]
I tried hard to look like others and hide my true self	[ ]	[ ]	[ ]	[ ]	[ ]
I accepted who I am	[ ]	[ ]	[ ]	[ ]	[ ]
I hated who I am	[ ]	[ ]	[ ]	[ ]	[ ]
I desperately wanted to be like everybody else	[ ]	[ ]	[ ]	[ ]	[ ]
I tried to hide who I am because of bullying and teasing	[ ]	[ ]	[ ]	[ ]	[ ]
I connected with others on the spectrum, and felt like I belonged	[ ]	[ ]	[ ]	[ ]	[ ]
I am ashamed of my autism	[ ]	[ ]	[ ]	[ ]	[ ]
I am proud of my autism	[ ]	[ ]	[ ]	[ ]	[ ]
I get depressed about social discrimination of autism	[ ]	[ ]	[ ]	[ ]	[ ]
Other	[ ]	[ ]	[ ]	[ ]	[ ]

Other: please specify:

Provide whatever detail you can to explain your answer:

DEGREES #8-9

223

49) *HEALING AND WHOLENESS*

Indicate at which points in your life each statement is true [or not]

	1. I don't know	2. Childhood	3. Teens & 20's	4. 30-50	5. 50+
Autism is a positive part of my life	[ ]	[ ]	[ ]	[ ]	[ ]
I love that I am on the autism spectrum	[ ]	[ ]	[ ]	[ ]	[ ]
I hate being on the autism spectrum	[ ]	[ ]	[ ]	[ ]	[ ]
I have autistic friends	[ ]	[ ]	[ ]	[ ]	[ ]
I'm involved in an autism support group	[ ]	[ ]	[ ]	[ ]	[ ]
I am active in an autism community	[ ]	[ ]	[ ]	[ ]	[ ]
I'm involved in a community of disabled	[ ]	[ ]	[ ]	[ ]	[ ]
I try to hide my autism	[ ]	[ ]	[ ]	[ ]	[ ]
I feel proud of talking about my autism	[ ]	[ ]	[ ]	[ ]	[ ]
If I could get rid of my autism, I would	[ ]	[ ]	[ ]	[ ]	[ ]
I wouldn't give up my autism even if I could	[ ]	[ ]	[ ]	[ ]	[ ]
I'd like to see a cure for autism	[ ]	[ ]	[ ]	[ ]	[ ]
I'd like to see autistic people have greater acceptance	[ ]	[ ]	[ ]	[ ]	[ ]
I get angry when people try to change me	[ ]	[ ]	[ ]	[ ]	[ ]
I try to help others on the spectrum	[ ]	[ ]	[ ]	[ ]	[ ]
I do volunteer work in my community	[ ]	[ ]	[ ]	[ ]	[ ]
I'm usually too depressed/ tired to do volunteer work	[ ]	[ ]	[ ]	[ ]	[ ]

I have been content since knowing about my autism	[ ]	[ ]	[ ]	[ ]	[ ]
I get depressed about discrimination against those on the spectrum	[ ]	[ ]	[ ]	[ ]	[ ]
I get angry about discrimination for those on the spectrum	[ ]	[ ]	[ ]	[ ]	[ ]
It empowers me to work towards changing discrimination	[ ]	[ ]	[ ]	[ ]	[ ]
I have some type of spirituality in my life	[ ]	[ ]	[ ]	[ ]	[ ]

Provide whatever detail you can to explain your answer:

50) *Do you feel you have reached a point in your life where you are comfortable with being on the spectrum and consider it a positive part of your life?*

[ ] Yes
[ ] No

If "yes" what do you want to share with others about how you got to that point?
Provide whatever detail you can to explain your answers above:

Have you ever participated in "Social Thinking" or other types of behavioral-cognitive programs? If so, Were they helpful?

51) *How do you think things are different for our generation - growing up before "Asperger's" was a term and when there was little understanding of autism?*

How do you think things are different for younger generations on the spectrum?

52) *What else would you like to add? What do you want readers of this future book to know about you and your life with autism?*

Thank you very much for participating in this survey!!!

ABOUT THE AUTHORS

Wilma Wake has been a licensed clinical social worker for over 40 years She is also an ordained minister, now retired after 28 years of active ministry. She has an M.Div. and D.Min. in Feminist-Liberation Theology and has published 4 books on spirituality. Her first love is education and she has a Ph.D. in Social Foundations of Education. She has taught on many levels, including 9 years as Associate Professor of Practical Theology at the Swedenborg School of Religion.

In her mid 60's she was diagnosed by a neuro-psychologist with Autism Spectrum Disorder. After absorbing this shock, she became active in an autistic adults' peer support group and now is co-facilitator. Her social work practice is devoted primarily to working with older autistic adults, neuro-diverse couples, and with autistic children and their families. She is committed to helping train other service providers to work with autistic adults.

She is trained and certified as a neurodiverse couples' therapist by AANE. [The Asperger/ Autism Network]. She has a post-graduate certificate in Play-Family Therapy from the Family & Play Therapy Center of Philadelphia.

Eric Endlich, Ph.D., clinical psychologist and founder of Top College Consultants®, helps neurodiverse students worldwide transition to college and graduate school. Dr. Endlich is on the Learning Differences/Neurodiversity Committee of the Independent Educational Consultants Association (IECA), and was recently honored by IECA with a "Making a Difference" award for resources he provides such as an autism-friendly college list. He is also on the Clinical Advisory Board of the Asperger/Autism Network (AANE) and helped found AANE's Neurodiverse Couples Institute. He is the co-admin for a Facebook group, Parents of College Bound Students with Learning Disabilities, ADHD and ASD, currently numbering over 600 members. Dr. Endlich has presented nationally at numerous events including the Harvard Medical School Continuing Education annual autism course, the Southern Maine Autism Conference and the CUNY Neurodiversity Conference. He has written articles for Autism Advocate Parenting Magazine, Different Brains, CollegeXpress and LINK for Counselors. He has taught undergraduate and graduate psychology courses at Boston College, Tufts University, Suffolk University and UMass/ Boston. Dr. Endlich has been interviewed by media including WGBH Radio, Forbes, Business Insider, College Confidential and U.S. News & World Report. Lastly, he is an autism dad and an autistic adult.

Rob Lagos is a computer programmer analyst and statistician. He has a Bachelor of Science degree from UCLA majoring in chemistry and computer science. He has worked for many years as a programmer/analyst and developer for several institutions in the New England area including United Health Group, Health Dialog, and New England Research Institutes. He served as a statistical consultant for Dr. Ramona Dvorak at the Joslin Diabetes Center, Harvard Medical School. He also tutored students from Harvard and Boston Universities in statistics, mathematics, and computer science. He has been the head facilitator for the Autistic Adults group that meets in Portland, Maine, for over 10 years. He has been a presenter and co-presenter of numerous talks and workshops dealing with autism, at Sweetser Training Institute, New Hampshire Mensa Regional Gathering, Asperger/Autism Network, and other institutes. He is a virtuoso classical pianist and has taught adult piano students.

Printed in the USA
CPSIA information can be obtained
at www.ICGtesting.com
JSHW061644160224
57523JS00012B/321